JERRY GRAHAM'S
MORE BAY AREA BACKROADS

JERRY GRAHAM'S
More Bay Area Backroads

by Jerry and Catherine Graham

PERENNIAL LIBRARY

HARPER & ROW, PUBLISHERS, NEW YORK
Grand Rapids, Philadelphia, St. Louis, San Francisco
London, Singapore, Sydney, Tokyo, Toronto

FIRST EDITION

Designed by Barbara DuPree Knowles

Maps by Ron Lang

LIBRARY OF CONGRESS CATALOGING-IN-PUBLICATION DATA

Graham, Jerry, 1934–
    [More bay area backroads]
    Jerry Graham's more bay area backroads/by Jerry and Catherine Graham.
      p.   cm.
    ISBN 0-06-096452-9
    1. San Francisco Bay Area (Calif.)—Description and travel—Guidebooks. I. Graham,
Catherine, 1955– . II. Title. III. Title: More bay area backroads.
F868.S156G7 1990b
917.94'610453—dc20

89-45660

90 91 92 93 94 DT/RRD 10 9 8 7 6 5 4 3 2 1

Contents

North Bay

South Bay

East Bay

Beyond the Bay

Acknowledgments

We would like to begin by expressing our gratitude to the thousands of readers of our first book, many of whom urged us to write more and more editions. Thanks also to the loyal viewers of "Bay Area Backroads" on KRON-TV, San Francisco, who were the first to embrace the book as well.

No words are adequate to thank the TV station crew for their continued support and encouragement. The "Backroads" group has become something of a close-knit family in four years and has gone through an orderly progression. Jessica Abbe, the original researcher, has become coproducer of the weekly program. Paul Ghiringhelli has been joined by Peter Hammersly as associate producer. Dave Vandergriff remains our editor, and Jeff "Kid Charlemagne" Pierce and Stan Drury are still our terrific cameramen.

Thanks to Amy McCombs, general manager of KRON-TV, who has brought new energy and success to the station, as well as to David Salinger, the program director. Special thanks to our dear friend Bob Klein, who conceived of the TV show "Bay Area Backroads" and remains its most ardent supporter.

We entered into a publishing contract with a certain amount of trepidation, having heard horror stories from friends whose books had been lost in the shuffle, edited to smithereens, and whose dreams of having a best seller (or at the very least a good seller) were dashed. Our experience could not have been more different. From the first meeting with our executive editor, Larry Ashmead, we have been treated with respect and consideration, and everyone at Harper & Row has been wonderful to work with. Belated thanks to Gideon Bosker of Portland, Oregon, for introducing us to Larry and to our agent, Peter Ginsberg. Special thanks to John Michel, our constant New York–to–Berkeley phone companion when it gets down to crunch time. Thanks also to Sayre Van Young for her indexing, Jean Haseltine for her invaluable research and fact checking, Ron Lang for his maps, and Bruce ("Rick") Emmer for his copyediting.

Most of all, thanks to you for picking up this book. We hope it helps open up many roads to discovery and adventure.

Preface

Eleven days after the massive earthquake, it is already clear that the Bay Area has bounced back. The resumption of the World Series showed millions of viewers that San Francisco and its neighbors were not destroyed and that the beauty and vitality that symbolize the Bay Area are intact. The cable cars are running again, Bay Bridge service is due to be restored in a few weeks, and the tourists are returning. For most of the area, things will be back to normal by the end of the year. For areas that were hardest hit, such as parts of Santa Cruz County, the recovery might take longer.

Because of the deadline demands of publishing, we, the authors, must complete our manuscript to the best of our abilities at this time. We have checked our locations since the earthquake and have tried to keep information as current as possible. A few of our locations were forced to close for a while but expect to be open by the spring of 1990, when this book will be released. As we recommend often in the book, it's always a good idea to call ahead before making a long trip. This is especially important for the Santa Cruz area.

If any good has come from this disaster, it is proof of the strong character of the people of the Bay Area. The spirit of friendliness and cooperation is apparent everywhere; volunteers have emerged from every walk of life to help those in need. Everyone expresses a desire to rebuild and get things back to normal. Few residents consider leaving.

So come ahead to the Bay Area. It's still one of the most beautiful and entertaining spots in the world. We want to prove it to you now more than ever.

Jerry Graham
Catherine Graham

OCTOBER 29, 1989

INTRODUCTION: Before You Hit the Road . . .

Since the publication of our first book in the summer of 1988, we have introduced viewers of the KRON-TV program "Jerry Graham's Bay Area Backroads" to more than 200 new places. This book consists of many of the best of those new destinations and will hopefully take off where our first book ended. Use them as companion guides or separately.

Now, as we said in the first book, let's assume that you've seen the Golden Gate Bridge, Coit Tower, and the cable cars. What else is there to do around San Francisco? Plenty. Whether you are visiting the area or have lived here all your life, you'll be amazed by what you'll find on the Bay Area's backroads. With this premise in mind, the television series was born in the summer of 1984, and it's still going strong. Broadcast each Sunday at 6 P.M. on Channel 4, San Francisco, it has consistently been the top-rated locally produced television show in the San Francisco Bay Area.

Each week, the show features four or five destinations plus recommendations of places to eat and sometimes places to spend the night. We have accumulated so many special restaurants and inns to tell you about that we have now written a separate guide for food and lodging. In this book, our emphasis is on the offbeat locations and the unforgettable local characters that most people could find if they took the time to slow down and look around for a while. The comment heard most often from viewers goes something like this: "I've lived here twenty-five years, and you're showing me places I didn't know existed in my own backyard!" Like the show, this book is about the pleasure that is easily lost in our modern, fast-paced society, the simple joy of roaming around and just looking. It requires getting off the main highway, slowing down, and forgetting about time. Traveling the backroads is as much a state of mind as it is an activity; it means being a visitor or a guest instead of a tourist.

The San Francisco Bay Area is the best place in the world to experience the backroads. We have lived in many parts of the United States and have traveled extensively around Europe and have yet to find anyplace that offers so much diversity within two to three hours of a major city, with weather that is generally cooperative all year round. Whether one heads north to the Wine Country and the rugged Mendocino Coast, east to the Sacramento Valley and the Wild West towns of the Gold Country, or south to the beaches of Santa Cruz and Carmel, one can head out on the backroads every single weekend and still never see everything there is to see.

This book is not a list of tourist sites. It is a companion to the guidebooks that point out the usual places to go. As often as possible, we've included places and people not mentioned in other books about the area. For places that are found in other guidebooks, we've tried to add a new perspective. We assume that our readers are like us, people who would rather cruise down a beautiful country road at 30 miles per hour than speed down the highway at the limit, people who like to explore and are excited by the folks they happen to meet.

The best way to use this book is to pick no more that two or three destinations per day and then head out. When possible, we have included approximate driving times. Within each chapter, the stories are arranged geographically. Although maps are included in the book, it's a good idea to take along a larger, more detailed map that may show every road, no matter how small. Then take off and find some spots of your own. Throw the book in your car and keep it handy if you happen to find yourself in the country. Make notes in it. Use it.

Keep in mind that some of our destinations do not have street addresses. In some backroads towns, the residents do not use them; the place you're looking for is "just down the block from the post office" or "one road beyond the stop sign." We've included directions to each destination; if you get into town and the location is not obvious, just **ask** someone. You might even make a new friend.

Some words of caution: The backroads are ever changing. Country property has a way of becoming prime real estate, and charm has a tough time competing with potential profit. A wonderful farm or inn can become a shopping center

The Bay Area

almost overnight. Also, most of the destinations in this book are mom-and-pop-type operations; they do not have the heavy financial backing of major tourist attractions. As a result, hours can fluctuate, and if the kid at home gets sick, the business might be closed for the day. Please call ahead to see if hours, admission, or location have changed. We've provided a phone number for each destination (each one that has a phone, that is). This is particularly important for those of you who require wheelchair access. We have tried to provide information on places that have made a special point of access, but for many destinations, access may be only partial or even nonexistent. Call first.

Finally, a word about the writing of this book. The television show is about Jerry driving around in his convertible visiting places and meeting people. Though he is the field producer of most of the segments, the show is always a collaboration among his coproducer, the crew, and the research staff stuck indoors at the office. Writing the book version of the show was a similar collaboration between husband and wife. Our stories are not transcripts of television shows. We have tried to add a new dimension to each location and provide the kind of detailed information that television's time requirements prohibit. For simplicity, we decided that the book should follow the feeling of the show and use Jerry again as the voice. Thus many of the stories you will read are written in the first person, the *I* meaning Jerry. However, the book was a collaboration in the truest sense.

There is much to see out there, and we hope you find some new stories on your own. One final reminder: While you're out driving slowly to take in the sights, some motorists will be in a hurry. Pull over to let others pass, and drive defensively.

JERRY GRAHAM'S
MORE BAY AREA BACKROADS

North Bay

As mentioned in our first book, *Jerry Graham's Bay Area Backroads*, most Bay Area residents and visitors travel north when they head out on the backroads. Most go to the Napa and Sonoma wine regions, which continue to expand dramatically. In the past five years, the number of wineries in the Napa Valley alone has tripled. And with the growth of the wine industry, fine restaurants have followed. Why wouldn't that attract lots of visitors?

The North Bay counties are also blessed with a natural beauty that is difficult to match, whether it's the rugged coastline of Sonoma, the fertile valleys of Napa, or the protected forests and parkland of Marin. This region was also the least affected by the major earthquake that rocked the Bay Area in October 1989.

The drive to the North Bay takes you across the Golden Gate Bridge, which on the return trip offers a beautiful view of San Francisco, as seen from the hills outside Sausalito. Unfortunately, in the past few years, like the other major thoroughfares in the Bay Area, the Golden Gate Bridge has become more and more crowded with traffic; so be prepared for slowdowns. Try to think of it as having more time to enjoy the view.

CHAPTER **1** Marin County

AREA OVERVIEW

We'll begin by driving across the symbol of the San Francisco Bay Area, the Golden Gate Bridge, into Marin County. Just minutes from the city you can be in the famous waterfront town of Sausalito, and in an hour or so you can travel to the farthest points in the county. The two major roads are Highway 101, which is the freeway on the Marin side of the bridge that cuts inland until reaching the coast 300 miles to the north, and Route 1, which snakes its way along the coast.

Marin County is one of the wealthiest counties in the Bay Area, but its population is a diverse mixture of folks from stylish towns like Sausalito to working-class cities like Novato. Perhaps most important of all, it is a county of exceptional beauty, thanks in great part to the huge expanses of oceanfront protected by the Golden Gate National Recreation Area. The main population centers are near Highway 101; the farther west you travel, the more countrified it gets. We will visit both sides of the county, starting off in Sausalito.

THE *WAPAMA*

In our first book, we suggested that a good place to get an overview of the entire Bay Area is the Bay Model, which is a huge indoor facility run by the Army Corps of Engineers. In less than an hour you can walk around several counties, over bridges, and above tunnels from Sonoma to San Mateo. This replica of San Francisco Bay and its interconnecting bodies of water is like a giant three-dimensional map that gives you a sense of where everything is in relation to San Francisco.

When you're at the Bay Model, you may notice a remarkable-looking antique steam schooner on the dry dock next door, to the east. That's the *Wapama*, built in 1915 and now the last wooden coastal steamer left in the United States. Once upon a time there were hundreds of such boats working the lumber route between the forests of northern California and the growing urban centers in central and southern California. The fleet was nicknamed the "Scandinavian navy" due to the abundance of Swedish and Norwegian immigrants working the line.

For years the *Wapama* had been docked at the Hyde Street Pier in San Francisco and was open to visitors. When time and the elements caught up with her, she was moved to Sausalito for a major restoration, still in progress.

There are two ways to get on board. One is to visit on Saturday mornings, when a guided tour is given. Another is to attend the on-board monthly party—work party, that is. Most of the restoration is being done by volunteers who show

Point Reyes Station

Novato

101

Sir Francis Drake
Blvd.

San Rafael

Marin

Mill Valley

Tiburon

Sausalito

up for these events, roll up their shirtsleeves, and take hammer or sandpaper in hand.

Whichever way you choose to see the *Wapama,* it's fun to go on board. Though there's still plenty of work to do to get her shipshape again, already you can see the fine workmanship that went into such vessels of yore. At one time these lumber-hauling boats were the only means of transportation up and down the California coast, so among the surprises is finding a grand staircase and an elegant passenger salon on the upper deck.

THE *WAPAMA, dry-docked just east of the Bay Model; look for the sign off Bridgeway near Spring Street. Guided tours are offered every Saturday at 11 A.M.; volunteer work parties are scheduled about every three weeks. Phone: (415) 332-8409.*

HOW TO GET HERE: *From San Francisco, take the Sausalito–Marin City exit off Highway 101, turn right off the ramp, and head south toward downtown on Bridgeway. At the third stoplight you will see a large supermarket called Molly Stone. Turn left and follow the signs to the Bay Model, and park in the lot next door.*

RICHARDSON BAY AUDUBON CENTER AND LYFORD HOUSE ②

Do you know what the fastest-growing spectator sport in America is? My guess was basketball, and when the ranger at the Richard Bay Audubon Center said the answer was "birding," I thought I was right (Larry Bird, Boston Celtics? Never mind). Anyway, here on the shores of Marin's Richardson Bay is the birdwatchers' equivalent of the Superdome.

This is a place where 80 species of water birds set up housekeeping at various times of the year—and close behind are the flocks of humans equipped with their binoculars and guidebooks. Most of this sanctuary is for the birds, literally. In fact, only 11 acres of this 900-acre sanctuary is dry and good for two-legged, nonwinged creatures to walk on; the rest is bayland, soggy to one degree or another at various times of the day and year. Human-type visitors are invited to wander along the trails past salt marshes and tide pools and to participate in the center's tours and programs (the latter include kayaking and children's outings).

One of the main attractions on this land is the Lyford House, a cheerful Victorian house that serves as a museum of sorts. Originally built nearby on Strawberry Point, this was the first house in Marin to have indoor plumbing. By the 1960s the house had fallen into abandoned disrepair and was going to be destroyed when the Point was being turned into a housing development. But a group of citizens pooled resources, floated the historic house across the bay on a barge, and helped fix the place up into its current condition. Inside is a surprisingly small but lovely home filled with antiques and furnishings of the Victorian era, plus several original prints of John Audubon's wildlife drawings. During a tour, you could be pressed into witness service, as the home is often rented out for weddings and receptions.

RICHARDSON BAY AUDUBON CENTER AND SANCTUARY, *376 Greenwood Beach Road, Tiburon. Phone: (415) 388-2524. The wildlife sanctuary is open Wednesday through Sunday, 9 A.M. to 5 P.M.; closed Monday and Tuesday. Admission: $2. LYFORD HOUSE open Sundays 1–4 P.M., November through April. Group tours by appointment. Admission included in sanctuary use fee. Wheelchair accessible.*

HOW TO GET HERE: *Take Highway 101 North from the Golden Gate Bridge to the Tiburon Boulevard–East Blithedale Avenue exit. Turn right off the freeway and continue to Greenwood Beach Road on your right. The Victorian home, visible from Tiburon Boulevard, is on the right side of the road.*

GREEN GULCH FARM ③

"Peace on Earth"—it's a phrase we hear often during the holidays. But here in Marin is a place where the noble concept is applied all year round. Green Gulch is a working farm, 15 acres of rolling hills and rows of fruits, vegetables, herbs, and flowers stretching from Shoreline Highway down to Muir Beach. It is also a Zen Buddhist community, a part of the organization that includes the San Francisco Zen Center and the Tassajara Monastery. Here you will see men and women attempting to live and work in perfect harmony with nature, practicing the concept that daily life is a form of meditation. Don't get the impression that Zen folks are holy hermits, cloistering themselves from the rest of the world. For years, they have operated the successful Tassajara Bakery, they open their remote center near Carmel to tourists, and they also run the immensely popular Greens Restaurant at Fort Mason. They know how to be good and successful hosts.

The beautiful farmland was purchased in the early 1970s from George Wheelwright, coinventor of the Polaroid Land camera. The Wheelwright home is the main building on the farm, with a large meeting room above and the dining hall below. Scattered throughout the property are various living quarters for residents and guests.

Those who live here are Zen Buddhist students and priests who work the land, tend to spiritual practices, and are dedicated to awakening "the spirit of kindness and realistic helpfulness." Not surprisingly, visitors travel from great distances, including Europe and Japan, to live and study in this tranquil and beautiful setting.

Visitors are pretty much left to set their own agenda. There is no pressure to think or dress the way the residents do (shaved heads on both men and women are not an uncommon sight). All that is expected of the visitor is respect toward others and the land. As you might imagine, it's usually very quiet here.

Although there are accommodations for a limited number of overnight guests, most visitors come to spend a Sunday at Green Gulch. You can stroll the grounds around the garden, hike the trails into the hills, or, if you wish, participate in the Sunday morning program, which includes meditation instruction at 8:30 A.M., a talk or sermon, followed by tea on the deck of the Wheelwright Center. You can also join in for a wholesome vegetarian meal, usually soup, salad, and bread, the vegetables grown on the farm, the bread freshly baked. The meal is served dining-hall style. You stand in line and serve yourself, then share a large table with others. A donation of $5 per meal is requested.

Another way to spend time at the farm is to take classes. A variety of workshops and seminars are offered all year round, including some of a spiritual nature and others about organic gardening and related crafts like making wreaths and drying herbs.

Good times to visit Green Gulch Farm include the Buddha's birthday, an annual celebration in early April that includes wildflower gathering and a picnic, and during the Christmas and Hanukkah season, when the shopping frenzy may drive you to seek some real peace on earth.

GREEN GULCH FARM ZEN CENTER, *Muir Beach. Phone: (415) 383-3134. The public is welcome on Sundays and for weekend workshops and celebrations; you can call for a schedule of activities and for information about overnight accommodations.*

HOW TO GET HERE: *From San Francisco, take the Golden Gate Bridge to Highway 101. Exit for Route 1–Stinson Beach, and follow the road toward the ocean. After several miles of winding, you will come to the entrance to Green Gulch on the left. (If you get to the Pelican Inn, you missed the turn.)*

POINT REYES BIRD OBSERVATORY ④

The Point Reyes Bird Observatory is not connected to the rest of the Point Reyes National Seashore (you get there by going through Bolinas), but other than that point of confusion, this is a fine place to visit on a clear day. You can walk on self-guided nature trails that wind along the ocean, through high grass, brush, and wildflowers. And though, as the name implies, there are a variety of birds to see, the main attraction here is watching scientists watch birds.

The Point Reyes Bird Observatory is a study center where long-term studies of landbird, shorebird, and seabird behavior are conducted. Since this center is located at the water's edge, this is the end of the line for landbirds that have lost their way. About 20 nets are set around the property to catch these birds for banding and study. Rest assured, the birds are not harmed by the nets and are detained only briefly. Tiny bands are attached to their legs and they are set free, to be caught again later for further study. No experimentation is done here.

When you visit the center, you will first come to a small and inviting museum where you can learn about the various projects, past and present. You'll probably see a group of schoolkids holding baby birds and listening to their heartbeats. Then you may go on a walk on your own or with staff members while they check the nets and bring stray birds back to the center for banding. It is a rare opportunity to see wild birds in the hand.

According to Dave De Santi, the observatory's scientific director for landbirds, these birds give us much information about the effects the changing ecosystem is likely to have on us. In effect, these fragile creatures offer us a preview of things to come. They are at the top of the animal food chain, and because they metabolize their food quickly, they eat large quantities of raw food from the oceans and forests of our planet. Hazardous elements in nature will show up in them long before humans are affected, like the canaries taken down into coal mines to warn humans of a low oxygen supply. In this age of concerns about the greenhouse effect and climatic change, studying these fragile creatures takes on increasing urgency.

Scientific importance notwithstanding, this is also a beautiful part of the shoreline. There are lovely trails from the center that wind through wildflowers and scrub brush, making for an ideal setting for a hike.

POINT REYES BIRD OBSERVATORY, *Mesa Road, Bolinas. Phone: (415) 868-1221. Open dawn to dusk daily, April 1 through summer; open Wednesday, Saturday, and Sunday, mid-November through March. Activities vary with the seasons. Most banding work is done in the summer months. Admission: Free.*

HOW TO GET HERE: *From San Francisco, cross the Golden Gate Bridge to Highway 101 North. Take the Stinson Beach exit and stay on Route 1 past Stinson Beach about 5 miles to a T-intersection at Bolinas Road. Be advised that the road is unmarked. Look for a big white farmhouse opposite the intersection. Turn left, and while heading into the center of town, look for Mesa Road on the right. Take Mesa all the way to the ocean and the observatory.*

The newest facility at Point Reyes National Seashore is the Environmental Education Center, located at the southern end of the park. Here weekend seminars for adults and children are held throughout the year. This is a "roughing it" facility, with cabins for dormitory-style sleeping, meals and classes held in a modern, attractive wood-and-glass main building, and outdoor sites set up for photography, bird walks, environmental awareness study, and lessons about understanding the food chain.

As the center's brochure says, "The camp has a kitchen but no cook; a woodpile but no wood carrier; lanterns but no lamplighter." You become all the above

POINT REYES ENVIRONMENTAL EDUCATION CENTER

for a weekend. Consider it a step above camping during a structured weekend with an educational goal in mind.

POINT REYES NATIONAL SEASHORE, *40 miles north of San Francisco off Route 1, west of Olema. Open 8 A.M. to sundown daily. Admission: Free. Main information number: (415) 663-1092.*

HOW TO GET HERE: *From San Francisco, cross the Golden Gate Bridge to Highway 101 North. Take the Sir Francis Drake Boulevard exit and follow it all the way to Olema. Turn right, and look for the signs for the entrance to Point Reyes National Seashore. Head for Limantour Road, and watch for the signs to the hostel.*

DIG THOSE CLAMS!

Here's an activity for those who have always wanted to wallow gleefully and guilt-free in the mud. I guarantee you'll get dirty, wet, cold, and tired, but you'll probably catch some clams, if you join one of the regularly scheduled clam-digging expeditions that take off from Lawson's Landing at Dillon Beach.

Dillon Beach is an unusual section of coastline; in contrast to the wide-open spaces of nearby Point Reyes National Seashore, Dillon Beach is privately owned. It is also Marin County's northernmost beach. Here you'll find huge sand dunes rising up from the ocean not far from rows of cottages and a trailer park. The land was originally purchased in the late 1800s by George Dillon, who thought this would be a dandy spot for a resort. And in fact, a hotel prospered here for several years. In the 1920s the Lawson family took over, and they still control the local concessions, including the grocery store, entrance gate ($2 car fee), and the offshore fishing, camping, and clam-digging operations.

The Lawsons run the five-minute barge ride out to the sand bar where the mollusks are. They'll also rent you a shovel and other necessary equipment. You'll quickly discover that the art of clam-digging involves wandering around looking down at the sand until you think you've found one under the mud. Then you stamp your foot. If a clam is there, it will squirt at you—in your face if you don't watch out. Then you start digging. Your catch will be 2 or 3 feet below the surface.

Most likely there will be some very experienced diggers in your group, and probably some first-timers, too. If you are of the latter category, the pros—probably one of the many members of the Lawson family—will show you the ropes. If you just want to watch, that's OK, too. This is not a serious enterprise; someone is always slipping or sliding or getting squirted, and folks laugh a lot. Everyone is brought down to the lowest common denominator of ugly clothes, thigh-high boots, and mud, mud, mud.

There are three kinds of clams to be mined here: Washington, geoduck, and horseneck. None is what you would call attractive. These are big, tough guys that are best used chopped up in chowder or ground for fritters and patties. The locals swear that these clams make the best chowder anywhere.

LAWSON'S LANDING AND DILLON BEACH, *on Dillon Beach Road off Highway 1, on Tomales Bay. Phone: (707) 878-2443. Open during the school year Thursday through Tuesday (closed Wednesday), 7 A.M. to 5 P.M.; during the summer, open daily; closed December and January.*

Day use fee for the dunes: $4 per person; camping, $9 a night. Barge rides out to the clamming area cost $2.50 per adult, $1.50 per child 12 and under.

HOW TO GET HERE: *From San Francisco, take the Golden Gate Bridge and continue on Highway 101 North until the turnoff for Route 1–Stinson Beach. Take Route 1 past the town of Marshall to Dillon Beach Road. Turn left. Follow the signs to Lawson's Landing. It's almost on the Sonoma county border.*

I'm wary of calling anything the "absolute best" of anything, but I'm tempted to use it here. I can safely say that I've never seen a better place to take kids than the Bay Area Discovery Museum. Children and adults can learn and play together in an atmosphere that looks more like a series of cozy playrooms than a stuffy museum.

BAY AREA DISCOVERY MUSEUM

The staff takes great pains to emphasize that this is not a day-care center but a real museum, defined by Director Diane Frankel as a place to preserve, collect, interpret, and display things. Most of the exhibits at the Discovery Museum are hands-on, learn-by-doing displays. The idea is to teach that learning is a lifelong process and that it can be fun. There are no computers, no video exhibits. Learning is encouraged by having the kids manipulate materials, not watch them.

The museum is divided into several areas. One is an architecture and design section set inside an environment resembling a Victorian house. Here you can draw your dream house at a drafting table using real tools of the trade, create a design on a "color shapes wall," then build a three-dimensional model in the Space Maze—the ultimate giant erector set.

The Discovery Theater is a place to introduce yourself and your kids to the sheer fun of the stage. Costumes and makeup are available for all, and there's a stage with several changing backdrops. Impromptu theatrical performances are encouraged. Heaven only knows how many future Oliviers and Streeps may get their start here.

The most popular area seems to be the Discovery Boat, a real rockin' re-creation of a Monterey Bay fishing vessel. Here kids can learn how to tie sailor's knots, fish for crabs, and generally get the feeling of being in a boat at sea. Adults are invited to crawl through the underwater adventure tunnel located below deck. Everybody can experience the sights and sounds of the sea, with starfish, herring, and kelp visible through the aquarium-style windows.

There are several more "learning environments," but I think you get the idea. Rules you should know about before you visit: All children must be accompanied by an adult (this is not a day-care center or an amusement park), and no running, eating, or smoking is allowed. Be prepared for, shall we say, a certain level of sound; all that learning does create some noise. Most of the exhibits are geared for ages 2 through 12. A new theme is established each month, and the theme is carried throughout the exhibits (thus you can return frequently and not get tired of the same old stuff). School groups are admitted free (with advance reservations), and special arrangements for birthday parties can be made (again, be sure to call ahead).

Note that there are plans to move the Discovery Museum elsewhere in Marin sometime in late 1990. Do call ahead to check the current address and admission price.

BAY AREA DISCOVERY MUSEUM, *428 Town Center Drive, Town Center Shopping Mall, Corte Madera. Phone: (415) 927-4722. Open Wednesday through Sunday, 11 A.M. to 5 P.M. Admission: $1 per person.*

HOW TO GET HERE: *From San Francisco, cross the Golden Gate Bridge and stay on Highway 101 North to the Tamalpias Drive exit. Cross over the freeway to the Town Center Mall. The museum is located between Thrifty Drug and World Savings.*

MAD DOGS AND STICKY WICKETS ⑧

Noel Coward was probably not thinking about Marin County when he wrote that "Mad dogs and Englishmen go out in the midday sun." Poor Noel never made the acquaintance of the Marin Cricket Club. Try not to make the same oversight, especially if you'd like to be party to an afternoon of British charm and tradition. While their colonial neighbors are playing or watching baseball, the Cricketeers are showing up at Piper Park in Larkspur for a ripping round of cricket. Decked out in their whites, these lads are a touch of Rex Harrison and Leslie Howard with a dash of Monty Python. Jolly good fun!

The Marin Cricket Club begins the game around 11:30 A.M. each Sunday between April and October. After an often lively debate about who will be the captains and who will be on which team, there are warm-ups, as in baseball. However, in cricket, the pitcher throws a wooden ball toward a batter holding what looks like a fraternity paddle. The idea is to hit the ball where the fielders can't get it and then to run between the wickets (posts instead of bases) to score runs. It does sound a lot like baseball, but the rules are so involved that to explain them all takes an afternoon—or at least the length of a game. Not that it matters. The entertainment for those of us on the sidelines is to hear the lines these expatriates throw at each other and to witness the obviously wonderful time they are having.

Visitors are sometimes asked to join in, or at least to have a try at hitting the ball. Afterward, everyone is invited to head over to a nearby English pub for some suds and a few rounds of darts. If you are an Anglophile, you will enjoy seeing the club in action. Besides, the regulars appear to be good cricket players, and at the very least you get to see a lively game free of charge in a beautiful park. The club has been going for more than 50 years now, and the players can't believe their good luck in having California weather to play in.

MARIN CRICKET CLUB, *Piper Park, Larkspur. For more information, call the Larkspur Parks and Recreation Department, (415) 924-4777. Club meets around 11:30 A.M. Sundays, April to October.*

HOW TO GET HERE: *From San Francisco, take the Golden Gate Bridge to Highway 101 North. Continue to Lucky Drive. As you exit, turn right at the stop sign, which will take you under the highway overpass. Stay on Lucky Drive through the three-way stop and a stoplight. Around Redwood High School, Lucky Drive automatically becomes Dougherty Drive. Continue along Dougherty Drive past the high school athletic fields until you come to the police station on the right side of the road. (If you reach the Lucky Shopping Center, you've gone too far.) The entrance to the police station is also the entrance to Piper Park. Continue straight to the softball field.*

Bernie Fogarty lives in a typical-looking home on a typical-looking street in San Rafael. You would never know from the outside what goes on in his basement. . . . That's where Bernie creates his art using things most people would rather do without, such as spider webs and worms. Yes, worms. And who knows, by the time you read this, he may be onto some new idea.

ART FOR BERNIE'S SAKE

You've got to meet Bernie. He's a robust man with a flowing white mustache and beard and a constant sparkle in his eyes. Now retired from a life as a carpenter, he seems to laugh his way through his days, making things and then showing them to people who stop by. He also writes and publishes books about his creations.

While living in Australia, Bernie got the idea to create "peg" art. Clothespins are called pegs Down Under (and in a lot of other countries). So he started making designs by taking the clips off the pins and putting the two pieces of wood together. Some of his creations will amaze you: intricate boxes that look like fine Oriental carvings, windmills with working lights, cosmetic cabinets, chairs . . . whatever strikes his fancy. It doesn't sound like it would be much, but these pieces are impressive, especially when you realize that Bernie never cuts a clothespin. They must fit together whole.

If your tastes run to the bizarre, you might be interested in Bernie's arachnid room. Here you will see 60 or more plaques on the wall made from spiders' webs.

Bernie stalks the webs all around the house, trying not to disturb the spider, and then spray paints the intricate web onto a lacquered board.

For the ultimate, ask to see his worm paintings. Bernie's latest venture is letting large worms wiggle through an oil-based paint, then putting them on a canvas. After they're done "painting," he has devised a way to allow the worms to roam back through sand and clean themselves off unharmed, before returning to his dirt-filled wheelbarrow. Is it art? You'll have to be the judge.

This is not a gallery. Nothing is for sale. Bernie says if he sold his creations, he wouldn't be able to look at them, which would defeat the purpose. The reason to come here is to be entertained and fascinated by one of the many original characters that make the backroads and the Bay Area so special.

BERNIE FOGARTY'S ART, *319 Bayview Street, San Rafael. Phone: (415) 453-3494. Call first to make sure he's home. Bernie will tell you how to get there.*

MARIN WILDLIFE CENTER

Think of the Marin Wildlife Center as a combination zoo, hospital, and school. It has some permanent residents, but mainly it's a temporary home for about 4,000 animals each year. Most of them have been orphaned, injured, or left homeless due to suburban development. The main goal at the center is to rehabilitate them and return them to the wild.

The setting is not what you might expect for an operation of this kind. Instead of being out in the woods, the center is located a few minutes from downtown San Rafael, in a parklike setting across from a stream and several playing fields. The main building serves as the hospital and administration headquarters, with several pools and cages with paths connecting them. The place was originally built as a petting zoo for exotic animals, but with the expanding consciousness of the 1970s, the focus was changed to protecting animals instead of entertaining humans.

As Director Marsha Mather-Thrift explained, "People began to see animals arrive on their doorstep. As more people moved in, more animals were injured and in need of care." With the building boom in the area, it was time to help the animals and to teach new Marin residents how to live with wild creatures. And the main lesson is that wild animals should be left wild.

Visitors to the center come away with an increased awareness of what is in their own backyards. They are urged to know what might be hiding in the bushes and underneath the weeds and who might be roaming around at night. Many examples of such animals are in the Wildlife Center, including bobcats, raccoons, possum, and an assortment of birds.

The permanent residents are animals that can never return to the wild for one reason or another. Examples of these are long-legged snowy egrets and a large bear. The latter had been adopted as a cub by a logging family; when the bear grew up, it ran away and was found wandering in a park, unable to fend for itself. Rarest is the 31-year-old golden eagle that lives at the Wildlife Center; since its kind is becoming extinct, this may be your only chance to see one.

There is a touching irony for the many volunteers who help run the center. Though they are motivated by a love for animals, they must take care not to become attached to the transient residents. In fact, tricks are employed to prevent the animals from becoming attached to people. Volunteers intentionally make frightening noises outside the animals' cages and occasionally spray them with hoses. These are not sadistic acts; it's for the purpose of making sure the animals will want to stay in the wild and never encounter another human again. However, inside the hospital building, a few pets are kept around to satisfy the volunteers' need to cuddle some of their wards.

Whether you talk to Marsha Mather-Thrift or to any of the staff or volunteers, you will learn something at the Wildlife Center. You'll also get a closer look at some of your wildlife neighbors who usually scatter as soon as they sense your presence.

By the way, if you were struck by the name Mather-Thrift, so was I. Marsha acknowledged to me that she is a direct descendant of the ultraconservative New England Mathers, Cotton and Increase; but she says she would rather be known as a descendant of another relative, Stephen Mather, the founder of the National Park Service.

MARIN WILDLIFE CENTER, *76 Albert Park Lane, off B Street, San Rafael. Phone: (415) 454-6961. Open Tuesday through Sunday, 9:30 A.M. to 4:30 P.M. Admission: Free.*

HOW TO GET HERE: *From San Francisco, take the Golden Gate Bridge to Highway 101. Follow 101 North to the Central San Rafael exit. Turn left on Third Street and continue to B Street. Turn left on B Street and continue to Albert Park Lane. Turn left and continue to the Wildlife Center.*

THE ORIGINAL BOYS' TOWN

When driving north of San Rafael on Highway 101, you will pass the striking Frank Lloyd Wright–designed Civic Center on the right side of the road. A few minutes farther up the road, you can see off in the distance another architectural wonder, a tribute to the past and to glories on high. Set back from the freeway in the rolling, wooded hills of Marin, St. Vincent's School, with its Italian Renaissance towers, magnificent chapel with towering stained-glass windows, and formal gardens, was built with the idea that the presence of grandeur would rub off on pupils and help them develop high ideals.

With all due respect to Father Flanagan, Spencer Tracy, and Mickey Rooney, St. Vincent's was the original Boys' Town. Its story begins in 1855, when the Daughters of Charity of St. Vincent de Paul came to Marin to establish a school.

The first boarders were girls, but the home soon became a residence for orphaned, abandoned, and court-dependent boys. By 1890 some 600 boys aged 7 to 13 were living at St. Vincent's.

The spectacular buildings and lovely gardens were built in sections, under the aegis of Monsignor Francis McElroy, who did not have the money to build everything at once. As a result, a variety of styles are present, from the stucco, tile-roofed California mission—type buildings to the intricacies of the carved white marble inside the chapel. Originally the boys lived in the ornate buildings, but recently new housing has been built for them on a distant hillside overlooking the main area. The school is now run by the Catholic Youth Organization and continues to serve wards of the court, many of them emotionally or developmentally handicapped.

The ornate original buildings of St. Vincent's are the real attraction for visitors. If you call ahead, you can arrange for a docent-led tour that includes the magnificent chapel and its 15 beautiful windows, the courtyard garden, and the Depot, a large thrift shop run by a women's auxiliary. Father David, who runs the boys' program, is a real charmer who sets the mood of warmth and welcome for all visitors. He and his colleagues will make you feel right at home.

One example of the sense of whimsy that prevails at St. Vincent's is the entrance to the place. You enter via a long drive up a eucalyptus-lined dirt road that has a posted speed limit of 9½ mph. They figured if the sign said "Drive Slowly" or "Speed Limit 10 mph," no one would pay attention. Everyone is so struck by the odd number that the sign works.

ST. VINCENT'S SCHOOL, *St. Vincent's Road, Marinwood. Phone: (415) 479-8831. Tours by appointment; you can attend Mass on Sunday, 8 to 10 A.M. No admission charge to visit the campus.*

HOW TO GET HERE: *From San Francisco, take the Golden Gate Bridge and Highway 101 North to the Marinwood exit. Head east (to the right) for ⅓ mile and you will come to the entrance. You can see the tower from the freeway exit.*

OLD DIXIE SCHOOLHOUSE ⑫

Believe it or not, there's a bit of Old Dixie in Marin County. Just a few blocks off the main drag, in the center of a suburban neighborhood, stands a lovely little schoolhouse, vintage 1864. It was built by one of Marin's pioneers, an Irish immigrant named James Miller. As the legend goes, many of Miller's construction workers were Confederate sympathizers, and they dared him to name the school Dixie. Miller was a man who liked a dare, so he accepted the challenge. Thus we have a place named the Old Dixie Schoolhouse right here on the Bay Area's backroads.

Today the one-room schoolhouse stands in front of the modern Miller Creek Middle School. The old building stands as a monument to the days when ranch children of all ages traveled miles and miles to get some learnin', all of them in the same classroom. One step inside, and it feels like you've gone back in time. You'll see a 37-star flag, McGuffey readers, and little school desks, the ones in the front row designed for the youngest children and larger desks in back for the older kids.

Most interesting is the list of punishments. Little boys were subject to punitive action for such activities as profane language (10 lashes) and putting little girls' pigtails into inkwells (8 lashes). There don't seem to be any punishments listed for little girls, who, presumably, never misbehaved in those days. But the school-marm had to watch her step. She was subject to dismissal for any unseemly behavior, including frequenting a pool hall, marriage, or joining a women's liberation group, particularly the suffragettes.

A good time for you to visit the Old Dixie Schoolhouse is on one of the frequent "Living School Days," when youngsters from local grammar schools come to learn about the good old school days from a docent dressed like an 1870s school-marm, apron, cap, and all. The visiting schoolkids are encouraged to dress in period costume, too. It's wonderful to see how excited they can get when they enter the past, before they head back to their computers and Star Wars lunch boxes.

OLD DIXIE SCHOOLHOUSE, *Las Gallinas Road, Marinwood. Phone: (415) 479-8678. Open on the first Sunday of each month; special tours can be arranged. Call ahead to find out when the next "Living School Days" event will take place. Admission: Free.*

HOW TO GET HERE: *From San Francisco, take the Golden Gate Bridge and continue on Highway 101 North to the Lucas Valley Road exit. Take Lucas Valley Road back over the freeway and head west until you come to the first stoplight. Turn right on Las Gallinas Road and go about 100 yards until you see the schoolhouse on the left. Park in back.*

CHAPTER 2 Sonoma County

Sonoma County is directly north of Marin, bordered on the east by Napa County and on the west by the Pacific Ocean. The nearest destinations to San Francisco, such as Petaluma, can be reached in less than an hour from the Golden Gate Bridge; some of the more distant stops, such as Fort Ross, require about a two-

AREA OVERVIEW

hour drive. As in Marin, Highway 101 provides the most direct inland route, and Route 1 takes you along the coast.

Sonoma is one of the great playgrounds of the Bay Area. While next-door neighbor Napa draws visitors from around the world to its famous wine country, Sonoma goes about its quieter, less chic ways. There are just as many wineries and good places to eat in Sonoma as in Napa; they're just more spread out in Sonoma. In fact, there is probably a little bit more of just about everything in this large and scenic county, including ocean beaches, mountains, parks, resorts, farms, and boomtowns.

Santa Rosa, a solid hour's drive from San Francisco, is the major city; the towns of Sonoma, Petaluma, Sebastopol, Healdsburg, and Occidental highlight unique facets of Sonoma life.

In almost any town, you can stop off at the local Chamber of Commerce or visitors' center to pick up a Sonoma Farm Trails map. This is a list of the farms in the county that are open to visitors and feature everything from animals you can pet to produce you can pick yourself. Or you can write away for a Farm Trails map. Send a legal-size self-addressed, stamped envelope to Farm Trails, P.O. Box 6032, Santa Rosa, CA 95406.

SEARS POINT RACEWAY

Having grown up in Indianapolis, I've always had a special place in my heart for race cars. Though nothing feels as exciting to me as the famous Speedway, here in the Bay Area you can get a taste of raceway action at Sears Point.

In case you're not familiar with the place, Sears Point Raceway is a popular racetrack for various classes of cars. The races, held on weekends during the racing season (usually spring through October), draw thousands, jamming the available space around the 2½-mile track and its 12 tricky turns. The track is also the home of the Bob Bondurant School for high-performance driving, famous for its James Bond–ish program designed for chauffeurs of politicians and high-level executives. The Bondurant School is in operation during the week, teaching drivers of various calibers and interests how to get the most out of their cars, including such skills as steering safely out of a spin on an oil-slicked road.

You can take a self-guided backroads-style tour of the place on weekdays. You drive right in, sign a liability waiver at the front office, and then take a behind-the-scenes look at high-performance driving.

For insurance reasons, common folk like us are not allowed on the track itself. But there's still plenty to do and see. You're free to walk or drive to the various vantage points around the track—closer than you might be on a crowded race day—and to wander into the shops where mechanics, designers, pit crew members, and drivers are working on their dragsters, classic racers, Indy types, for-

Healdsburg

Santa Rosa

Sebastopol

Petaluma

Sonoma

Sonoma

mula racers, and motorcycles: making major and minor adjustments, timing how long it takes to change a tire, perhaps completely rebuilding a machine.

In the morning you will find the Bondurant drivers going through their paces: weaving around an obstacle course of rubber barriers to test their navigating skills or screeching to a sudden stop to test their reaction time. At noon or thereabouts the Bondurant folks take a lunch break, and the track is turned over to the racers; the car you saw disassembled in the shop at 10:30 A.M. might be out on the track being tested at 200 mph.

This is the kind of destination where you might spend a half hour or most of the day, depending on your fascination with the subject. There is a snack bar on the premises, and plenty of rest room facilities. The best time to go is right before a big race weekend; the shops will be filled with cars, and the lunch break will be quite a show.

SEARS POINT RACEWAY, *located at the junction of Routes 37 and 121, where Sonoma, Napa, and Solano counties meet. Phone: (707) 938-8448. Open 8 A.M. to 5 P.M. Monday through Friday; weekend hours vary. Admission just to look around during the week is free; racing events on weekends can cost as much as $35.*

HOW TO GET HERE: *From San Francisco, take the Golden Gate Bridge to Highway 101 North. Exit at Route 37 and head east toward Vallejo. At the intersection of Routes 37 and 121, look for signs to the Raceway entrance, which will be on the left, clearly marked.*

SAMI'S LI'L HORSE RANCH ②

If you happen to be driving down the Lakeville Highway that runs along the Petaluma River, you'll probably see some cars pulled over by the side of a farm. The attraction? Sami's li'l horses, or more properly, miniature horses, a special breed that reaches full height at 2 to 3 feet. These are car- and showstoppers. When the babies are around—mini-miniatures—a new dimension is added to the word *cute*. You can just pull off the road and watch for a while, or call ahead for an appointment and a tour of the place.

Sami is Sami Scheuring, who runs this miniature horse-breeding farm with her husband, Ron, a veterinarian in Marin County. Sami is a delightful and funny hostess who will introduce you to your tour guides, her children, John and Tui. They will show you around the ranch and tell you whatever you want to know about miniature horses. Be forewarned: These critters are sold as rather expensive pets, and once your guides show you how easy it is to love them, you could get hooked. In fact, that's how the Scheurings happen to be here. They used to have a lovely suburban home in Marin, complete with a backyard swimming pool. But then they got a miniature horse; now they have a horse-breeding farm in Sonoma.

It's easy to agree that they made the right decision. As you drive down Lakeville Highway, you will pass one horse ranch after another, intermingled with an occasional dairy farm that has been around for generations. It's a bucolic setting. Next door to the Li'l Horse Ranch is a million-dollar facility called Pegasus, where thoroughbreds are raised for the likes of the Kentucky Derby. Although Pegasus is not open to the public, you can occasionally see a beautiful specimen roaming the grounds.

SAMI'S LI'L HORSE RANCH, *near Petaluma, off the Lakeville Highway. Phone: (707) 762-6803. Tours by appointment. No admission charge.*

HOW TO GET HERE: *From San Francisco, take the Golden Gate Bridge to Highway 101 North. Continue to Route 37, which is also marked as the turnoff to Vallejo and Napa. Follow 37 East for a few miles to the Lakeville Highway. Turn left and continue until you find Lakeville Road 3 on your right. Turn right, and the ranch will be the first driveway on the right. The horses are usually clustered near the highway, which is where you are likely to see cars and people clustered to have a look at them.*

Exotic animals have always been a mainstay on the "Backroads" TV show. We have come across herds of llamas, camels, and worms, but I can't remember seeing a more remarkable sight than a gang of ostriches racing pell-mell out of a barn at the Circle M Ranch, just south of the town of Sonoma.

OSTRICH FARM

If you have never seen an ostrich up close, you are in for a treat. These birds are natural comics, with their long gangly legs, wide-eyed heads that swivel on endless necks, and squat middles covered with feathers that seem to grow in all directions. They probably think *we* look ridiculous.

Other ostrich facts: They grow to 9 feet tall, weigh 400 pounds, and can run at 40 mph. Though they are birds, they cannot fly. And like most animals, the babies are adorable: huge eyes that take up most of their head; their brains can't quite figure out how to coordinate the long neck and legs, except maybe to run in circles for hours on end.

As of this writing, the Circle M is the only ostrich farm in the Bay Area. Carolyn and Bob McKean are the ostrich keepers, and they've become experts. They've even written a little pamphlet about the care and feeding of ostriches, which they hope will promote their breeding business.

Until a few years ago, the Circle M Ranch was mainly used by the McKeans for raising quarter horses. They decided to try their hand at ostrich parenting after reading an article in the *New York Times*. In late 1987, seven adult "big birds" arrived at the ranch, and the breeding operation began. Now just about any time of year you might want to visit, you'll see all sizes and shapes of ostriches.

There's no sand here for the ostriches to stick their heads into, but these animals are shy and might run away at the first sight of a stranger. Eventually, though, their curiosity tends to get the best of them, and they might come up to check you out. Though they are not overly aggressive beasts, their kicks can kill, so there will always be a sturdy, high fence between you and any curious ostrich.

You can see the birds from the road, but the McKeans do welcome visitors. I should warn you that Bob makes a living selling ostriches, and he can be a very persuasive talker. (If you leave the Sonoma area with a miniature horse and an ostrich in the back of the family bus, don't say we didn't warn you.) Carolyn, however, is a softie; she admits that she gets attached to the birds and hates to see them go. She'll also show you the eggs. Each weighs about 3½ pounds, and the females can lay as many as 60 of these in a season (no wonder their feathers go in all directions!).

CIRCLE M RANCH, *1340 Napa Road, Sonoma. Phone: (707) 938-2881. Call ahead for an appointment.*

HOW TO GET HERE: *From San Francisco, take the Golden Gate Bridge to Highway 101 and continue north to the Route 37 exit. Turn right toward Napa and continue east. Bear left onto Route 121 to the Sonoma turnoff on Route 12. At Napa Road, turn right and continue to 1340.*

TRAINTOWN
④

Even though the trains stopped coming to Sonoma years ago, there is still activity on the rails at Traintown, 1 mile south of the Sonoma Town Plaza. Billed as the best-developed miniature railroad in the nation, this is an elaborate park built around a ride on small trains pulled by steam-powered locomotives.

Traintown was built in the 1950s, back when it was possible for jus' folks to buy 10 acres of land in the heart of what is now a busy Wine Country town. It was the kind of project that rail buffs have put their hearts into, creating a great ride through tunnels and over bridges on the one-quarter-scale train. It was the idea of the late Stanley Frank, who started in Oakland, building the equipment piece by piece. He bought an old cow pasture south of the town of Sonoma and built his park. The concept was to re-create the feeling of a Sierra town in the 1850s. Recently the founder's son, Robert Frank, completed a bright new station complex complete with a 50-foot clock tower. It's a sight that grabs your attention as you drive into town from the south or out from the north. But you still would have no idea how extensive the place is until you take a ride.

To give you an idea of how visitor-oriented this place is, not too long ago a local mother with a wheelchair-bound daughter told the owners she wished her little girl could enjoy the train. A special flatcar with a ramp was built for handicapped persons and dedicated at a ribbon-cutting ceremony during Barrier

Awareness Week. The very impressed mother called us to make sure Robert Frank's efforts were acknowledged.

The train trip takes about 20 minutes. The landscape is designed to give you the feeling of traveling through the countryside. Everything is in miniature, except for the 2,500 trees that were planted in the 1950s that are now grown, generously providing a shaded ride in the hot summer months. The midway point of the ride features a stop at a small town with authentically designed historic buildings, a petting zoo, and even a miniature outhouse.

Obviously this is a place for kids—for adults who love to show children the way things used to be. Traintown is very well designed and maintained, and it keeps growing. Frank hopes to install a series of waterfalls to add even more drama to the ride. All aboard!

TRAINTOWN, *20264 South Broadway (Route 12), Sonoma. Phone: (707) 996-2559. Open 10:30 A.M. to 5:30 P.M. weekends all year; 10:30 A.M. to 5:30 P.M. daily from June 15 through Labor Day. Admission: $2.40 for adults, $1.80 for kids. Wheelchair accessible.*

HOW TO GET HERE: *From San Francisco, take the Golden Gate Bridge to Highway 101 and continue north to the Vallejo turnoff at Route 37. Take Route 37 eastbound and turn left onto Route 121. Take Route 121 to the Sonoma turnoff on Route 12, which is South Broadway, and continue to Traintown, which will be on your right.*

While we're on the subject of trains, if you're a history buff or a wine lover who's had enough, you might want to visit the Depot Museum, located a block off the Sonoma Town Plaza. This cheerful yellow train depot was built in the 1880s and played an important role in the development of Sonoma. It was the northern terminus for businessmen and vacationers from San Francisco who came up for the resorts, spas, and historical sights.

DEPOT MUSEUM

The local historical society has turned this into a charming spot to visit. The depot office has been restored to look just like it did when train tickets to San Francisco cost a quarter. Other rooms have displays of what various homes in the area were like, featuring mannequins wearing period costumes. Outside is a collection of cattle cars, a refrigerator car, and a caboose, with a nice parklike area, including some picnic tables. It's a good place to spend a half hour or so.

SONOMA DEPOT MUSEUM, *270 First Street, Sonoma. Phone: (707) 938-9765. Open Wednesday through Sunday, 1 to 4:30 P.M. Admission: Adults, 50 cents; children 12 to 18, 25 cents; free under 12 if accompanied by adult.*

HOW TO GET HERE: *From San Francisco, take the Golden Gate Bridge to Highway 101 and continue north to Route 37. Take Route 37 eastbound. At Sears*

Point, turn left onto Route 121 and continue to the Sonoma turnoff on Route 12. Turn left and follow South Broadway to the Sonoma Town Plaza. From the plaza, go north on First Street West. The Depot Museum will be on your right.

VELLA CHEESE COMPANY

The Sonoma Town Plaza is so inviting that you might be tempted to spend your entire visit in the park or strolling around the square. As pleasant as this might be, you're cheating yourself by not extending your walk by just two blocks to the north, where you will find a lovely historic brick building that is the home of the Vella Cheese Company. Stop in for a tour and a taste.

Vella has been in business since 1931, making cheese based on family traditions that started in Sicily. Ignazio Vella is the big cheese here. Ig, as he's called, seems to be constantly on the prowl, checking the cheesemakers in back, sweeping up, urging his young employees behind the counter to give a customer a taste of this or that. Ig loves visitors, especially when they'll listen to him tell stories about life in Sonoma and, specifically, his products. He'll probably tell you that Cary Grant was a steady customer who used to send wheels of Vella's jack to friends around the country. Or he'll bring out his newspaper clippings to show you his raves.

The pride and joy of Vella cheese is the famous dry Monterey jack, which has been aged from seven months to two years. It tastes much like Parmesan, created by Italo-Californians who could not get their beloved cheese from their homeland during World War I. In the 1930s many cheesemakers produced this dry jack; however, since it is a handmade, labor-intensive product, most cheesemakers have given it up. Vella is one of the few places in the world you can get this delicious grating cheese.

When you enter the Vella Cheese Company, you will first be greeted by the friendly folks behind the retail counter. They will offer you samples and describe the various kinds of cheese made here, including Fontinella, raw-milk cheddars, and the dry Monterey jack. Don't be shy about asking to see more—the real show is in back. You can watch the workers use garden rakes to stir huge vats of curds, scoop them into muslin sacks, then squeeze out the moisture by squishing the sacks against their bellies. Ig or one of his employees will explain the entire process, from milking the cows to coating the wheels of cheese with cocoa, oil, and pepper.

Perhaps you will be curious about the Vella Cheese logo. The bear on the label is in honor of the Bear Flag Revolt, which established California as separate from Mexico and took place just two blocks away. Apparently this explanation was not sufficient for Ig's father, whose reply is now part of the Vella family legacy. "That's fine," he said. "But do bears give milk?"

VELLA CHEESE COMPANY, *315 Second Street, Sonoma. Phone: (707) 938-3232. Open 9 A.M. to 6 P.M. Monday through Saturday; 10 A.M. to 5 P.M. Sunday. Admission: Free.*

HOW TO GET HERE: *From San Francisco, take the Golden Gate Bridge to Highway 101 and continue north to Route 37. Take Route 37 eastbound. At Sears Point, turn left onto Route 121 and continue to the Sonoma turnoff on Route 12. Turn left and follow South Broadway to the Sonoma Town Plaza. Turn right at the plaza onto East Second Street. Take East Second to the factory, which is on the left side of the street.*

Most of the wineries you see in the Sonoma and Napa valleys are fairly new. Hacienda is one of the exceptions. The land is where European grapes were first planted in the mid-1800s by Count Agoston Haraszthy. His spread has since been divided between Hacienda and the larger, more famous Buena Vista Winery.

MORGUE-TURNED-WINERY

The winery building at Hacienda was Sonoma County's first hospital. On a casual visit you would not be aware of the building's past, unless you go downstairs. Here, behind a creaky old door, is the former morgue—a series of little rooms and catacombs that makes for an unusual attraction, to say the least. Appropriately, this area is now used as a—excuse the expression—cooling room.

Most visitors, however, opt for a trip to the tasting room and the surrounding grounds, which are some of the prettiest you'll find at any winery. Picnic tables overlook a valley of vineyards; horses from a nearby ranch amble over to check out what's going on. A pond stocked with catfish is often surrounded by hopeful people with fishing poles.

This is a destination worth building your schedule around, especially if you enjoy gardens and the great outdoors while exploring the Wine Country.

A recent addition to the property is a re-creation of Count Haraszthy's Hungarian villa, which you will pass on the long road up to the winery. At this writing, it is not open to the public, but that may change by the time you visit. Inquire at the tasting room.

HACIENDA WINERY, *1000 Vineyard Lane, Sonoma. Phone: (707) 938-3220. Tasting room hours 10 A.M. to 5 P.M.; tours by appointment. No admission or tasting charge.*

HOW TO GET HERE: *From San Francisco, take the Golden Gate Bridge to Highway 101 and continue north to the Route 37 exit. Take Route 37 eastbound. At Sears Point, turn left onto Route 121 and continue to the Sonoma turnoff on Route 12. Turn left and follow South Broadway to the Sonoma Town Plaza. Head east on East Napa Street (bordering the plaza) and turn left on Seventh Street.*

Follow Seventh Street to a stop sign, and take the less extreme right turn onto Castle Road. Follow Castle Road until you come to two pillars. Go between the pillars, and you will be on Vineyard Lane. Continue to the winery.

PYGMY GOATS
⑧

Truly, the backroads are becoming a breeding ground for the terminally cute. More and more I'm finding farms dedicated to unusual animals, many of them miniatures. Well, you ain't seen nothin' until you've watched a baby pygmy goat wobble around on its spindly little legs. These critters are natural comedians, leaping around in fits and starts, moving all four legs at once, often in opposing directions. And the babies are just part of the ongoing show at the Primrose Pasture Farm.

This is yet another stop on the Sonoma County Farm Trails map, which means that the operators, Al and Loretta Maynard, make it easy for folks to drop by on the weekends and roam around. They have organized their backyard and surrounding land as a place to show off and sell their pygmy goats. First you enter what Loretta calls the "kiddergarten," where the babies and their mothers roam freely. Then there's the shed where the young sleep at night, which leads out to the area where the adults are separated by sex—until it's time to produce more unspeakably cute baby goats. In addition to the living quarters, you can see the "goat aerobics" area, a jungle gym of sorts where the goats can climb and jump and develop proper muscles.

Loretta has names for all of her goat family, except for the neutered baby males, which are put up for sale. She doesn't name them because she's afraid she'll get too attached to sell them. It's easy to see why she'd fall hopelessly in love. They're about the size of a small dog, and they don't bark. Of course, they do have the tendency to chew everything in sight, but Loretta says they can be trained not to. The Maynards swear that many of their customers keep these goats as house pets.

How does one get into the business of selling miniature goats? For Loretta and Al, it was an accident. They started out with dairy goats, but that was too much work. For fun, they bought a couple of pygmies. Two goats suddenly became 11, and they were in business. Now they usually have about 50 goats out back, raised as show animals and for sale. Prices range from about $75 to $200. The Maynards have set up a special program for 4-H students, who can buy a goat by working for it. The Maynards also welcome seniors and the disabled and will bring the goats to the vehicles if visitors are not mobile.

Yet another warning to those who fall in love too easily: Before you visit Primrose Pastures Farm, make a firm decision about whether or not you are willing to drive away with a new pet in your backseat. This is one place I'm glad my wife didn't visit with me, or else we'd now have a tiny goat sharing the backyard with our cats.

PRIMROSE PASTURES PYGMY GOATS, 4327 Primrose Avenue, Santa Rosa. Phone: (707) 585-0696. Open weekends 10 A.M. to 5 P.M.; by appointment during the week. No admission charge.

HOW TO GET HERE: From San Francisco, take Route 101 North toward Santa Rosa. After Rohnert Park, exit at Todd Road. Exit right, then cross back over the highway; immediately turn left onto Frontage Road, which becomes Scenic Road. Follow Scenic to Primrose Avenue; turn left. Continue for about ½ mile, and look for the sign for Primrose Pastures Ranch on the right side of the road.

Celebrity wineries are not an unusual sight north of San Francisco. Pat Paulsen had one; in fact, he used to own an entire town, Asti, until he sold most of it when his marriage ended (the product, however, still bears his name). Film mogul Francis Coppola has a winery north of St. Helena, but it is not open for tours. One of the first and certainly the most accessible show biz–related wineries is the Smothers Brothers' place in the Valley of the Moon, right on Route 12 in the town of Kenwood.

SMOTHERS BROTHERS WINERY

Tom and Dick Smothers began dabbling in viticulture back in the 1960s, with the help of the proceeds from their popular CBS television show. Today they run a well-established operation with a very popular tasting room. They are serious but not somber about their product. So in addition to such premium wines as Smothers Chardonnay, Sauvignon Blanc, Cabernet Sauvignon, Gewürztraminer, and White Riesling, you can also pick up inexpensive table wines called Mom's Favorite Red and Mom's Favorite White.

Lots of folks drop in with the hope of meeting the famous duo. In fact, according to the employees, one of the first questions people ask when they walk through the door is, "Where's Tom and Dick?" The usual reply is, "Oh, they just left." The truth is, it would be rare to find either brother in, since their show biz career has taken off again and they are usually on the road. But you can see vestiges of them throughout the tasting room. In fact, this is probably the first winery in history to decorate the walls with gold records and notices from Variety. It's also the only winery in the world that posts a notice telling where the owners will be performing next. Last but not least, there's a little "while you were out" form with the message "Tom, Mom called" pinned up on display.

This is the kind of place you stop for a quick visit. There is no winery tour, just a tasting room and a gift shop. One of the most popular items is the T-shirt with the message "Mom likes me best." Good old Mom.

SMOTHERS BROTHERS WINERY, corner of Highway 12 and Warm Springs Road,

Kenwood. Phone: (707) 833-1010. Open daily 10 A.M. to 4:30 P.M. Picnic tables available.

    HOW TO GET HERE: *From San Francisco, take the Golden Gate Bridge to Highway 101 and continue north to Route 37. Take Route 37 eastbound toward Vallejo and Napa. At Sears Point, turn left onto Route 121 and continue east to the Sonoma turnoff on Route 12 into Sonoma. At the Sonoma Town Plaza, turn left to stay on Route 12. The winery is on Route 12 in the town of Kenwood.*

BEES, BEES, BEES
⑩

Watching thousands of bees swarming around in someone's backyard may not be your idea of a great way to spend the afternoon. If, on the other hand, you are fascinated by these colorful, buzzing creatures who are capable of producing one of life's sweet mysteries, then head to Earth Grown Honey Farms, which is located in a nice suburban area outside Santa Rosa.

Matthew Jamison is the resident apiculturist, aka the beekeeper, and he has turned his backyard into a regular bee-in. In addition to tending the hundreds of thousands of busy, energetic insects, Matthew bottles and sells honey and teaches classes to all who want to know about the bees without the birds. According to Matt, the California bee is indispensable to the state's agricultural industry, for bees pollinate more than $12 billion worth of crops each year. What's more, they have a fascinating society.

To illustrate bees and their lifestyle, Matthew has designed several displays, including glass cases surrounding hives with as many as 50,000 residents in each, and a large tent with cutaways of hives; those who dare can put on protective gear and walk into a swarm with Matthew.

For the less adventurous, myself included, the value of a visit is simply learning about bees and how they follow their queen. It's a fascinating societal story, and Matthew is a good storyteller. His mission is to see that you leave knowing more about bees than when you came and that you are less afraid of them, too. He will also assure you that there is a great unlikelihood of your getting stung here. The bees are busy doing other things, and the only time they sting is when they are threatened by being swatted or breathed in. Sometimes they are upset by a strange aroma, usually a perfume or hair spray, and I don't know how you could determine ahead of time whether your particular brand would annoy the creatures. However, I can report that our television crew spent several hours among the bees without incident.

If you'd simply like to purchase some honey, there is an "honesty" box out in front by the entrance to the driveway. It's usually stocked with several jars of fresh Earth Grown honey; you can leave your money in the box and move on. Apparently the honor system works well. Matthew says he's never been stung.

EARTH GROWN HONEY FARM, *4640 Valley Quail Lane, Santa Rosa. Phone: (707) 823-8590. Open all year, Saturday and Sunday only. Please call ahead.*

HOW TO GET HERE: *From San Francisco, go up Highway 101 North toward Santa Rosa. Exit at Guerneville Road–Steele Lane, and head west toward Guerneville. Continue on Guerneville Road for about 5 miles, then turn right onto Laguna Road. Go ⅓ mile to Valley Quail Lane, and follow it to the last house on the right.*

Of all the tasting rooms in the Sonoma Wine Country, Shoffeitt's may be the most unusual. Certainly it's the spiciest. This is the home of Shoffeitt's California Seasonings, little bottles filled with things like lemon pepper and salt-free herb blends that you sprinkle on your food.

The Shoffeitt (pronounced "shah-fit") family has been making seasonings since 1966. The business began with the patriarch, William Shoffeitt, creating a variety of seasonings by blending as many as 25 herbs and spices until he got a mixture he wanted.

When William passed away in 1988, he left behind a growing concern as well as a growing family of spicemakers, and they are the main reason a visit to the seasonings factory is so interesting. First of all, they're all women, led by William's widow, June, their three daughters, and their daughters' daughters. And they all look alike.

Add in a cousin or two plus a few friends, and you have an entire work force of enterprising women. They greet guests at the door, take them on tours, blend the seasonings, and bottle and package them, having designed and printed the labels. And when the time came to take advantage of all the folks coming to the neighborhood to taste wine, they built the tasting room, even though they had never tried their collective hands at carpentry or construction before. (Photos of the work parties are proudly displayed in the tasting room.)

The building itself is not terribly inviting from the outside. The fading yellow industrial exterior suggests nothing but a drab warehouse inside. But when you drive around the back to the parking lot, the entrance to the tasting room is much more attractive (for neophyte builders, the Shoffeitts have done a very nice job).

If you're planning to take a tour of the operation, be sure to allow enough time to see the lab, with its test tubes filled with herbs and spices, the bottling line lined up with granddaughters who cap and label, and last but not least, the heart of the operation, the upstairs mixing room. This is where the herbs and spices are measured into giant vats, then sent down a tube to the bottling line below. One warning: If you visit while they are making a batch of pepper, be prepared to hold back your sneezes!

Down in the tasting room, visitors are encouraged to snack on cheese balls, pasta, and dips flavored with various Shoffeitt blends. When a group schedules a tour in advance, a real spread is laid out.

Aside from the chance to get a quick snack and to tour an unusual business, the best part of a visit is a chance to meet the family. They are a remarkable group.

SHOFFEITT'S TASTING ROOM, *420 Hudson Street, Healdsburg. Phone: (707) 433-5555. Open 10 A.M. to 4:30 P.M., Monday through Saturday. Tours and tastings are free.*

HOW TO GET HERE: *From San Francisco, take the Golden Gate Bridge and continue on Highway 101 North past the city of Santa Rosa. Take the first Healdsburg exit, which is Healdsburg Avenue, and bear right. As soon as you cross the metal bridge, turn right onto Front Street. Take the next left onto Hudson Street, and look for the yellowish building on the left-hand corner. Go up to the first driveway and park in the back.*

IF CHICO MARX OWNED A WINERY . . . ⑫

Don't bother to look for Nervo wines at your local store. Nervo is one of those tiny wineries that only sells at the source, which in this case is a little old stone building right off Route 101. I should tell you right away that this is not the sort of place to visit for award-winning wines or esoteric conversation about bouquet and insouciance. The attraction is the cast of characters inside and the fact that you can get a decent bottle of wine for $5 or less.

A visit here is like dropping into a family winery in the Italian countryside. Two guys named Ralo and Bruno hold forth in the tasting room, where they are most likely shooting the breeze with the *paisanos* who drop by every chance they get. This is an unofficial community center, and the community is based on drinking wine and telling stories. It's not unusual for a song to break out, too. Italian flags and photos of the old country adorn the place, and the ceiling and walls are covered with hundreds of business cards left by former visitors; Bruno swears these keep the building up.

Whatever your ethnic background, you will become an honorary Italian if you spend a few minutes with the gang.

A few facts about the wine: They don't age it. The idea is to sell it young and let the customer age it. That way their operating costs are kept down, and they can pass the savings on to the consumer. The winery itself dates back to 1888, when the Nervo family arrived from Italy and set up a winemaking operation. It is now owned by the large neighbor down the road, Geyser Peak, but the corporation leaves the place alone and lets the Nervo gang run it as they please.

Hours are 10 A.M. to 5 P.M. every day except major holidays and the birthdays of the folks who work there. If you have your heart set on a visit, you might want to call ahead. Picnic tables and rest rooms are available.

NERVO WINERY, *19550 Redwood Highway, Geyserville. Phone: (707) 857-3417. Open 10 A.M. to 5 P.M. daily, except holidays and staff birthdays. Admission: Free.*

HOW TO GET HERE: *From San Francisco, take the Golden Gate Bridge and continue on Highway 101 North past Healdsburg. Take the Independence Lane exit about 4 miles north of Healdsburg. Turn right on East Frontage Road, then take the first left, which is the Redwood Highway. Head north to Nervo, which will be on the left.*

As another alternative to wine tasting, how about apple tasting? And I'm not talking just pippins and Granny Smiths. At Walker Apples you get the chance to taste such unusual varieties as the Bellflower, Northern Spy, Arkansas Black, and Winter Banana.

WALKER APPLES
 13

"Try before you buy" is the motto at this family-run operation located deep in Sonoma County's backroads. The Walker family settled in Sonoma in the 1840s; Grandpa Walker planted the first apple orchards in 1912. Today the family farm and business are run by Lee and Shirley Walker; during harvest time you'll find at least four generations on hand around the packing line.

Don't expect to find an elegant tasting room. When you arrive at the Walker farm, after a seemingly endless drive up a hill on a very narrow road, you'll make your way to a large open-air shed where the apples arrive by the truckload from the nearby orchards and are sent down conveyor belts for sorting, inspection, and packing. Lee or Shirley will stop what they're doing and greet you. The tasting area is a little table surrounded by bushels of the kinds of apples that have just been picked: Gravensteins and MacIntoshes in August; Red Delicious, Jonathans, and Bellflowers in early September; Northern Spys and Baldwins in late September; Granny Smiths and Rome Beautys in October; pippins and Arkansas Blacks in November. A paring knife will emerge from Shirley's purse, and you'll be invited to taste as many as you like.

Obviously this is not a formal affair, but you can educate your palate to the subtleties of the "forbidden fruit." For example, the prettiest, the Winter Banana, tastes the worst (but you might want to buy a bag for a lovely centerpiece at home). The variety of flavors is truly amazing.

You can also learn about the reality of farming in this day and age. Growing apples is not a way to get rich in Sonoma County; as Lee will tell you, many apple orchards have given way to the more profitable grapevines. But Lee says he will stick to what he knows. "Apples have been good to us," he says. Taste a couple of slices fresh from the tree, and you will be glad he made the right choice.

WALKER APPLES, *Upp Road, Graton. Phone: (707) 823-4310. Open 9 A.M. to 5 P.M. during harvest time, August 1 through November 15, give or take a few days depending on the year's growing season. Be sure to call ahead. Admission: Free.*

HOW TO GET HERE: *Take Highway 101 North to 116 West, go through Sebastopol, and continue for 4 miles to Graton Road; turn left. Follow Graton Road down into Graton, then turn right and go up the hill that is Upp Road. Don't worry about the sign that says, "Danger, guard chicken on duty." Continue ¾ mile up the narrow road, and you will come to Walker Apples.*

BODEGA HEAD MARINE LAB

The proud joke around Bodega Bay is that this is a town with a hole in its head. That's because at one time there were plans to build a nuclear power plant on Bodega Head, a piece of land across the bay from Route 1 and the main part of town; construction had progressed as far as digging a hole for the foundation before a citizens' group blocked the project, thus leaving the now famous hole in Bodega Head. Less well known is the world-class marine laboratory, run by the University of California at Davis.

The folks who run the Bodega Head Marine Lab have a bit of a dilemma. They attract scientists from around the world to this unique facility, and they would like the public to know what they're doing out here. But since they do their work on a protected reserve, there is concern about letting people wander off to places they should not go. So visits are rather tightly controlled, but they are permitted. An open house with docent-led tours is held every Friday between 2 and 4 P.M., and group tours for other days can be arranged in advance.

The lab is situated on prime oceanfront land, with sweeping views of the shoreline. Inside, scientists research the effects of our modern industrial society on the ocean. Several buildings house a variety of research projects. As Director James Clegg told me, here they study everything from great white sharks to pulp mill effluents. He added that while sharks are more interesting to most people, it is important to know what happens when that nasty waste material is pumped into the water.

The lab is like a cross between a hospital and an aquarium. As you are led through the buildings, you'll see clusters of scientists in their white lab coats peering into tanks filled with ocean creatures. In one aquaculture room is a large tank with a dozen or more Eastern lobsters (which apparently provide a tasty snack after the experiments are over), and there are touch tanks for visitors who like to feel small denizens of the deep.

There is much to see here, better described by the volunteers on the scene than on this page. But Director Clegg doesn't want you to expect a splashy,

Marine World—type show either. "Our work here is basic science," he says, "not very visible or dramatic, but a key to knowledge."

UC BODEGA HEAD MARINE LAB, *Bay Flat Road, Bodega Bay. Phone: (707) 875-2211. Free open house held Fridays, 2 to 4 P.M.; group tours on other days by advance appointment only. Be sure to call ahead to let them know you're coming.*

HOW TO GET HERE: *From San Francisco, take the Golden Gate Bridge and continue north on Highway 101 to the Central Petaluma exit. Go under the freeway and into downtown Petaluma. You will be on Washington. Continue on that road until it becomes Bodega Avenue. Follow Bodega to Valley Ford Road. Bear to the right onto Valley Ford, and it will join Route 1 and take you into Bodega Bay. At the only stop sign in Bodega Bay, turn left and go to the bottom of the hill. Then veer to the right on Bay Flat Road and follow it all the way past the marina to the lab.*

Once upon a time, llamas were a rare sight in northern California. Now several llama farms adorn the Bay Area. There's even a llama bed-and-breakfast place in the Gold Country, the Llamahall Guest Ranch in Sonora.

In the first edition of this book we wrote about Chuck Warner's Pet-a-Llama, formerly of Petaluma; Chuck was one of the first breeders in the area, and business got so good that he needed more room. Now he's located farther north in Sebastopol.

For sheer beauty of the surroundings, few sites can compare with the Llama Loft, also known as the Big Trees Farm of Valley Ford. This is the home of Beulah, Jim, and Tyrone Williams. You can't beat the setting: a Victorian farmhouse set on lush, rolling countryside. And then there's Tyrone. Beulah calls Tyrone the sales manager. He's an incredibly friendly llama who happily greets every visitor. As soon as you get out of your car and start walking toward the house or barn, there is he, nuzzling up to you. If you'll let him, Tyrone will give you a kiss. Believe me, you haven't lived until you've been kissed by a llama. It's an experience that defies description. Mercifully, it's more of a hirsute peck than any kind of lingering romantic expression.

The Williamses started their llama-breeding business in 1975 with just four animals. Actually, Beulah wanted buffalo but is now happy to have Tyrone and the wide-eyed and woolly gang instead. She has learned to make even the largest llamas obey. It seems that llamas have extremely sensitive ears; by holding one ear firmly, the largest of the beasts becomes putty in Beulah's hands. She has also learned how to communicate with them by blowing on their noses, though I have no idea what she's saying.

There are dozens of llamas besides Tyrone that you can visit. They're friendly

LLAMA LOFT
(15)

and nonaggressive, and if they feel threatened, they'll simply back away shyly. The Loft part of the Llama Loft operation is a gallery inside the Williamses' Victorian home. You can buy garments and other items made from the wool of the llamas. They'll aso sell you a llama for about $750 up. There are at least 14,000 llamas in the United States now. Though they originally came from the Andes in Chile, they adapt well to the northern California climate.

THE LLAMA LOFT, *Route 1, Valley Ford. Phone: (707) 795-5726. Open Friday through Sunday, noon to 5 P.M.*

HOW TO GET HERE: *From San Francisco, take the Golden Gate Bridge and continue north on Highway 101 to Petaluma. Take the Central Petaluma–Washington Street exit, and go through the center of town. Washington Street will become Bodega Avenue. Continue west on Bodega Avenue, which will become Valley Ford Road. The Llama Loft is on the right, perched on a small hill.*

GROWING GOOD ROSES

Just about everyone has a childhood memory about roses: the smell, the beauty, the little old lady next door who grew them. Rayford Reddell remembers seeing his first roses—buttery yellow bushes growing in a neighbor's yard in Louisiana. He asked his mother why they didn't have roses in their yard, and her reply was, "They're too much trouble."

Reddell grew up to be a professional rose grower, the operator of the largest commercial rose garden in the United States, supplier to the stars (1,500 roses for Caroline Kennedy's wedding, roses for a bash in New York thrown by designer Calvin Klein, that sort of thing), and author of a beautiful and informative text, *Growing Good Roses* (Harper & Row, 1988). In the introduction to his book, Reddell admits that his mother was right: Roses *are* a lot of trouble.

They are also beautiful, fascinating, and seductive, as you will discover when you visit Garden Valley Ranch, the place where Reddell grows his good roses. If he were an ordinary rose farmer, Reddell would sensibly tend his flowers inside a greenhouse. But no; he is a rosarian, whose relationship to the flower might be compared to a gourmet's to food, a connoisseur's to wine. Thus Reddell tends his roses outdoors in a garden, leaving them and himself open to the ravages of nature. The result is worth the effort: The flowers are spectacular.

And for backroads travelers, here is an opportunity to visit one heck of a rose garden graced by 4,000 bushes, including 150 different varieties, all planted on about an acre of the 7-acre ranch, all surrounded by rolling hills and neighboring dairy farms.

But that's not all: Another acre of land is occupied by the fragrance garden, tended by Reddell's partner, Bob Galyean. Together they have published the book *Growing Fragrant Plants* (Harper & Row, 1989). The two adjacent gardens make for a lovely visit, especially in summer, when almost everything will be in bloom.

Visitors are welcome Thursdays through Sundays to wander through the gardens, walk across the chamomile lawn, feed the *koi* in the fragrance garden's pond, and visit the nursery, where you can purchase live rosebushes, cut flowers, dried wreaths, and brewed potpourri made from plants grown in the fragrance garden. Both Reddell and Galyean love what they do and are happy to swap stories with everyone even remotely interested in gardens.

GARDEN VALLEY RANCH AND NURSERY, *498 Pepper Road, Petaluma. Phone: (707) 795-5266. Ranch and nursery open Thursday through Sunday, 10 A.M. to 4 P.M. Closed in December. Admission: Free.*

HOW TO GET HERE: *From San Francisco, take the Golden Gate Bridge and continue north on Highway 101 to Petaluma. Take the Central Petaluma exit, and head for the main part of town. At Petaluma Boulevard North, turn right and continue to Stony Point Road. Turn left and continue to Pepper Road. Turn left and look for the Farm Trails sign and a huge field of roses.*

In most places in the world, a visit to the town museum can tell you a lot about the community. This is certainly true in Petaluma, and a visit to the Petaluma Museum has a bonus: a chance to meet Vangie Ruiz. I wouldn't miss this opportunity. Vangie is the director of the museum and is one of the most fascinating people I've met on the backroads. Vangie was a museum vounteer for years after retiring from her job as a state highway patrol dispatcher. When the staff director left the museum, Vangie was offered the job, which she sandwiches into her busy schedule, which also includes attending classes at Sonoma State University.

PETALUMA LIBRARY AND TOWN MUSEUM

When you visit, you will probably be greeted by Vangie or her husband, Bob. They'll tell you about the building itself, which is imposing indeed. It was built as a Carnegie library, part of the literacy program through which the steel baron donated money to small towns to build free libraries. When Petaluma built a new library in the 1970s, the Carnegie building was turned into the town museum. In keeping with the original grant, it remains open as a library, too, featuring a small supply of historic texts. Even a benevolent photograph of Carnegie himself graces one of the walls, lighted by rays through the stained-glass dome in the center of the structure.

But mainly the space is used for historical displays. As you enter, the first exhibit is the town's old fire wagon, a horse-drawn beauty that had to pull water from the Petaluma River. Downstairs, small exhibits show the original inhabitants of the area, the Miwok Indians, followed by the Mexican settlers and their leader, General Vallejo. Since the displays are not what one would call spectacular, Vangie will tell stories to bring them to life, all told with a sparkle befitting her colorful serape and snappy knit hat.

On the second floor are displays concerning modern history. A fun area is the re-creation of Petaluma when it was known as the "egg basket of the world." From 1918 until World War II, chicken was king in Petaluma. Vangie tells the story about moving up from Santa Barbara and thinking the Petaluma hills were white with snow, only to discover that they were blanketed by chicken feathers.

The city of Petaluma has done a good job of holding on to its history. The downtown area is alive and growing, making use of its historical buildings. The Chamber of Commerce has designed a self-guided walking tour of notable buildings, which includes the site of the world's only chicken pharmacy and, of course, the old Carnegie Library, now the town museum.

PETALUMA HISTORICAL LIBRARY AND MUSEUM, *20 Fourth Street, Petaluma. Phone: (707) 778-4398. Open Thursday through Monday, 1 to 4 P.M. Admission: Free.*

HOW TO GET HERE: *From San Francisco, take the Golden Gate Bridge and continue north on Highway 101 to Petaluma's Washington Street exit. Go into town and turn left on Petaluma Boulevard North. Continue past the Plaza Theater and turn right onto B Street. The library is one block away, at the corner of B and Fourth.*

TRASH CAN ART

This is the story of a suburban revolution—well, maybe not a full-scale overthrow of authority, but certainly a pie in the face of the bureaucratic powers that be.

It all started in 1986, when the residents of Petaluma were informed that their friendly, familiar metal trash cans would be replaced by new 90-gallon polyethylene containers, identical for all households. This announcement outraged a retired Pacific Gas & Electric photographer named Dick Hoorn. "I protest this regimented thinking," he said as he got out a box of paints. Hoorn drew a colorful dragon face with snarling eyes and a down-turned mouth onto his new trash container and set it out by the curb on trash collection day. When the city "sanitation engineers" arrived, Hoorn watched their reaction from behind his curtains.

The trashmen loved it, and Hoorn decided that art and a sense of humor were the highest form of protest. Hoorn organized his neighbors on Petaluma's Halsey Avenue, and they painted their trash receptacles, too. Soon other neighborhoods caught on. So today as you drive through the neighborhoods of Petaluma on trash collection day, you'll see some pretty wild-looking garbage cans.

Some imaginative folks have used the lids to create faces of alligators; others stud theirs with stars, create rather elaborate portraits of their kitties, or depict their favorite TV cartoon characters.

And what does Dick Hoorn think of the revolution, er, revolt he hath wrought? He loves it and sees this one small step as a giant leap for humanity. He suggests that the American leaders get together with Russian leaders in the same spirit; he thinks that if they painted our nuclear weapons in bright colors, they would seem ridiculous and we could all laugh and be friends. Hey, maybe he's onto something.

GARBAGE CAN ART OF PETALUMA can be seen in May as part of the city's annual Butter and Eggs Day Parade and in driveways all around town. One of the best blocks for artistic cans is Halsey Avenue. For more information, call Dick Hoorn at (707) 763-1497.

CALIFORNIA COOPERATIVE CREAMERY ⑲

Remember the good old days when milk was delivered to your door in bottles? Remember the bottles, with the glass bubble filled with cream on top and the skim milk below? Even if you don't, you'll still get a kick out of a visit to the Creamery Store, the first stop on a tour of the California Cooperative Creamery.

Here you can graze through a collection of antique milk cans, bottles, and various dairy machines. If you've got the muscle and the patience, you can churn some butter. A 10-minute slide show is presented to anyone interested in the history of the dairy co-op, which includes nearly 500 member farms in California and Nevada who pool their resources for the distribution of milk and the production of cheese.

The tour continues across the street, where cheese is made. For health reasons, visitors are not allowed inside, but large windows allow you to see state-of-the-art equipment like the 24-foot towers that spew out huge blocks of cheese. You'll also see large tanks where cheese is stirred by giant mixers. If you're like me, you'll learn a thing or two about the dairy biz; for example, when Little Miss Muffet sat on her tuffet, she was probably eating not curds and whey but cottage cheese. Curds and whey are the basic by-products of cooked milk. The curds are the solids, and the whey is the liquid waste, which is whooshed down large drains in the tanks.

There is no difference in taste between yellow and white cheddar. Food coloring, extracted from a bean, is usually added because consumers associate that orangy color with that kind of cheese.

The cheese market has saved the California dairy industry. Until recent years, California imported 85 percent of its cheese from the East Coast. Now California makes most of its own cheese, and this place alone produces more than 20 million pounds of it a year.

You might want to begin or end your tour with a visit to the downstairs of the Creamery Store, where you can purchase such items as a cow sweatshirt or a milkshake. Tours are given daily, every half hour beginning at 10 A.M., and can accommodate up to 20 persons at a time. Large groups must call ahead. It's a very low-key, folksy place worth visiting for a half hour or so.

CALIFORNIA COOPERATIVE CREAMERY, *711 Western Avenue, Petaluma. Phone: (707) 778-1234. Open Monday through Friday, 10 A.M. to 6 P.M.; Saturday and Sunday, 10 A.M. to 5 P.M. Admission: Free.*

HOW TO GET HERE: *From San Francisco, take the Golden Gate Bridge and continue on Highway 101 North to the Petaluma Boulevard South exit. Follow Petaluma Boulevard into town, and turn left onto Western Avenue. The creamery is at the intersection of Western and Baker, just a few blocks from downtown.*

UNCLE GAYLORD'S ICE-CREAM MUSEUM ⑳

I don't know who comes up with these statistics, but supposedly people in the Bay Area consume more ice-cream per capita than any other region in the country. True or not, the Bay Area certainly is a haven for ice-cream companies, each creating and packaging its own special frozen desserts. One of these competitors calls himself Old Uncle Gaylord, and to my knowledge he's the only ice-cream maker to have his own ice-cream museum. It's in his main plant on the outskirts of Petaluma.

First, let me tell you about Gaylord. Yes, Virginia, there really is an Old Uncle Gaylord, and though he's not particularly old, he is everyone's kindly uncle, straight from central casting. He says he's an old-fashioned guy from a very poor family in Illinois. But he did get a 5-cent allowance, and he'd always spend it on ice cream. As an adult in San Francisco, he worked 9 to 5 in a suit and tie and hated it; he remembered his Midwestern roots and decided to open a simple little ice-cream shop of his own. His gimmick was to create an old-timey atmosphere and an old-timey product: ice cream from basic, natural ingredients.

Soon Gaylord had a hit on his cold hands and began opening stores all over the Bay Area. At last count there were 20, and he has been talking to Japanese businessmen about starting an international operation.

He is headquartered in a small ice-cream shop and ice-cream plant 45 minutes north of San Francisco, and this is where he keeps his collection of antique ice-cream paraphernalia. At last count he had 300 pieces, including cartons from the Bing Crosby and Hopalong Cassidy brands of ice cream; a malted-milk machine made by Adolph Coors during Prohibition; two-handed ice-cream scoops from 1880; a water-driven ice-cream maker; plus various buckets, dishes, and spoons. One of my favorites is a contraption called an Auto-Vac. It was designed to make ice cream by being strapped onto the side of a Model T; the motion of the car shook up the ingredients much like turning a crank would.

Keep in mind that this is not a typical museum, with display cases and labeled exhibits. It's basically one man's collection that you can enjoy while savoring an ice-cream cone or a banana split.

OLD UNCLE GAYLORD'S, *824 Petaluma Boulevard South, Petaluma. Phone: (707) 778-6008. Store hours: 11 A.M. to 6 P.M. daily.*

HOW TO GET HERE: *From San Francisco, take the Golden Gate Bridge and continue north on Highway 101 to Petaluma. Exit at Petaluma Boulevard South, and follow the road toward town for 1½ miles. The museum will be on your left.*

CHAPTER **3** Napa County

AREA OVERVIEW

Napa County is sandwiched between Sonoma County to the west and Solano county to the south and east. The closest destination from San Francisco is the city of Napa, about an hour's drive from the Golden Gate Bridge. It will take another 45 minutes in moderate traffic to get up to Calistoga, home of popular hot springs and health spas. The county includes a few lakes and valleys at its east and, to the west, a small mountain range that separates Napa from the Sonoma Valley. Most of the action, however, is concentrated along the center of the Napa Valley.

The Napa Valley has literally exploded with small wineries in the past few years. A major no-growth movement is developing in reaction to it, and at this writing, a "wine train" that would take visitors by rail to many of the best-known wineries is making trial runs, although without stops at any wineries. Some say the train would alleviate the heavy traffic on Route 29; others say it will be the ruination of the valley, damning it forever to commercialism rather than agriculture.

In the meantime, countless winery tours are available from such major names as Domaine Chandon, Robert Mondavi, Beringer, and Sterling, but don't miss the smaller operations or some of the other attractions. In this chapter we will concentrate on the latter, with a unique winery thrown in here and there.

Despite the size of its international fame, Napa is one of the smallest counties in the Bay Area. The best time of the year to visit is the fall, when the weather is ideal and the annual grape crush is on. This is when the wineries are bustling with energy and the grapevines themselves light up the roadside with brilliant reds and yellows. Finally, if you're tasting wine and planning to continue behind the wheel, don't swallow the samples. Most wineries provide buckets or drains so that you don't have to drink and drive.

THE GRAPE CRUSHER
(1)

There is no doubt that you have entered the Wine Country when you hit the outskirts of the city of Napa, thanks to the Grape Crusher. He stands there on one foot, pulling mightily on the lever of an old-fashioned grape barrel. The Grape Crusher also happens to be 16½ feet tall and weighs 3 tons, and since he's built of steel beams and covered with bronze, he's going to be around for a while. This statue, located at the intersections of Routes 29 and 121, was a gift from the Napa Corporate Industrial Park and Caltrans and made its debut in the spring of 1988. There is some obvious irony here in that the statue is a reminder that this was once farm country and that the labor of the worker is responsible for what is now a booming tourist and industrial area.

The artist is Gino Miles, a sculptor from Santa Fe, New Mexico. Gino got the commission from Bedford Properties, which owns the industrial park. He designed and built the Grape Crusher as a tribute to the laborers who built this valley. The statue is incredibly realistic, down to such details as belt loops and stitching on the man's jeans. To give you a sense of the Grape Crusher's size, the names of the crew who assisted the artist are carved into the label on the back pocket. The giant sculpture was spread out in 15 sections in Gino's Santa Fe studio, then trucked to Napa and put together on the site.

There are two ways to see the Grape Crusher. You can drive by at 50 mph and point at it from the highway; it was designed so that drivers entering the Napa and Sonoma valleys could see it from the road. A better idea, though, is to go right up to it. Although not obvious from the highway, it is possible to drive up to the site, where you'll find a nice little park complete with benches and a garden path; it's a pleasant place to rest or have a picnic.

Two bits of safety advice: First of all, don't just pull off the highway to look, as reentry onto the highway is dangerous. Also, if you happen to be the adventurous, athletic type, don't climb the statue. Not only is it damaging to the work, but wasps have found it a lovely spot to nest, and they are not friendly to interlopers.

THE GRAPE CRUSHER, *south of the town of Napa, near the intersection of Routes 29 and 12.*

HOW TO GET HERE: *From San Francisco, take the Golden Gate Bridge to Highway 101 North. Exit at Route 37 toward Vallejo. Follow the signs to Napa, turn left onto Route 29, and head north until you come to a fork in the road. Route 29 goes to the left. Route 12 to Napa goes straight. Go straight for a short distance, then turn left into the Napa Corporate Industrial Park. Follow the main road*

Napa

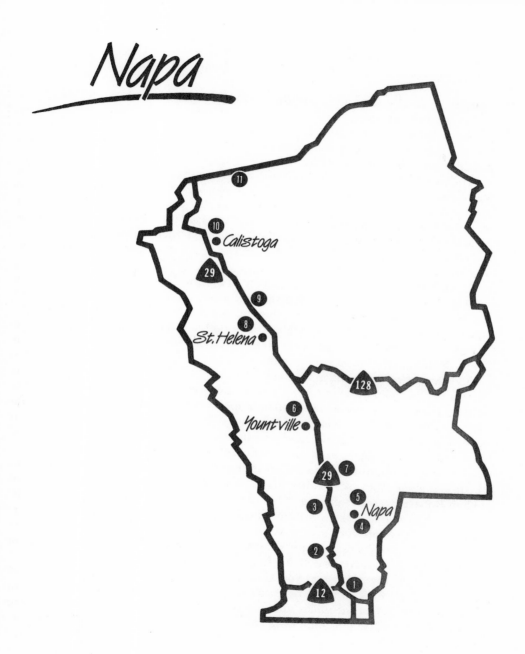

Calistoga

St. Helena

Yountville

Napa

around to the left and up the hill until you come to Vista Point. Turn right, and the road will take you to a parking area just below the statue.

DON'T CALL IT COGNAC
(2)

One of the more unusual Wine Country tours is available at the RMS Vineyards. The product made here is called California alambic brandy; however, the same stuff made in France would be called Cognac. But as is the case with champagne, the French name their products after their region of origin. Thus this brandy bears the name California.

The next part of the name, alambic, refers to the unusual pots in which the spirits are distilled. These alambic pots are made of copper, and they are gorgeous. The distillery resembles a museum or fine art gallery, with its series of alambic vats lined up like domes on Greek Orthodox temples. In fact, the process was discovered centuries ago by the Greeks and then adopted by the Arabs, hence the name (*ambic* is Greek; *al* is an Arabic prefix) and the Middle Eastern–looking vats.

Eventually this process found its way to Spain, France, and now California. The design of the vats and the basic technique have never changed. In brief, local wine is cooked and distilled, then aged in French Limousin oak barrels for about five years, then bottled. California alambic brandy is made by RMS Vineyards, a collaboration between Rémy Martin, the French company, and Schramsberg, the Napa Valley concern. Here in Napa, this lovely brandy is made exactly as it's made in Cognac.

Tours are given all year round, but the best time is in the fall when the stills are all fired up and the heady aroma of spirits is in the air. Through your guide and a collection of old photos and memorabilia, you'll learn everything you've ever wanted to know about brandy in about a half hour.

Unlike most winery tours, this one doesn't end with a complimentary tasting. Because of the high alcohol content in brandy, RMS is prohibited from offering tastes. Instead, they offer sniffs. In fact, you might be lucky enough to be there when Robert Leaute is on one of his frequent consulting visits from France. He gives a marvelous lesson on how and how not to sniff, his accented English making him sound very much like a good-humored Inspector Clouseau. Here are some of Leaute's major points: Never—or *"nevair"*—swirl the brandy before sniffing; it will disturb the delicate balance of the aroma. Place your nose exactly 2 inches from the glass and you should detect the aroma of oak, vanilla, and cigar box. Yes, he said cigar box, and by golly, you can smell it. Then put your nose up to the top of the glass, and you should sniff flowery spices, and hazelnut or almond. Finally, put your nose into the glass, and you should pick up the essence of licorice. Now, and only now, may you swirl.

The final test is, of course, the taste. Leaute assured me that even though I was not allowed to taste the brandy, he was because he is the quality control expert. He sipped and after a long pause pronounced it very good. Then he took another sip to make sure.

RMS VINEYARDS, 1250 Cuttings Wharf Road, Napa. Phone: (707) 253-9055. Tours Monday through Friday by appointment at 10:30 A.M. and 2:30 P.M.; Saturday by appointment. Group tours can be arranged in advance.

HOW TO GET HERE: From San Francisco, take the Golden Gate Bridge and continue north on Highway 101 to the Route 37 exit for Vallejo and Napa. Continue east (right) on Route 37 to the intersection of Route 121. Turn left onto Route 121, and continue past the Sonoma turnoff to Cuttings Wharf Road. Turn right, and RMS is 1.3 miles down the road.

I deliberately avoid superlatives when describing the various places to visit on "Backroads," but I must use them to do justice to this extraordinary winery and art museum. A visit to the Hess Collection is so much more than a visit to any other winery that it belongs in a category all its own.

Let's begin with the setting. Swiss-American entrepreneur Donald Hess put his personal collection of art into the Old Mont LaSalle winery that was operated by the Christian Brothers until they sold recently to Heublein, Inc. The original stone buildings were re-designed to create an ultra-modern facility that still shows off the original architecture. The entire complex sits alone off a country road on Mount Veeder.

Even though the business of the operation is wine, the modern art collection is the highlight of the visit. It is beautifully displayed on three floors and features the works of American artists like Frank Stella and Robert Motherwell, as well as European artists like Francis Bacon and Georg Baselitz. Hess is a passionate art lover and collector who tries to get to know each artist personally, then acquires a body of their work. So instead of seeing an isolated painting or sculpture, you get to see miniexhibitions of each of the artists. More than 160 works are displayed, and the effect is staggering.

Hess, whose Swiss holdings include real estate, hotels, wineries, and the Valser Mineral Water Company, told me that when he leased the old Christian Brothers property he suddenly realized that he had more space than he needed for his winery. After a lifetime of squeezing into small spaces in Switzerland, he decided to take advantage of all this room by creating an American home for his art.

There are subtle reminders that you are indeed in a winery. Windows are strategically placed throughout the exhibition halls showing the bottling line,

HESS COLLECTION
③

the open top fermentation tanks, and even a view of the vineyards for the Hess Chardonnay and Cabernet Sauvignon. And, of course, there is a tasting room, which consists of a huge rectangular wooden bar, plus a window with views of the barrel room. Unlike the white walls that display works of art through the rest of the place, the walls here are the original stone with no paintings or sculpture in sight. Hess says he wants the wine to be the focus in this room and not compete with anything else.

This is a one-of-a-kind operation that is tastefully done at every turn. A pamphlet outlining a self-guided tour is handed to visitors at the reception area. You can start by watching a brief audiovisual presentation describing the winery and the Hess concept, or you can simply follow the Roman numerals which mark the various stages of the tour. Guided tours are also available by appointment.

HESS COLLECTION, *4411 Redwood Road, Napa. Phone: (707) 255-1144. Visitors Center is open daily from 10 A.M. to 4 P.M. Admission: Free to the art exhibition area; $2.50 charge for wine tasting.*

HOW TO GET HERE: *From San Francisco, take the Golden Gate Bridge to Highway 101 North to Route 37. Take Route 37 East toward Napa and Vallejo to Route 29. Turn left and take Route 29 until you come to Redwood Road in Napa. Turn left and stay on Redwood Road as it winds up Mount Veeder, approximately 4½ miles to the winery.*

NAPA BOXING MUSEUM ④

You know you're in for something different when you head down Action Avenue and see a large building named Joe. Next door is a building called Missy. In fact, all the buildings in this complex a few minutes from downtown Napa are on a first-name basis.

But the real surprise comes when you enter the building named Joe and you find the place full of historical boxing memorabilia and a 73-year-old man working out in shorts, a T-shirt, and boxing gloves and using the moves of a 20-year-old. That's the owner of the buildings and the Boxing Museum, "Newsboy" Joe Gavras. Joe has to rank as one of the top 10 characters we've ever met on the backroads, a real contender.

In the 1930s Joe was a big draw in San Francisco boxing circles. He used to pack them in and had a lifetime record of 89 wins and 9 losses. His nickname came from his day job as a newspaper hustler, selling the *San Francisco Chronicle* on the streets. According to Joe, nobody could hawk papers like he could.

But Joe also learned a few other lessons about business and life. When he was a headliner, making as much as $200 a fight, he was the king of the streets. People stopped him and asked for his autograph. But if he lost, nobody would talk to him. He saw too many broke fighters, so he decided to start saving everything he made and invest it in real estate.

Today Joe has millions of dollars in holdings, but he says he hasn't ever changed his lifestyle. He wears old clothes, drives an old jalopy, and is only interested in working out. He spends six days a week in his museum, which is also a training facility for amateur boxers. Only his pals can work out there, but everyone can come and look around, and there is much to see. First off, there is the ring in the center of the one-room museum. The great heavyweight champ Rocky Marciano fought on it in Kezar Stadium in San Francisco's Golden Gate Park. It's also been the stage for many title and Golden Gloves fights. Below it are director's chairs with the names of boxing champs. On the walls are photos and posters of the famous and not so famous, including several shots of Newsboy Joe in his prime. In fact, if you just walk past the photos, you'll get a pretty good history of American boxing, from the 1920s to the present. To the side of the ring are punching bags and exercise machines where Joe and his pals work out. A genuine boxing ring bell sounds every three minutes.

If at all possible, engage Joe in a conversation. He has stories upon stories. Although his voice is raspy and his teeth were sacrificed in the service of pugilism, this is no punch-drunk boxer. Joe is shrewd and colorful and is obviously revered by his tenants and friends.

BOXING MUSEUM, *Action Avenue, Napa. Phone: (707) 224-4977. Call before you visit to make sure Joe is there.*

HOW TO GET HERE: *From San Francisco, cross the Golden Gate Bridge to Highway 101 North to Route 37 East. At Sears Point, go left onto Route 121 into the city of Napa. It will become Soscol Avenue. Continue on Soscol over two sets of railroad tracks, and look for Vallejo Street on the left. Turn onto Vallejo, and then take an immediate right turn onto Action Avenue. Look for the building marked "Joe." It's well marked.*

There's more to the Napa Valley style than great wine and fine restaurants. There is also a flourishing art community, and it will grow in recognition if Jessel has anything to say about it. Based on her track record, it would not be wise to bet against her. Jessel is an artist-dynamo who moved to the Napa Valley from Oakland in 1987 bent on setting up a cultural center. She bought an old whiskey distillery building not far from the posh Silverado Country Club and set up shop.

JESSEL

Originally she used most of the space as a studio for her watercolor work, with the rest maintained as a gallery. But her idea has been so successful that her studio has now been moved to a nearby building, and the entire original space is devoted to the cultural center and gallery. This includes three rooms of exhibit space, also used for musicales and occasional aerobics classes (Jessel also happens to be a musician and an aerobics instructor).

Maybe this is a good time to deal with the matter of her name. At first one might wonder why anyone would choose to honor the former Borscht Belt comedian. But as it turns out, Jessel is her real last name. She always hated her first name, so she simply dropped it. Maybe Cher and Liberace are more glamorous one-name names, but Jessel has enough charm and talent to get away with calling herself whatever she likes.

Jessel has been painting for many years, and each of her canvases now commands thousands of dollars. This success is even sweeter because one of her early and influential instructors told her she would never make it. With the determination to prove him wrong, Jessel stuck to her art and now tries to encourage local artists who need a showcase. Currently the gallery features a roster of some 35 artists.

The gallery is a hospitable place for backroads travelers to visit. You can browse through the collection and sit on the front porch, where you can picnic or simply take a load off your feet. Something new always seems to be happening, whether it's a performance or the opening of yet another room. This is a place that will keep growing and developing. It's also a comfortable place for people who are usually intimidated by art and galleries.

To illustrate the optimistic spirit of the founder of the gallery, Jessel was first disappointed when 95 condominiums started being built in the parklike setting across the street; then she decided that this was good news: Think of all the white walls that would need paintings! The new homes could keep a lot of Napa artists very busy.

JESSEL GALLERY, *11019 Atlas Peak Road, Napa. Phone: (707) 257-2350. Gallery open Thursday through Monday, 11 A.M. to 4 P.M. Admission: Free.*

HOW TO GET HERE: *From San Francisco, cross the Golden Gate Bridge and continue up Highway 101 North to Route 37. Turn right toward Napa and take Route 37 to Route 29. Turn left and continue on Route 29 to Trancas Street. Turn right and continue until you get to the Silverado Trail. Turn left on Silverado. The gallery is the first building on the left.*

CARMELITE MONASTERY
⑥

This is the kind of place I'm talking about when I use the motto of my television show, "You never know what you'll find on the Bay Area's backroads." If you have ever traveled Route 29, the main artery of the Napa Valley, you may have noticed the imposing mansion at the foot of the Oakville Grade. Many visitors mistake it for a winery, and no wonder. It's surrounded by a glorious 28-acre estate, complete with a pond and a lovely garden.

Actually this is where a half dozen Carmelite monks live cloistered as hermits six days of the week, living quietly in their brown robes. On the seventh day they may indulge in the worldly activity of their own choosing. For example, Father Albert, who took me on a tour of the place, likes to don a pair of Bermuda shorts and play a round of golf.

Though no formal tours are offered, guests are welcome daily. You can walk around in the gardens, sit peacefully by the pond, contemplate great thoughts in the chapel, and shop in the gift store (where you will find T-shirts with a smiling monk and the legend "Oh, Heavenly Daze"). It's not a bad idea for each of us to become hermits now and then, to take the time to get away from the usual sounds, sights, and schedules of our lives, to collect our thoughts.

Whatever your reason to visit, you will be impressed by the beauty of the place and its unusual history. The mansion was originally built in 1921, complete with a carriage house and swimming pool. In the 1950s, long before the real estate boom hit the valley, the Carmelites purchased the whole shebang for—hold on to your tonsure—$60,000.

Occasionally someone will try to buy the place. Father Albert told me about the visitor who asked what it would take to get the Carmelites to sell, and the father in charge jokingly answered, "Four million dollars." When the visitor reached for his checkbook, the good father had to explain that he was just kidding.

I should mention that the interior of the house is rather sparsely decorated. All trappings of wealth and ostentation left with the previous owner. Even the chapel is simple and unadorned. This is a house of prayer, sitting in stark and peaceful contrast to the booming valley below.

CARMELITE MONASTERY, *Oakville Grade Road, Oakville, about one mile off Route 29. Phone: (707) 944-2454. Open daily, but be sure to call ahead first. Admission: Free.*

HOW TO GET HERE: *From San Francisco, cross the Golden Gate Bridge and take Highway 101 North, following the directions to Route 29 and the Napa Valley. Turn left off Route 29 onto Oakville Grade Road. About a mile down Oakville Grade Road, you will see the entrance to the monastery on the right. (If you come to the Oakville Grocery on the right, you have gone too far.)*

MONTICELLO CELLARS

Although Sonoma County's Count Haraszthy is considered the father of the northern California wine industry, the man responsible for introducing fine wines to America is none other than Thomas Jefferson, the third president of these here United States. Though he never made it to the West Coast, Tom's presence is felt in the Napa Valley at Monticello Cellars.

You probably remember Monticello from your elementary school history books or from the backside of a nickel. A scaled-down version of Jefferson's Virginia estate has been strikingly re-created for use as winery offices—red bricks, stately white columns, and all. Though the tasting room and gardens are open all year, the mini-Monticello structure is open to the public only a few times a year. The major annual event is an open house around Jefferson's birthday, April 13.

The Jeffersonian theme extends to the tasting room, where the pourers have been schooled in the incredible story of America's first Renaissance man and gourmet. They can tell you that Jefferson brought grapes from France to Virginia and that he first introduced to the colonial states such foods as pasta, ice-cream, waffles, and almonds. Along with bottles of wine, you can purchase books on Jefferson from the tasting room.

If you visit Monticello on an open-house day, you can visit the extensive library that holds the winery owner's private collection of rare books. Most fascinating is Thomas Jefferson's Garden Book, a daily diary of his flower and vegetable adventures spanning decades.

MONTICELLO CELLARS, *4242 Big Ranch Road, Napa. Phone: (707) 253-2802. Visits by appointment, seven days a week. Call to inquire about annual open house in April, plus special dinners.*

HOW TO GET HERE: *From San Francisco, cross the Golden Gate Bridge, and follow the signs to the town of Napa. Stay on Route 29 past Napa for about 4 miles, then turn right onto Oak Knoll Avenue. After about 1 mile, turn right onto Big Ranch Road, and continue until you think you've suddenly arrived in Virginia.*

GREYSTONE WINERY
(8)

With so many attractions in the Napa Valley, every winery needs a hook. How about this: the oldest building west of the Mississippi built with the Ransome Patent method of construction? If that doesn't grab you, perhaps just the fact that Greystone is among the most spectacular buildings in the Wine Country will. We couldn't include it in our first book because it was closed for five years to bring it up to modern earthquake-proof standards.

For many years, this was the home of the Christian Brothers, a Catholic order that ran the famous Christian Brothers winery. The revenue generated went toward educational works, such as helping fund St. Mary's College in Contra Costa County (see story, page 119). Then, in 1989, the Christian Brothers sold the winery to the Heublein conglomerate. At this writing it is uncertain whether the name of the winery will remain the same. Regardless, public tours will be continued.

Greystone was built in the 1880s by William Bourne, the man who brought water to the South Bay peninsula after striking it rich in the Gold Country. Bourne built Filoli, an elegant manor house and spectacular gardens located in

Woodside in the South Bay; today Filoli is National Trust property, and the exterior of the house is known for the opening of the television show "Dynasty." Here in the Napa Valley, Bourne wanted to create a cooperative storage facility for local wine producers. In his usual grand style, Bourne built a 90,000-square-foot building, 75 feet wide and 400 feet long, more than 3 acres of covered floor space. The decorative material was hand-hewn volcanic rock. The aforementioned Ransom Patent construction, by the way, involves a second floor of concrete with the support of a series of steel arches.

As you tour the facility, the size and scale of the building is nearly overwhelming. You enter through massive arched doors into a huge foyer with a seemingly endless ceiling. On both sides are tasting rooms. Everywhere you look, you will see a type of craftsmanship that is rare in modern construction. Seemingly no expense was spared in the use of materials, such as the rich, lovely mahogany paneling.

The guided tour will take you to several sections of Greystone, past laboratories, storage facilities, and some of the original tunnels that were cut into the hillside to create a kind of natural air conditioning. In the good old days when the Christian Brothers ran the winery, visitors would be shown Brother Timothy's collection of more than 1,500 corkscrews, as well as many displays showing the development of the brothers and their works. No matter what new touches the Heublein company adds, the building is the main attraction here, and the tours will certainly continue to be popular.

GREYSTONE WINERY, *2555 Main Street, St. Helena. Phone: (707) 967-3112. As of this writing, tours are held daily, 10 A.M. to 4 P.M. and are free; be sure to call ahead to see if things have changed under the new ownership.*

HOW TO GET HERE: *From San Francisco, cross the Golden Gate Bridge, and follow the signs to Napa. Stay on Route 29 beyond downtown St. Helena. You will come to Greystone on the left side of the road, immediately after the Victorian Beringer facility.*

TEMPLE TO WINE

Just minutes away from some of the oldest wineries in the Napa Valley is a stark, postmodern gem designed by architect Michael Graves. It is the dream come true of owner Jan Shrem, what he calls "a temple to the art of winemaking and the pleasure of drinking wine." The story behind the Clos Pegase winery is as interesting as the wine itself.

Shrem, born in Colombia, raised in Jerusalem, and educated at the University of Utah and UCLA, is an internationally known art collector. He made his fortune in real estate and publishing scientific texts in Japan, thus providing the means to indulge his enthusiasm for Japanese and European art. While living in

Paris, Shrem's interest in wine grew along with the size of his art collection. He decided to give up his other occupations to create a landmark winery, and he chose the Napa Valley as the place to build.

In 1984, the San Francisco Museum of Modern Art sponsored an architectural competition, and from the 95 designs submitted, Shrem chose Michael Graves's design for his dream winery. However, local building codes and fiscal reality eventually tempered the original plans (which included a hillside amphitheater, a sculpture garden, and a waterfall), and the modified version opened in June 1987.

The result is a multihued winery wrapped around a 300-year-old oak tree, the tree symbolic of tradition, the colors symbolic of the present. As Graves told Shrem, "We can't build with stone like in the old days, so we will build with color." The stucco and tile villa with Italianate columns is divided into areas for production and for enjoyment, hence it has two grand porticoes—one to "welcome the grapes into a crush pad" and another for guests.

Inside, Shrem's art collection is displayed throughout, with Venetian glass chandeliers in the tasting rooms and paintings and tapestries hung between the oak barrels in the aging rooms.

Several paintings depicting the winged horse Pegasus hang in the tasting room. Symbolist Shrem never seems to tire of telling the myth of Pegasus, which links wine with pleasure, inspiration, and art—a concept Shrem wishes to promote in his Napa Valley temple.

Like anything new in the Napa Valley, Clos Pegase has stirred controversy; one man's temple may be another man's eyesore. When the winery opened, one wine publication heralded Clos Pegase as perhaps "one of the most important architectural accomplishments of the decade." Meanwhile, neighbors and various critics described it "Hollywood's version of Egypt" and compared it aesthetically to both Disneyland and an atomic waste plant.

Meanwhile in France, a major art exhibition on winery architecture is in large part dedicated to Clos Pegase, considered by the organizers of this show to be a significant achievement balancing tradition and modernity. This traveling show opened in Paris in November 1988 and will travel internationally for four years.

It's worth a trip to the lovely 60-acre site just to judge the building for yourself. Admission is free, but, like many of the better champagne makers in the area, Clos Pegase charges $3 for tasting its product (Chardonnay, Cabernet Sauvignon, Merlot, and Sauvignon Blanc).

CLOS PEGASE, *1060 Dunaweal Lane, just south of Calistoga. Phone: (707) 942-4981. Open Monday through Saturday, 10:30 A.M. to 4:30 P.M. daily. Building tours are free; tastings cost $3, and you get to keep the glass. Wheelchair accessible.*

HOW TO GET HERE: *From San Francisco, cross the Golden Gate Bridge and follow the signs to Napa. Stay on Route 29 north of St. Helena until you come to Dunaweal Lane. You will see the large, white Sterling winery on a hill on the right before you come to Dunaweal Lane. Turn right on Dunaweal, which will also be marked as the entrance to Sterling. Pass the Sterling entrance and look for Clos Pegase on the left; believe me, you can't miss it.*

Would you like to know the best spot for a picnic in the entire Napa Valley? Would you like to visit the winery that put California on the map as a serious wine producer? It's the same place. Chateau Montelena is a real chateau, built in 1882 by State Senator Alfred Tubbs, for whom Tubbs Lane is named. The good senator was a wealthy businessman and Francophile who wanted to own a chateau like the ones he had seen in the French countryside. He hired a French architect, imported French stones, and brought over a Frenchman to be his first winemaker.

THE WINE THAT FOOLED THE FRENCH
⑩

In the 1950s the property was purchased by an Asian couple who installed a huge garden to remind them of their ancestral home in northern China. They created Jade Lake—a little paradise on earth, with arched bridges leading to little islands, surrounded by weeping willows and lush greenery and populated by swans, ducks, and geese.

About that picnic. On one of the little artificial islands is a lovely red-lacquered pagoda. I can't imagine a more lovely, serene place to unload a basket of goodies and enjoy a leisurely lunch. (However, such an outing does require some advance planning; people call ahead to reserve the pavilion well in advance, so be sure to do so to make sure that this idyllic spot is available before you arrive.) Picnic or no, everyone is welcome to stroll around this lakeside setting, and I recommend that you do.

Now about the wine. In 1976, when California wines were pooh-poohed as second-class citizens in the wine world, a blind tasting of 10 top-of-the-line French white burgundies and California chardonnays was held in Paris. Chateau Montelena's Chardonnay was awarded first place. This caused quite a scandal, with some members of the all-French judging panel claiming that they had made a mistake and trying to change their votes.

It was too late; both first and second places had been awarded to California wines, and Chateau Montelena's Chardonnay returned home with the gold medal. The California fine wine industry took off from there.

You can taste Chateau Montelena's Chardonnay, Cabernet Sauvignon, Zinfandel, and Johannisberg Riesling in the hospitality room located inside the chateau. There you're in for an additional treat—Kippy the cat, a story in himself. This enormous furball of a beast melts visitors' hearts as he drinks milk from a wine glass and mugs for their Polaroids. He's developed an unofficial fan club; in the tasting room you can see Kippy's scrapbook, filled with snapshots, postcards, and fan mail sent by visitors.

The cat in the tasting room is a good way to explain the kind of place this is: a beautiful, historical setting with award-winning wines and a lighthearted, fun atmosphere. There's no snobbish attitude here. The staff is young and friendly, headed up by the winemaker, James P. "Bo" Barrett. Though his dad owns the place, Bo started working at the winery at age 16 from the ground up, literally—his first job was picking up rocks on the property. Now in his thirties, he loves to tell about his wedding in the pagoda on the lake; he says it was a helluva party, and he runs the entire operation so that the fun never stops.

CHATEAU MONTELENA, 1429 Tubbs Lane, Calistoga. Phone: (707) 942-5105. Tasting room open 10 A.M. to 4 P.M. daily; tours of the winery by appointment. The gardens and lake are open during tasting room hours. Call ahead if you plan to picnic.

HOW TO GET HERE: From San Francisco, cross the Golden Gate Bridge and follow the signs to Napa. Stay on Route 29 past Calistoga to Tubbs Lane; turn right. Continue about 1½ miles to the chateau.

SMITH TROUT FARM

One of my memories from childhood is of a cross-country trip I took with my parents from Indiana to the West. From the car I saw a solitary fisherman standing by a clear, rushing stream waiting to catch a dinner of fresh mountain trout. Though I've never had the urge to don a pair of hip boots, I do remember that fisherman. I thought about him again when I dipped my borrowed fishing pole into the pond at the Smith Trout Farm.

Technically, this place is located in Sonoma, just above Calistoga, but you get there on Napa roads, so we thought it would more logically be part of a Napa excursion.

For folks like me who rarely fish, the Smiths make the experience easy and pleasant. Their farm, also called Lake Mount St. Helena, is off in the woods, the kind of place where you could just sit and relax and enjoy nature. They've provided picnic tables, and there are lots of trees and roaming-around room for the kids.

The major attraction, of course, is the fishing, and success is more or less guaranteed. The Smiths provide the pole and bait, and you simply stand by the lake and wait for the unsuspecting trout to tug on the line. What is especially nice for a nonfisherman like me is the absence of squiggly worms. This bait, which works every time, consists of soybean and sardine meals, the feed the trout grow up on—the Cheerios of the fish world.

The Smith family has been running this farm since 1942. In one pond, eggs are hatched, and the trout grow to 8 inches. Then the main fishing pond is stocked with the fish, which keep growing until someone catches them. The largest ever caught here had grown to 27 inches. There's no charge for fishing, only for what you catch. The fish are priced by size, with the biggest going for $3. The really good news is that the Smiths will clean the fish and get them ready for cooking. You can take them home or use the barbecue grills there and have a picnic.

Why do people come here instead of heading out to remote mountain streams? For one thing, you don't need a license; for another, there is no limit. It's also a nice place to go with the whole family, with easy access and the secure knowledge you won't go home empty-handed.

SMITH TROUT FARM, *off Ida Clayton Road, north of Calistoga. Phone: (707) 987-3651. Open Friday through Monday, February 1 to Labor Day; weekends, Labor Day through November 1.*

HOW TO GET HERE: *From San Francisco, take the Golden Gate Bridge to Highway 101 North and continue to Route 37 West. Take Route 37 to Route 29 and continue north to Calistoga. Get onto Route 128 and take it north for about 6 miles to Ida Clayton Road. Turn right and continue for 7 miles to the trout farm.*

Highways 101 and 280 are the two major roads connecting you to the backroads of the South Bay. Whenever possible, use Route 280, which offers some of the most beautiful scenery of any freeway in the country.

In our first book, this region was divided into two sections: South Bay Inland and South Bay Coast. For this edition, the South Bay section has been expanded. To make it easier to plan trips, the South Bay has been divided by county. San Mateo County is the closest to San Francisco; you can drive to the San Mateo coast in less than an hour from Union Square. Santa Clara County is the home of the sprawling city of San Jose, which features a spectacular new downtown, highlighted by a striking ultra-modern convention center. Figure on at least an hour's drive between San Francisco and San Jose.

Santa Cruz County is known for its namesake city, its beaches, and its mountain communities. This community was the hardest hit during the October 1989 earthquake, yet this area is already bouncing back and being rebuilt. As with all our destinations, we urge you to call ahead before you visit places in the Santa Cruz area to be sure they and the roads leading to them have been reopened. The city of Santa Cruz can be reached in about 90 minutes from San Francisco. The southern sections of the county are about two hours away.

CHAPTER 4 San Mateo County

AREA OVERVIEW

San Mateo County begins where the city of San Francisco ends and includes some of the most expensive communities and some of the most secluded beaches in California. San Mateo County is also the flower capital of the Bay Area, with the most activity centered around the ocean at Half Moon Bay. Farther down the coast, along Route 1, there are farms that grow such California cuisine as artichokes, brussels sprouts, and kiwifruit. The San Mateo coast also offers nine state beaches, some very rocky and rugged, others good for sunbathing and surfing, and most of them good for tidepooling and beachcombing.

Along Highway 101 are the county's heavy population centers as well as San Francisco International Airport. Route 280 takes you to the woodsy hill country with its tony suburbs.

RALSTON HALL

The suburbs of the Peninsula are sprinkled with lavish estates of the people who struck it rich during the Gold Rush days. These lucky folks built luxurious summer places where they could escape the fog of San Francisco and bask in the sunshine of the South Bay. William Ralston, who made his fortune in mining and then went on to found the Bank of California, built his getaway in the town of Belmont.

In 1864 Ralston bought a 100-acre estate with a small villa for the then princely sum of $1,000. Over his lifetime Ralston built and added on, turning the modest home into a four-story, 80-room Victorian mansion, just right for entertaining 120 overnight guests or 75 of his closest friends for a sit-down dinner. These guests usually included the likes of Mr. and Mrs. Leland Stanford, Mr. and Mrs. Charles Crocker, and Mr. and Mrs. Mark Hopkins, as well as visiting dignitaries such as Ulysses S. Grant.

Nothing delighted Ralston more than inviting to dinner a snobbish Easterner who thought the West was a desert populated by cowboys and Indians. He proved them wrong by the dazzling interior of his home. Ralston was a fan of palaces (in fact, he built the ornate Palace Hotel, now the Sheraton-Palace, in San Francisco). Here in his home in Belmont, he built a long mirrored ballroom modeled after the palace at Versailles and a grand staircase leading to a gallery of second-floor sitting areas that look like opera boxes overlooking the foyer and ballroom.

The first floor was set up so that it could be made into one huge open space. The doors that separated the various rooms were built to slide up and out of the

San Mateo

Half Moon Bay

Redwood City

Woodside

Palo Alto

way into archways reaching toward the high ceilings. Other doors, with hinges made of silver, could open in either direction, out of the way of the flow of gowns and tuxedos.

Over the years the mansion changed hands several times. Then in 1922 it was purchased by the Sisters of Notre Dame de Namur to be the main building of their College of Notre Dame, a private four-year college and graduate school. It is open for tours by appointment, and of all the mansions in the South Bay open to the public, it is my personal favorite.

Why is the house so special? Mainly due to the overall architectural design and the small details. This place is not as grand a setting as other South Bay gems like Filoli or Villa Montalvo. Only a few of Ralston's original furnishings are still on display, and parts of the house are used as college administration offices. But if you are interested in interior design and genuine style, you won't be disappointed. Be sure to save time to stroll around to see the rest of the campus and the gardens.

Another way to enjoy the mansion is to attend one of the regularly scheduled classical music concerts sponsored by the college. You can call for a printed schedule of events.

RALSTON HALL, *Campus of the College of Notre Dame, 1500 Ralston Avenue, Belmont. Phone: (415) 593-1601. Tours by appointment, 9 A.M. to 4 P.M. Wednesday and Thursday. Admission: $5 per person for groups of four or less, $3 per person for groups up to 40; student and senior rate: $2 per person for groups of 5 to 40.*

HOW TO GET HERE: *From San Francisco, take Highway 101 South to the Ralston Avenue exit in Belmont. When you approach the campus, look for the stone pillars on the left side of the driveway. Go between the pillars and follow the one-way road all the way to the parking area on the side of the mansion.*

BEHIND THE SCENES AT THE RACES ②

Have you ever been on a movie set or backstage at the theater? If so, you have an idea of how much goes on that the audience never sees. Bay Meadows Race Track offers an unusual opportunity to see what it takes to put on a horse race. It happens on Saturday mornings during the race season, and it's free.

It's surprising to discover that there's an entire city back there, with a row of stores for equestrian supplies, a small café for workers, and a medical facility. You'll get to see the grooms, jockeys, horseshoers, and vets at work. And of course there are the horses. They're treated like royalty. If you time it right, you'll see their trainers walking them through a series of exercises; you can sense how close the workers are to the animals. Finally, watch the horses go out for trial runs around the track to loosen up—their version of batting practice before a baseball game or shooting hoops before a basketball game.

All you have to do is show up at the clubhouse at 8 A.M. Tours are led by an employee of the track, which each week hosts a different guest speaker, usually a jockey or a trainer. You can have breakfast if you wish (that's the only part of the tour that costs money); then you'll be guided behind the scenes. Usually the tour lasts until about 11 A.M., and if you want to stay for the races, you can get a discount pass.

BAY MEADOWS RACETRACK, 2600 Delaware Street, San Mateo. Phone: (415) 573-4617. Saturday morning tours during racing season, August through January, 8 A.M. Admission: Free.

HOW TO GET HERE: From San Francisco, take Highway 101 South. Exit at Delaware Street and head south. Follow Delaware into the racetrack parking lot.

As I shoot more and more stories for the "Backroads" television program, I am constantly reminded that the backroads really are a state of mind. You can find a hidden treasure almost anywhere. A case in point: the American Gaming Museum. For starters, it's located on a side street off El Camino Real where you'd never expect to find anything interesting. Then your suspicion grows when the address leads you into the real estate offices of the San Bruno Investment Company. But once you're inside, you know you've stumbled onto something special.

You are greeted by life-size statues of W. C. Fields and Oliver Hardy that double as slot machines. One glance around the room and you will see that the workers share their office space with a collection of mechanical gaming devices. In fact, there are more of these machines than there are typewriters or telephones. And you haven't even arrived at the collection yet.

If you want to sound like you know your way around, ask to see Joe. He's the head real estate honcho and the "curator" of the museum. Joe says he has the largest collection of antique gaming devices in the country, and when he takes you upstairs, you'll believe him.

It's a staggering sight, 2½ very large rooms filled from floor to ceiling with slot machines, fortune telling machines, gumball machines, music-making machines, air-conditioning machines—examples of just about everything that was manufactured to be coin-operated, the only exceptions being pay toilets and electronic games.

Joe, a burly pixie who taught himself how to get rich in real estate, says he was bitten by the collecting bug early in life. He started by collecting cars, but they needed too much storage space, and besides, lots of people collect cars. Gaming machines were a more esoteric field of interest. Joe smiles when he says he got many of the one-armed bandits from Chicago; these are relics of the Capone era. The Fortune Teller and the machine that delivers an electrical shock ("For that much-needed energy lift") came from the old Playland at the

SLOT-MACHINE HEAVEN
③

Beach in San Francisco. Another machine claims to be the "Eighth Man-Made Wonder of the World." It's a machine that plays three minutes of excruciating music of a screeching violin and a tinny player piano. I suggest that you save this one for last because you will want to leave before the three minutes are up.

AMERICAN GAMING MUSEUM, *San Bruno Investments Company, 338 West San Bruno Avenue, San Bruno. Phone: (415) 589-1262. Open Monday through Friday, 9 A.M. to 5 P.M. Admission: Free.*

HOW TO GET HERE: *From San Francisco, take Highway 101 South to the San Bruno Avenue exit. Head west and continue past the railroad tracks to 383 West San Bruno (the cross street is Easton). (If you reach El Camino Real, you've gone too far.)*

AMPEX MUSEUM OF RECORDING ④

This little-known museum is a must stop for anyone interested in audio or video recording. Peter Hammer, the curator, is quick to point out that this is an important stop for anyone who wants to understand the development of our culture of the past 80 years. To illustrate his point, Hammer suggests imagining what would happen to all of us if a giant antimagnetic force swooped down on earth and erased all the data and impressions recorded magnetically. In less than one second, all government, medical, and financial records, not to mention the Brandenburg Concerto tape you keep in the car and that final episode of *M*A*S*H* you videotaped years ago, would be gone forever.

The museum is located in the huge home office of Ampex, the company that manufactures magnetic recording tape. Grim scenarios aside, this is a fascinating collection of machines and inventions that have changed our lives. Starting with the first wire recording device (invented by a Norwegian, by the way), you walk through the history of magnetic recording, including the latest in video machines. Interestingly enough, that first wire recorder was a telephone-answering device invented in 1911; the cute messages that plague us today didn't come along until the 1970s.

As you walk through the three-room gallery, you'll see how the wire recorder gave way to the tape recorder and that Bing Crosby was responsible for tape catching on. At the time, Der Bingle was one of radio's mainstays, broadcasting his weekly program live for various times zones. When he heard about the new development of tape—the invention of German scientists—he realized that he could work in a more leisurely manner by prerecording his shows and not worry about appearing live. Crosby backed the development of American tape recording and helped Ampex grow from a tiny manufacturer of small motors to the recording giant it is today. On hand at the museum is a copy of one of Bing's early radio shows.

More than 200 pieces of recording equipment are on display here, including one table of tape recorders. Chances are you'll see one that touches off a wave of nostalgia. My first Webcor is there, and so is the first cassette machine. Surprisingly, the cassette machine hasn't changed much since this 1964 Phillips model was invented. Also on display is the famous "Mission Impossible" playback device, though the tape did not self-destruct, at least not while I was there.

In the video section you'll see the first VCR, an object much like the first computer in that it is a far cry from the sleek, modern home versions we're now used to. This machine is a behemoth half the size of the average TV control room, and the tape is 2 inches wide. You'll also see the first home models, still a far cry from the compact devices of today, but so much easier to program.

This museum started with Hammer's private collection of a few machines and is still growing. People call in all the time to ask if the old gizmo they found in the attic is worth anything. Hammer urges everyone not to throw away old equipment. "This is history," he says, "and a disposable society is in danger of destroying its valuable records and artifacts." Besides, that dusty old reel-to-reel tape recorder could be worth a fortune someday.

Special tours are available by prior arrangement, though a drop-in, self-guided tour is easy, thanks to the signs placed throughout the museum.

AMPEX MUSEUM OF MAGNETIC RECORDING, *411 Broadway, Redwood City. Phone: (415) 367-3127. Open 11:30 A.M. to 1:30 P.M. Monday through Friday. Admission: Free.*

HOW TO GET HERE: *From San Francisco, take Highway 101 South to the Woodside Road exit in Redwood City. Upon exiting, bear left onto Broadway. Follow Broadway a few blocks to the south and look for the huge Ampex sign. Look for the sign for the cafeteria and museum building.*

U.S. GEOLOGICAL SURVEY OFFICE

Now, really, a visit to a government office is usually not anybody's idea of a good time. But for a "Backroads" person, the USGS headquarters in Menlo Park is like a candy store. This is a major regional office where mapmakers, scientists, and what appear to be hundreds of federal employees study and chart the world around us. Though you can't go behind the scenes to tour the labs and drawing tables, you can reap the fruits of their labor.

If you're interested in anything having to do with land in the United States, chances are you will find a map of it here. Along with displays explaining geology and cartography, you will find just about every kind of map imaginable—mineral maps, topographical maps, aerial maps, agricultural maps, everything but your basic garden-variety road map. If you're a hiker, you can pick up a map of the region you wish to visit; a mapmaker will help you scope out the terrain. If you are interested in earthquakes, you can get a map showing every major tremor that has rocked California. Best of all, these colorful maps, many suitable for framing, cost just a few dollars each; some are available free.

If you are really crazy about maps and are willing to spend some time here, you can go to the library behind the service counter. One of my favorite maps, which is also displayed on the wall, shows the expansion of the United States, charting the original colonies, the Louisiana Purchase, the annexation of Texas, and so on. Though I had learned all about it in grade school history classes, the scope of the expansion hadn't come to life for me until I saw this.

UNITED STATES GEOLOGICAL SURVEY WESTERN REGIONAL OFFICE, *345 Middlefield Road, Menlo Park. Phone: (415) 853-8300. Open Monday through Friday, 8 A.M. to 4 P.M.*

HOW TO GET HERE: *From San Francisco, take Highway 101 South to the Marsh Road exit in Redwood City. Follow Marsh Road to Middlefield Road; turn left and continue to 345 Middlefield. Go down the long driveway to the USGS building on the right.*

PHIPPS RANCH
6

It comes as a surprise to many visitors, Easterners in particular, to find farms thriving in abundance on the rugged coastline from Half Moon Bay down to Santa Cruz. In spite of the fog and the bracing ocean air, the weather is fairly mild, constantly moist, and ideal for growing flowers, artichokes, broccoli, cauliflower, lettuces, berries, and a variety of other fruits and vegetables. Many of the big growers are open only to wholesale buyers, but down Pescadero Road is Phipps Ranch, a place set up specifically for visitors.

At first glance, Phipps Ranch seems to be a large farm stand, with fresh produce from the area and beyond. Behind the stand is a barnyard with several pens of horses, sheep, goats, mules, rabbits, pigs, and other barnyard animals, including lots of cute baby animals most of the time. Some parents begin a visit by dropping the kids off at the animals while they shop at the farm stand at leisure. But eventually the parents usually end up in back, oohing and aahing at the incredible cuteness.

The barnyard area is more than just a diversion to help shoppers. The Phippses are very concerned about the state of farming in America. Their mission is to introduce kids to farm life before the lifestyle goes the way of the horse and buggy. The Phippses offer tours to school groups and anyone else interested in what they have to say and show, including trips out into the fields for lessons about how things grow. As Carolyn Phipps says, "So many kids have never been on a farm. Too many kids think food comes from the supermarket or the freezer."

Every attempt is made to have the farm be as accessible as possible to the public. During the summer berry season, you can grab a bucket at the stand and then charge out to the fields to pick your own produce. Picnic tables are set up so that you can enjoy your purchases on the spot. You can see the planting areas devoted to specialty items, such as miniature vegetables, which the Phippses sell directly to Bay Area restaurants.

PHIPPS RANCH, *2700 Pescadero Road, Pescadero. Phone: (415) 879-0787. Open 10 A.M. to 7 P.M. during Daylight Savings Time, 10 A.M. to 6 P.M. the rest of the year. Berry-picking season is mid-June to late August. Tours, by appointment only, cost $1 per person; or you can wander around on your own for free. Closed on major holidays.*

HOW TO GET HERE: *From San Francisco, take Route 1 South to Pescadero Road. Turn left and follow Pescadero through town. Continue for about 3 miles, and you will come to the ranch on your right.*

CHAPTER **5** Santa Clara County

AREA OVERVIEW

Santa Clara County is the center of Silicon Valley. This is where you'll find computer terminals in coffeeshops and floppy disks next to the pantyhose in supermarkets. Stanford University is here, on former farmland. Now there's a strong movement to preserve what remains of the area's fruit-farming past. The surprise for many people is that Santa Clara goes far south from San Jose. That's where you'll find more wide-open spaces and a still active agricultural center. There's a booming wine industry in the south near Gilroy, which is also known as the Garlic Capital of the World. Again, Highway 101 and the more scenic, less crowded Route 280 take you south to the major population center, San Jose. Plan on an hour to reach some of the northernmost destinations.

JUNIOR HIGH EXPRESSIONISTS

Graffiti has become something of a national problem. Ever since Kilroy started appearing all over the place in the 1950s, people have taken to splashing messages and pictures on subway cars, buses, walls, and just about any other surface that can act as a free billboard. Graffiti-itis knows no economic boundaries. You will see it in the New York ghettos and in affluent suburbs like Los Altos. In Los Altos, however, they were also lucky to have Michael Durkett.

In 1972 Durkett was the art teacher at Blach Junior High School. One day the walls of the school were spray-painted with what he considered ugly messages, so he devised a plan. He took the vandals by the ears, gave them paintbrushes, and challenged them to fill the walls with the works of the great masters. Instead of a message like "School lunches are poison," suddenly a pretty good version of Rembrandt's self-portrait was featured on a wall. Other words chosen to shock were replaced by works inspired by Michelangelo.

His plan worked. The walls of the school remained grafitti-free. Though Durkett has since retired, the fine arts program has continued at the junior high. The program has become so popular that most eighth graders choose to work on the murals as part of their mandatory art class. Drive past the school for a sight to behold. You see colorful mural after mural of the art classics, from Da Vinci's Mona Lisa to Van Gogh's "Starry Night." More than 60 great works are on the walls, and the hits keep coming. And all because one teacher figured out a way to turn vandalism into creative energy and a town treasure.

Though many of the paintings are visible from the street, if you would like to see more, you must call the school for an appointment to enter school grounds. Since schools must keep track of adults on the grounds, you are not invited to just walk in and start browsing.

BLACH JUNIOR HIGH SCHOOL MURALS, *1120 Covington Street, Los Altos. Phone: (415) 964-1196.*

HOW TO GET HERE: *From San Francisco, take Highway 101 South to Route 280. Follow 280 South to the Magdalena Avenue exit (about an hour south of San Francisco). Exit to the east and cross over the Foothill Expressway. Bear left onto Springer Road. Follow Springer until you come to Covington. Turn right to the school.*

SHIRLEY TEMPLE'S DOLLS ②

I don't know what it is about Palo Alto that attracts dolls, but I find it curious that two major collections are to be found in the same university town. One is the world's most complete collection of Barbies (see "Barbie Hall of Fame" in *Jerry Graham's Bay Area Backroads*). The other is a huge display of antique dolls from around the world, featuring the (enormous) personal collection of child star Shirley Temple. These are displayed in the halls and lobby of Children's Hospital at Stanford. This remarkable pediatric facility, a story in itself, really, is an independent, nonprofit hospital affiliated with the Stanford University School of Medicine and dedicated to the care of acutely and chronically ill and disabled children. It is located at the eastern end of the campus of Stanford University and just a few minutes from the busy Stanford Shopping Center.

The hospital's remarkable doll collection began in 1938 when an heir to the Mark Hopkins fortune donated the family's accumulation of dolls from around the world. Over the years, friends of the hospital contributed toys, each with an interesting past. There's a Normandy doll, smuggled out of Paris in the 1920s; a Polish doll, sent in return for clothing donated to the Dutch after World War II; a German doll dismantled by customs officials looking for narcotics; and, one of the most valuable in the collection, a 26-inch French beauty with a bisque head, brown glass eyes, satin slippers, a brocade and satin dress, turquoise earrings,

Santa Clara

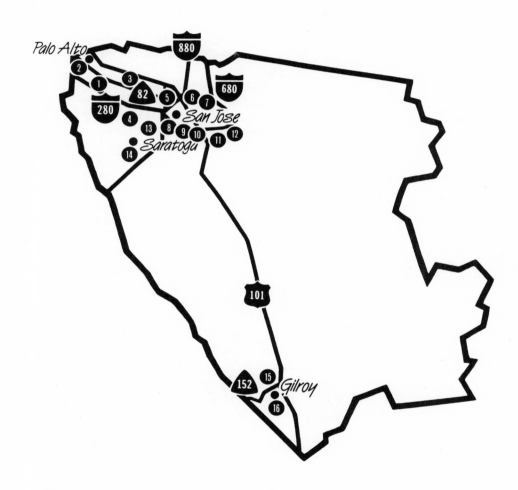

and a large green velvet hat with blue ostrich plumes. However, the main attraction arrived in 1971, when Shirley Temple donated her personal collection of dolls.

Shirley Temple Black (or "Mrs. Black," as she likes to be called) lives nearby in the community of Woodside; she and her husband have been longtime supporters of Children's Hospital. As you can imagine, young Shirley had more dolls than your average American girl. When she was the toast of Hollywood, her family took her on vacation to Hawaii, and a press agent put out the word that Shirley was lonely for her favorite doll back home. That set off a flood. Adoring fans sent dolls from all over the world.

Among those she received are a 5-foot-tall Japanese bride and some very tiny French grandparent dolls made of bread crumbs and seated on miniature chairs. Over the years her collection grew to include carvings of costar Bill "Bojangles" Robinson and several that bear her likeness. These are on display in climate-controlled glass cases, so they still look brand-new. The doll historian might also be interested in the examples of the work of famous dollmakers on display, including Lenci of Italy, Tête Juneau of France, and Bernard Rauca, a Russian who worked in Paris. For the more media-minded visitor, the collection of celebrity dolls includes the Dionne quintuplets and a 1938 Princess Elizabeth.

For the Shirley Temple dolls, this is a visit that does not involve a tour or a reservation, and there is no admission charge. Just gaze at the cases in the main lobby. The rest of the collection is in cases throughout the halls of the hospital. Since that's where the patients are, you must be accompanied by hospital staff or volunteers. Advance reservations are required.

CHILDREN'S HOSPITAL AT STANFORD DOLL COLLECTION AND SHIRLEY TEMPLE BLACK DOLL COLLECTION, *located in the hallways and lobby of Children's Hospital, 520 Sand Hill Road, Palo Alto. Phone: (415) 327-4800. Advance arrangements necessary to see the entire doll collection; no advance arrangements required to see Shirley Temple's collection. Admission: Free.*

HOW TO GET HERE: *From San Francisco, take Highway 101 South to the University Avenue exit in Palo Alto. Follow University through town and onto the campus, then follow the signs to the hospital.*

OLSON'S CHERRY FARM ③

It is tempting to say that life is just a bowl of cherries at the Olson Farm in Sunnyvale, but that would obscure the incredible struggle that has gone into preserving the last fruit farm on El Camino Real. In case you're not familiar with El Camino, it is the main drag through much of the Peninsula, running from South San Francisco through San Jose. Actually, the road cuts a path all the way to southern California, but the portion we're concerned about here is in the heart of Santa Clara County. Once this road was lined with grain and fruit farms; today it's stores, restaurants, gas stations, and one remaining fruit farm.

Charley and Deborah Olson are running things these days. They are the third and fourth generation of the Olson family in Sunnyvale, and despite their surroundings, they produce and sell some of the sweetest cherries you'll ever taste. Charley's grandparents started the farm in 1899, and he says he's determined to stay in business to celebrate the centennial in 1999. Charley runs the farm, which is spread out in back, hidden from El Camino Real. Daughter Deborah runs the fruit stand by the road. Usually she'll be decked out in cherry earrings, cherry-decorated socks, and cherry-colored lipstick. She creates a general atmosphere of fun, and most visitors never bother going beyond the fruit stand. But you are welcome to stroll around in back and see some of this last-of-its-kind property.

Out back you'll see rows and rows of cherry trees, mostly Bings. You'll also see the original Olson home plus many buildings that once housed workers and are now used for storage and processing. You'll also see one of the most unusual headquarters you can imagine—the offices of Sunnyvale State University, right there in Charley's office, which looks like a hot-dog shack. Charley created this mythical institution several years ago, and it has grown to have a prestigious faculty and staff of locals and friends who have joined in the act. For example, Bill Walsh, ex-coach of the San Francisco 49ers, is listed as SSU's assistant tennis coach. John Madden, the sports broadcaster who travels only by train or bus, is the aeronautics instructor, and Peter Ueberroth, the former baseball commissioner, is listed as university travel adviser.

What's the purpose of Sunnyvale State? Charley, president of the university, uses it to establish credentials so that he can get special seats for college athletic events. He hasn't missed the NCAA basketball finals in years, and he gets invited to all the parties.

Sure, this tomfoolery doesn't have much to do with growing cherries, but it does have a lot to do with the kind of spirit that's willing to preserve the last farm in the neighborhood. Face it, they could get millions for their land, but the Olsons have been fighting the encroachment of the highway and new buildings for years, and they intend to keep up the battle. It is quite a responsibility to be the last holdout; and since they also produce such great fruit, it is quite an accomplishment.

OLSON'S CHERRY FARM AND STAND, *El Camino Real, Sunnyvale. Phone: (408) 736-3726. Open May 15 through August 31, 7 A.M. to 7 P.M. daily. Olson cherries are available May through July 4; Washington State cherries arrive in late June and are sold after the Olson crop is sold out.*

HOW TO GET HERE: *From San Francisco, take Highway 101 South past Palo Alto to the Mathilda Avenue exit in Sunnyvale. Exit to the right and continue on Mathilda to El Camino Real. Turn left on El Camino and look for the cherry stand on the right.*

CALIFORNIA HISTORY CENTER ④

Here's an ideal place to visit in combination with a stop at Olson's Cherry Farm. One of the great surprises of the Bay Area is right on busy Stevens Creek Boulevard, on the campus of De Anza College. Le Petit Trianon, alias the California History Center, is a jewel of a building that houses a museum, a regional history library, a learning center, and a glorious setting for special events.

The building predates the college, and it played a part in the history of the Santa Clara Valley. Built around 1895, Le Petit Trianon was the home of San Francisco financier Charles Baldwin and his wife, Ella Hobart. They commissioned the famous architect Willis Polk to build a glittering showplace for entertaining the San Francisco social set. Polk was urged to evoke the feeling of the palace at Versailles. The result is this stately building, with its white columns and arched windows, its pools and gardens.

Later the property was sold to become the site for De Anza College, with the stipulation that the home be preserved. To make room for the Flint Center Auditorium, Le Petit Trianon was moved to its present location, and restoration began. The California History Center Foundation stepped in to continue the work of not only saving this architectural treasure but creating a community resource as well.

When you visit the center, you have several options. You can concentrate on the museum, which features well-researched and nicely displayed exhibits on the various phases of valley history. The displays change periodically but may include such subjects as the contributions of a particular ethnic group or the passing legacy of farms in the area.

Or you may choose to concentrate on the resources of the Regional History Library, which is a stately, skylit room filled with books, photographs, videotapes, recorded oral histories, and other material related to the Santa Clara Valley. This noncirculating library was the room where the Baldwins probably read the evening newspaper or the latest novel by Jack London.

You can tour the mansion on your own, or groups of 10 or more can sign up for a docent-led tour of the mansion, which still contains some of the Baldwins' original furniture. When you visit, the emphasis will be on the rich history of the area. If you're lucky, you'll meet Yvonne Jacobsen, who is a lecturer and a board member of the center. Yvonne became a History Center booster in a very personal way. In 1979 Yvonne, who holds a master's degree in English from Columbia, took time off from her teaching job to research the story of her father, who was nearing the end of his life. He had farmed in the Santa Clara Valley, and Yvonne realized that her family story was typical of all the valley farms. She wrote the book *Passing Farms, Enduring Valleys*, published by the California History Center.

Yvonne and her colleagues believe that it is very important for Californians, most of whom have come from someplace else, to have a sense of history of their home. "Learning about the past gives roots and a sense of place," she says. Yvonne also wants newcomers to realize that there were prunes and cherries in this valley long before there were Apples—computers, that is. In fact, her family runs the last cherry farm in Santa Clara County (see Olson's Cherry Farm, page 64). She says that one thing history teaches you is that nothing is permanent, and thus Silicon Valley may just be a passing phase, to be replaced one day by farms.

CALIFORNIA HISTORY CENTER, *De Anza College Campus, 21250 Stevens Creek Boulevard, Cupertino. Phone: (408) 996-4712. Open 8 A.M. to 4:30 P.M. Monday through Friday, 10 A.M. to 2 P.M. Saturday. Closed during summer vacation. Groups of 10 or more can call ahead to arrange for docent-led tours. Admission: Free.*

HOW TO GET HERE: *From San Francisco, take Highway 101 South to Route 280 toward San Jose. Exit at Stevens Creek Boulevard in Cupertino and head toward the De Anza College campus. Park in the Flint Center parking lot, and walk down the path to the Trianon building. From Olson's Cherry Farm, take the Sunnyvale-Saratoga Road (Route 85) from El Camino Real to Stevens Creek Boulevard and turn right to the campus.*

Santa Clara is one of those overlooked communities. People usually know that the Great America amusement park is there, and others have heard of Santa Clara University, but that's about it.

TRITON MUSEUM

The Triton Museum of Art could change that.

I should point out that there has been a Triton Museum in town for 20 years, but it was not the world-class facility that opened in late 1987. Thanks to some grants made by those who made their fortunes in the Silicon Valley (most notably the Packards, of Hewlett-Packard), the new, improved Triton Museum is an architectural gem, arguably the most attractive art facility in the entire Bay Area.

The building design consists of a series of pyramids finished in stucco, with a lovely courtyard and sculpture garden. Inside, you experience a sense of space and light. Each gallery is equipped with state-of-the-art lighting along with louvered ceilings that allow natural light in while protecting the paintings from the rays of the sun. All in all, there are six galleries and a series of rooms used for lectures and social gatherings.

The art on display is eclectic. The permanent collection consists primarily of nineteenth- and twentieth-century American art. Always on display are the works of California artists, past and present. Rotating exhibits, usually set for six-week runs, feature major national and international exhibitions. At least one gallery is likely to feature contemporary works.

This is a good destination for those who have been intimidated by the stuffy quality of some art establishments and a perfect spot for seasoned art lovers. The community of Santa Clara is proud of its showcase, and the staff of volunteers will be happy to greet you and answer your questions.

TRITON MUSEUM OF ART, *1505 Warburton Avenue, Santa Clara. Phone: (408) 247-3754. Open Monday, Wednesday, Thursday, and Friday, 10 A.M. to 5 P.M.; Tuesday, 10 A.M. to 9 P.M.; Saturday and Sunday, noon to 5 P.M. Admission: Free.*

HOW TO GET HERE: *From San Francisco, take Highway 101 South to the San Tomas Expressway South. Continue to Monroe Street. Turn left on Monroe and continue to Warburton Avenue. Turn right. The museum is between Monroe and Scott streets, on the left side, across from the Civic Center.*

AMERICAN MUSEUM OF QUILTS AND RELATED ARTS ⑥

I recall seeing several years ago a book or a pamphlet called *Quilts in Women's Lives*. Though I don't recall the actual publication, I do remember the central idea: that quilts and textiles have long been a medium for creative and political expression.

This idea comes to life in a little white house tucked away in a residential neighborhood near downtown San Jose. It's the home of the American Museum of Quilts and Related Arts, the nation's first museum dedicated to the preservation and exhibition of this cozy yet powerful art form.

It's a charming and inviting place, as warm and comfortable as the feelings evoked by these colorful textiles. The Santa Clara Quilt Guild founded the museum in 1977. Though the practice of quiltmaking dates back as far as 3400 B.C., it was American women who created patchwork quilts. These quilts provided a system of symbolic communication, often referring to the events of the day: the Lincoln-Douglas debates, westward expansion, the Gold Rush, the Underground Railroad, and women's suffrage. You can see examples of these on display.

In modern times, just as more traditional canvases have become media for abstract emotional expression, quilts have become very colorful and expressive and often funny. Last time I was there, on display was a quilt honoring the San

Francisco Giants, with team members' names included in various patches; when I stepped back, I could see that the entire design spelled out the team's battle cry, "H-m-m Baby."

Interestingly enough, quilting is no longer the domain of sweet little old ladies; it has become a very popular hobby among both men and women. Over 800 quilting guilds now exist in the United States, one of the largest of which is the Bay Area's own East Bay Heritage Guild. Perhaps the most famous quilt of our time is the AIDS Memorial Quilt, each patch memorializing a casualty of the disease.

Director Leach explains the current interest in quilts in terms of the comforting nature of the process, especially when using Mom's old apron, Dad's old shirt, and a piece of Brother's old jeans to make a family heirloom. In addition to the 100 or so quilts on display at the museum, the gift shop has an impressive collection of books and quilt-related gifts, You'll also find volunteers working on their own project as they tend the shop. Classes, lectures, and workshops are also offered on a regular basis.

Those in the know come from around the world to visit this collection. The average person has the chance to see some beautiful work, to talk to eager hobbyists, and to tap into the warm, cozy feeling generated by these canvases. "We want to show that quilts are much more than just bedcovers," says Leach.

AMERICAN MUSEUM OF QUILTS AND RELATED ARTS, *766 South Second Street, San Jose. Phone: (408) 971-0323. Open 10 A.M. to 4 P.M., Tuesday through Saturday. Admission: Free.*

HOW TO GET HERE: *From San Francisco, take Highway 101 South to Route 280 South and continue to San Jose. Take the Seventh Street exit and turn left onto Reed Street. Go south to Second Street and turn right. Follow Second back under the highway to the museum. It's on the corner of Margaret and South Second streets.*

THE CRUCIBLE

The main attraction at the Fine Arts Center in San Jose is the Crucible. Not the play by Arthur Miller but a large vessel for melting and pouring liquid bronze into artists' molds. This is the kind of scene you have witnessed in a dozen classroom and industrial films, but here in San Jose you can see it live.

The Fine Arts Foundry is at one of the most unlikely backroads locations you could imagine. But it is an off-the-beaten-path attraction, and the show is spectacular. The foundry is the headquarters for artists who make large artwork in metal. And big sculptures require big machines. There's a gallery at the entrance to the foundry; here you can see the fruits of the labors of the artists toiling in back, where the real spectacle is. Here you get to see skilled workers melting bronze and pouring the hot, hot liquid from the giant crucible into molds. The light from the molten metal is brilliant; you can feel the heat and smell the unusual aroma. If you time it right, you will see the artists remove the hardened sculpture from the mold and add the finishing touches.

Between the first spark of the artist's inspiration and the finished product unfolds a process that involves creating a design in wood or plaster, then making a series of molds. This is a centuries-old process, and artists from all over the state come here to work since this is one of the largest art-based foundries on the West Coast. The visitor has the opportunity to see all stages of the artmaking process, from the rough design in plaster to the finished product in bronze.

FINE ARTS METAL FOUNDRY, *825 North Tenth Street, San Jose. Phone: (408) 292-7628. Call ahead to see the foundry and the pouring process; this usually takes place three times a week, and the days and times vary. Visitors are welcome into the gallery 9 A.M. to 6 P.M., Tuesday through Friday, and weekends by appointment. Admission: Free.*

HOW TO GET HERE: *From San Francisco, take Highway 101 South to central San Jose. Exit on Thirteenth Street North and take the first right turn on Hedding Street. Go three blocks to Tenth Street and turn left. Look for number 825 on the right.*

MUMMIES FROM NIEMAN-MARCUS (8)

The Rosicrucian Museum attracts people from all over the world. Some 250,000 living souls find their way here each year, making this San Jose's most popular attraction. Oddly, very few of these visitors are from the Bay Area, which seems a shame. This is a remarkable museum, featuring the West Coast's largest collection of Egyptian and Babylonian artifacts.

The Rosicrucian order may sound like some arcane sect, aligned with the likes of witchcraft or voodoo. But as it turns out, it is a very active educational organization dedicated to exploring such philosophical issues as what life's all about and why we're here, and it is dedicated to preserving historical artifacts that may provide some clues to the answers.

The Rosicrucian Museum in San Jose is the international headquarters for the Rosicrucian order. Inside this Egyptian-style building are administration offices and a museum. The museum section started in 1929 as the personal collection of the order's director H. Spencer Lewis. Over the years more and more acquisitions were made, and a museum was formally established in 1932.

The present large facility was built in 1966, its façade a reproduction of the Karnak Temple at Thebes in Upper Egypt. The beliefs of the Rosicrucian order are quite similar to those of ancient Egypt, thus the interest in collecting things from the time and place of Cleopatra. Inside is a remarkable assemblage of statuary, amulets, and scarabs. Children in particular are fascinated by the mummy gallery. Here you'll see the tombs of priests, queens, and pharaohs, plus a mummified assortment of cats, birds, and other animals, including the head of a sacred bull.

There's an amusing story about the acquisition of a pair of his-and-her sarco-phagi. It seems that several years ago Nieman-Marcus offered a pair of 2500-year-old coffins for sale in its Christmas catalog. The museum curator put in his order and soon received a phone call from a chagrined representative of the store. The curator was informed that one of the coffins was not empty, and the store offered to dispose of the unsightly mummy inside. The curator quickly explained that an occupied coffin was perfectly acceptable. This unexpected guest turned out to be Usermontu, a priest who lived about 600 B.C. His mummy, his coffin, and the coffin of his wife, Irterau, are on permanent display in the mummy gallery.

The most popular exhibit is the museum's full-size replica of a walk-in rock tomb. This subterranean burial chamber is based on those dating back 4,000 years and is the only one of its kind in the United States. Among the hieroglyphics in the tomb is a drawing that summarizes much of the Egyptian and Rosicrucian philosophy. It is a judgment scene in which the heart of the deceased is weighed against the feather of truth. In other words, to be lighthearted and truthful are important balances in life. It's hard to argue with that.

If all this talk of mummies and burial chambers seems depressing, there are other treasures to behold, such as jewels, pottery, and an "authentic" figure of Cleopatra (meaning, I suppose, that she modeled for it).

One of the purposes of this museum is to expose the public to the accessibility of Egyptian art. Special tours of this educational, spiritual, and cultural center are offered throughout the year, especially to school and senior citizens' groups.

ROSICRUCIAN EGYPTIAN MUSEUM, *Rosicrucian Park at Park and Naglee avenues, San Jose. Phone: (408) 287-9171; on weekends call (408) 287-2807. Open Tuesday through Friday, 9 A.M. to 5 P.M.; closed Mondays. Admission: Adults, $3; teenagers 12 to 17, $1; seniors, $2.50; children under 12 and members, free.*

HOW TO GET HERE: *From San Francisco, take Highway 101 South toward San Jose. Exit at Route 17 (Santa Cruz). Take the Alameda exit south from Route 17, and follow Naglee Avenue; turn right. Take Naglee to the first stoplight, and turn left into the museum parking lot.*

Only a short distance from Silicon Valley and the intersection of Routes 680, 280, and Highway 101 lies a farm—certainly one of the most out-of-place farms in the world. Just the fact that it's there makes it worth a visit. But more important, the Emma Prusch Farm and Park offers much to see and learn.

Emma Prusch Park is 47 acres of fine Santa Clara land that was deeded to

FARM UNDER THE FREEWAY

the city of San Jose by Emma Prusch in 1962. She was the last member of a longtime farming family. Her gift came with one stipulation: that it continue to be operated as a farm. Evidently she foresaw the booming growth of the area.

Today on the farm you are never far from the roar of the freeway and jet planes, yet it is possible to ignore all that and step back in time. The original nineteenth-century, 10-room farmhouse has been restored and is used as an information center and offices. You'll also see a pond and a lively community of chickens, peacocks, ducks, and geese, all apparently unconcerned about the traffic jam on the cloverleaf behind them.

My advice is to make a beeline for the barn. I'm told this is the third largest in California. It is filled with cows, sheep, pigs, and other farm animals, cared for by local members of the Future Farmers of America and the 4-H.

The day we arrived to shoot the television story about the place, one of our cameramen, Stan Drury, focused just in time to capture on tape the birth of two baby lambs—not an uncommon sight here, especially in the spring. These unbearably cute little critters were born about noon, and by 1 o'clock, the little lambs were already nursing and trying out their legs, attempting to walk. The barn was also filled with little curly-tailed piglets who kept roaming from stall to stall, visiting the sheep and cattle.

This is truly a community farm. Local residents can come and raise vegetables in the garden. Most impressive is the fruit orchard, where 100 kinds of rare fruit from around the world are grown. The purpose of this is to serve the many ethnic groups who have moved to the area. Africans, Asians, or Central Americans can come to the farm to find foods they thought they would never see again. And they can get seeds and advice on how to grow the trees in the yards of their new homes.

Here you'll find fruits you may never have heard of, such as limequat (a cross between a lime and a kumquat), pawpaw, gumi, and sapote. In addition, exotic varieties of apples, cherries, guavas, persimmons, grapefruit, and other citrus are grown here. In the spring, the garden is an international fruit salad.

When I visited, Alice Valenzuela, a volunteer and a member of the farm's board of trustees who showed me around, expressed a concern that is growing in the Santa Clara Valley. "Generations of people are growing up in Silicon Valley," she said, "who think an apple is a computer. Here we can show them what country life is, and it's right in their own backyard."

EMMA PRUSCH FARM, *647 South King Road, San Jose. Phone: (408) 926-5555. Open daily 8:30 A.M. to 8:30 P.M. during Daylight Savings Time; 8:30 A.M. to 6 P.M. the rest of the year. Admission: Free.*

HOW TO GET HERE: *From San Francisco, take Highway 101 or Route 280 South to San Jose. From 101, exit on Story Road and turn left (east); the entrance to the park will be on your left. From Route 280, exit on South King Road and continue to the park; the entrance will be on your right. The white farmhouse is the visitor information center.*

So far I've talked a lot about the disappearing farm situation in Santa Clara County. Just as the Napa Valley seems full of wineries, the Santa Clara County Valley seems to have many last-of-its-type places.

Truth be told, once upon a time, all this area was agricultural, so the last farm stand and the last cherry orchard really are special places. As you drive up to J and P Farms, you'll learn how difficult it is to hold on to a farm. The first thing you will see are the signs leading up to the produce stand. Each sign tells a story: "Highway 85 will mean death to this orchard" and "Buy this property: Beautiful view of 8 wide lanes, fast-moving traffic, high noise level, polluted air, aroma of diesel fuel, blowing litter, blinding lights at night . . . starts someplace, goes nowhere."

These signs were put there by the owner of J and P Farms, Phil Consantino, who is waging a one-man war against a highway. More than that, he's fighting to save the farms that are left in the Santa Clara Valley. As Phil says, "It took nature a million years to make the most fertile valley in the world. It took only thirty to cover it with asphalt."

Phil and his family grow some of the best-tasting fruit you'll ever have in your life. They sell their walnuts, almonds, apples, kiwis, grapes, and persimmons at the family-run produce stand, and you can wander among the 1,000 trees on the 5-acre farm to see how they're grown. Phil's dad started this farm in 1945; today Phil grows nearly 60 varieties of nuts and fruits, some of them one-of-a-kind. He considers it his mission to grow types of peaches, pears, berries, and apricots that are no longer commercially viable for big-volume companies. This is the kind of fruit that tastes like fruit and reminds you what's missing from supermarket varieties.

When you talk to Phil, he sounds like one of those guys on TV who knows everything about fruits and vegetables. Take tomatoes, for example. According to Phil, most of the tomatoes we buy in the market have been picked green and then shipped to a warehouse for gassing. That's how they get their color and tough skin, the latter minimizing bruising during mass transportation in giant trucks.

Every year new housing developments move closer and closer to Consantino's farm, and the planned extension of the highway looms in the future. But for now, the family keeps working their land and keeping up the fight to preserve what they've got. Why doesn't Phil take the easy way out by simply selling his land and moving to Florida? "We take pride in growing fruit that tastes like this," says Phil. "You can't put a price tag on that." And when you taste it, you'll see his point.

J AND P FARMS, *4977 Carter Avenue, San Jose. Phone: (408) 264-3497. Fruits are ripe from mid-May, starting with peaches and berries, through mid-September, with grapes, prickly pears, and apples.*

HOW TO GET HERE: *From San Francisco, take Highway 101 or Route 280 South to Route 17 South. Take the Camden Avenue exit and stay on Camden until you come to a fork at Hillsdale Avenue. Bear right onto Hillsdale. Less than a mile later, turn left onto Branham Lane, then take a quick right onto Carter. Continue to the farm.*

NEW ALMADEN
⑪

Many people who happen onto the Almaden Expressway in San Jose assume they are on a road named after a winery. Wrong. The road and the nearby community of New Almaden are named not for a wine or a vine but for a mine, the largest mercury mine in the world, in Spain. New Almaden was the site of North America's first and richest quicksilver mine. Once upon a time, between 1847 and 1912 to be exact, there were three mining communities in the area, each pulling out tens of millions of dollars in quicksilver used in medicine, gold mining, and weapon manufacture.

Today, New Almaden is a picturesque historic community, a step back in time and tempo from citified San Jose and the busy namesake expressway. The entire village is a historic landmark of restored homes and community buildings. It should be noted, however, that the area is getting smaller every year as more and more housing developments crop up on Almaden Avenue.

There was a time when New Almaden was considered the roughest, toughest town in the West. It's said that only one murder on a payday was considered a quiet day. Law and order was finally established around 1870, in the person of the mine boss. He ran things from the Casa Grande, a red frame building that was built as a hotel but was so nice the mine boss decided to call it home. This was when emissaries from all over the world came here to negotiate for the mercury extracted from the ground. John McLaren, the landscape artisit who designed Golden Gate Park in San Francisco, created a beautiful yard outside the Casa Grande, complete with a gazebo sent by the emperor of China. The great house is now headquarters for an insurance company but has a public restaurant and an Opry House featuring weekend melodrama.

The hills around New Almaden are still honeycombed with tunnels; one is open to visitors and is run under the auspices of the county as part of a 3,600-acre park. For the best insight into what once went on in town, head for the New Almaden Museum, which is a few minutes beyond the Casa Grande, behind the

Clayton House. (Many of the homes in this area are named for the original occupants.)

For years the museum was the private property of Connie Perham, who grew up in town and began collecting things as the town started to disappear before her very eyes. The mines shut down in 1912, and many of the buildings were gradually demolished over the years. Connie accumulated several roomfuls of history, documenting early mine techniques, the history and uses of quicksilver, photos and artifacts of the various mining communities, and even personal items that were left behind. When she reached her eighties, operating a museum became too much for her, so Connie sold her collection to the county.

The park itself offers wild canyons, wildflowers, rolling hillsides, trails, and the opportunity to see one of the mines. You will be amazed to learn that in this quiet village, more than $70 million of mercury was taken from the hills.

NEW ALMADEN COUNTY PARK, *San Jose. For information about Casa Grande and performances at the Opry House, call (408) 268-2492; for mine tours, call (408) 268-1729. The museum is open Saturdays, noon to 4 P.M.*

HOW TO GET HERE: *From San Jose, take Route 280 East to the Vine Street exit. Turn right onto Vine Street and continue until it becomes the Almaden Express-way. Continue several more miles, past the intersection of Almaden Expressway and Camden Avenue, to Almaden Road, which will be on your right. Follow Almaden Road for 2½ miles to the center of town.*

VIRL NORTON'S ZEBRAS

You run into a lot of cowboy types out on the backroads. But for authentic der-ring-do, no one is quite like Virl Norton. Virl does things like race horses in 100-mile endurance contests and compete in New York-to-Sacramento mule races. His checkered career also includes climbing smokestacks and TV towers for a living. The most remarkable thing about Virl is that he still does it all, even in his seventies.

Of his many challenges, none was more adventurous than his decision to tame zebras. Everybody told him it was impossible, that zebras are the nastiest, most ornery animals. But he did it anyway. Now you can stop by his ranch and watch him in action.

While I visited Virl, he was recovering from a hernia operation. Still he in-sisted on saddling up an uncooperative zebra. After a struggle, Virl convinced the animal that he was the boss, all the while telling me the story of seeing zebras for the first time in Texas and deciding he wanted to take on the chal-lenge. It takes quite a while to break them, but now they are a part of his ranch, along with his horses.

How tough are zebras? Virl says that wild horses and grizzly bears are for kids compared to "the horses in striped pajamas." Still, Virl loves a challenge and has accomplished what he set out to do. If your timing is right, you might see him riding his zebra-drawn wagon down to the local supermarket, something he does just for the kick of seeing how people on the street react.

As for the ranch, it is the one holdout in an area loaded with housing developments. As you head up Virl's long driveway, you get farther and farther away from San Jose, physically and spiritually. His is a very large ranch on the edge of the state's fastest-growing city; it feels more like Oklahoma than northern California. Here Virl and his assistants carry on like it's still the Wild West, tending the land and working the horses, zebras, and other ranch animals. Virl owns some more land farther north, just in case the city gets too close, but he says he'd prefer to keep on ranching right here. Why doesn't he retire, or at least slow down? "I've seen too many other fellas sit in a chair and just stay there. I'm not going to do that," he says. And that is that.

Visitors are welcome to stop by, shoot the breeze, and look at the zebras. Just be sure to keep your distance. "They'll fight you till they die," warns Virl.

VIRL NORTON'S ZEBRAS, *20206 Harry Road, San Jose. Phone: (408) 268-1745. Call ahead to be sure Virl is around.*

HOW TO GET HERE: *From San Francisco, take Highway 101 South to Route 280 to the Almaden Expressway. Take it to Harry Road; turn left. Virl's driveway is the second on the left; it is unmarked. Drive all the way back.*

CAMPBELL MUSEUM

If you didn't know better, you might think Campbell was just another section of sprawling San Jose. That would make Benjamin Campbell—as well as many of the current residents of this quiet town—very unhappy. Campbell was a rancher who went west from Missouri as a young man of 19. In 1887 he subdivided his 160-acre ranch to create a community where folks were invited to flee the wild and woolly streets of San Jose. The only condition was that no saloons could be built on his land.

The city of Campbell was not officially incorporated until 1952. What you'll find today is small-town charm highlighted in the downtown section by the town historical museum. The building itself played a role in the town's history, first as City Hall, then as the Police and Fire Department. It opened as a museum in 1984, and it covers a wide range of subjects such as the early settlers, the growth of agriculture in this part of Santa Clara County, early businesses, the rise of new industry, and the effects of various wars on the community.

I have often said that a good way to get to know a town is by touring the town museum. The one in Campbell is very thoughtfully laid out, and the story of Campbell turns out to be the story of most small towns in California. The displays are beautifully presented, and most of the exhibits are hands-on. You'll see old ads from the days when this area was one large pruneyard, the clothing and household artifacts of the early settlers, plus changing exhibits of current interest. Much advance planning has gone into the design of the museum; you can walk through history in the large and well-lighted gallery.

CAMPBELL HISTORICAL MUSEUM, *First Street and Civic Center Drive, Campbell. Phone: (408) 866-2119. Open Tuesday through Saturday, 1:30 to 4:30 P.M.; closed holidays and the last two weeks of December. Admission: Free.*

HOW TO GET HERE: *From San Francisco, take Highway 101 or Route 280 South to Route 17. Continue south to the East Hamilton Avenue exit. Follow Hamilton Avenue to the right (west) to Winchester Boulevard. Turn left (south) on Winchester and continue to Campbell Avenue. Turn left and continue on Campbell to North First Street. Turn left and park in the large lot on the right. The museum is to the right of the parking lot.*

On the "Backroads" program we have visited many wonderful hostels, those overnight accommodations where guests can "rough it" and spend the night for next to nothing. Though many places are interesting, by far the most beautiful has been the one located in Sanborn Park, about 10 minutes from the town of Saratoga. In fact, it's worth visiting even if you're not planning to stay there. This is one of the few hostels in the official American Youth Hostel (AYH) system that welcomes day visitors.

Nestled in the woods near a pond, this hostel looks more like a country estate —probably because it was a country estate, or at least a summer "cabin" built by the county's first Superior Court judge, James Welch. Most of us would not call this place a "cabin." The rooms are large and airy, and the use of wood is lavish; most impressive is the curving redwood staircase leading to the second floor. There's a large, inviting kitchen, a hexagonal dining room, and beautiful grounds with acres of oaks and redwoods and a big, cool gazebo.

So how did this former county estate turn into a youth hostel? It wasn't easy —just ask Sylvia Carroll, who, with a dedicated group of friends, saved the house. After Judge Welch died, the place just sat there for years, falling into disrepair. The county decided that something had to be done, and that might have meant demolition. But Sylvia and friends led a drive to save the property, raised nearly half a million dollars to fix it up, and promised to keep it running as a hostel.

Sylvia still runs things, along with her menagerie of friendly dogs, cats, turkeys, and other animals. (I should mention that these animals get special treatment and peacefully coexist with the human population. Last time I visited I

SANBORN PARK HOSTEL

was amazed to watch a turkey descend the interior redwood staircase with all the aplomb of Gloria Swanson.) Sylvia gets to know all her guests, who come from all over the world.

Those interested in simply touring the house or roaming the grounds will find the welcome mat out most of the time; this is a busy place, so it's a good idea to call ahead.

SANBORN PARK YOUTH HOSTEL, *in Sanborn Park, Saratoga. Phone: (408) 741-9555.*

HOW TO GET HERE: *From San Francisco, take Highway 101 or Route 280 South. Near San Jose, exit for Route 17 South toward Santa Cruz. Exit onto Route 9 headed toward Saratoga–Los Gatos. Follow Route 9 into and through Saratoga; continue 2 miles up a winding, hilly road. Turn left onto Sanborn Road and continue for about a mile. Look for the AYH sign; follow the signs to the large redwood home.*

CARPET OF FLOWERS (15)

If you enjoy being dazzled by floral displays, drive toward the coast on Hecker Pass Road. Look to the left a little over a mile after you leave the city of Gilroy. If you time it right, you will see thousands of snapdragons, pansies, carnations, marigolds, and zinnias in bloom outside the Goldsmith Seeds test gardens.

You may never have heard of Goldsmith Seeds, but the company is one of the largest producers of flower seeds in the world. In addition to the spread in Gilroy, the Goldsmiths have facilities in other exotic locations like Kenya, Guatemala, Denmark, and Michigan. They sell their product to major marketers like Burpee and Park, who in turn produce those enticing glossy catalogs and sell the seeds to the public.

Fortunately for flower lovers in the Bay Area, visitors are welcome to drop by the company's 17 acres in Gilroy. What looks like a stunning garden is actually a carefully watched experiment. The Goldsmith folks are checking for things like uniformity of blossom, how early a certain plant might bloom, water consumption, and other horticultural considerations. Inside the greenhouses is where the relatively secret work of creating new plants and hybrids goes on, and guests are not invited in. As owner Glenn Goldsmith explains, this is modern science, taking Luther Burbank's vision into the 1980s and beyond.

But the outdoor gardens are much nicer than indoor science labs anyway. No formal tours are offered, but you are welcome to wander through the garden, which includes a shaded area with picnic tables and a pond stocked with colorful Japanese *koi*. The gardens are planted twice a year; they bloom from January to April and from July to September.

Here's something that may make you groan: At the end of the season, the rows of beautiful flowers are plowed under to make way for the new crop.

One word of caution: Because the fields of flowers are so eye-grabbing, some motorists stop to take a look. Don't! This is a potentially dangerous road with lots of truck traffic. Goldsmith has provided a large parking area with lots of room for visitors. Pull in instead of parking along the busy highway.

GOLDSMITH SEED COMPANY, *Hecker Pass Road (Route 152), Gilroy. Phone: (408) 847-7333. Gardens open to the public daily during daylight hours. You're welcome to stroll through the gardens any time of year, but you're most likely to find flowers in bloom January through April and July through September. Admission: Free.*

HOW TO GET HERE: *From San Francisco, take Highway 101 South through San Jose to Route 152 West. Follow the signs to Watsonville. Goldsmith Seed is about a mile and a half west of the city of Gilroy, on the left side of Route 152.*

THOMAS KRUSE WINERY
⑯

In a wine region known for its small, intimate wineries, none is so small or so intimate as the Kruse operation. In fact, you will probably miss it unless you look for the eye-catching cactus pear ranch next door on the south side of Route 152.

There is a sign, but it's likely to be on the ground or leaning against a tree. But when you finally find the driveway, just pull in and park, and walk around to the back. Suddenly you will find yourself in the production facility and tasting room of the Thomas Kruse Winery.

When you drop by for a tour and tasting, production might come to a screeching halt. That's because your tour guide is also the owner and chief bottle washer of this operation. Tom Kruse (not to be confused with Tom Cruise, the guy in Hollywood) will cheerfully show you his ancient equipment, the kind that might be on display elsewhere as antiques; here it's the production line. More than likely you'll see his son or his wife, Karen, putting labels on the bottle or a friend from a nearby farm dropping by with a box of peaches to hand out to winery guests. Or you might catch Tom out in the yard next to the barbeque wearing a welder's protective visor as he performs the tricky and potentially explosive job of corking the champagne by hand. In other words, this is a casual place, full of warmth and humor, not a stuffy wine boutique. It is also one of those making-dreams-come-true places.

Once upon a time, Tom worked in the financial world in Chicago. But he dreamed about making wine. One day he headed west, and, as the legend goes, when driving over Hecker Pass Road, he noticed a man putting up a "For Sale" sign on the site of the old Roffinella Winery, a family-run business that had been in operation from 1910 until 1946. Kruse took it as an omen, bought the place, and corked his first bottle in 1971.

Today the winery produces a mere 3,000 cases of wine per year. Two of his most popular wines, Gilroy Red and Gilroy White, are named for the nearest town, best known as the Garlic Capital of the World. He also makes French colombard, chardonnay, cabernet sauvignon, zinfandel, and pinot noir, plus a bottle-fermented champagne with the tongue-in-cheek moniker Insouciance. Tom writes the labels himself, often using them as an editorial platform to put down wine snobbery and pretense.

Bargain hunters' alert: Kruse sells wine by the case on the premises at a 50 percent discount. If you taste the wine and like it, this is an opportunity to bring home an inexpensive souvenir of Gilroy. Anyway, it's worth dropping by to meet Tom; he will gladly extoll his philosophy about the pleasures of wine and turning a hobby into a way of making a living.

THOMAS KRUSE WINERY, *4390 Hecker Pass Highway (Route 152), Gilroy. Phone: (408) 842-7016. Open daily, 11 A.M. to 6 P.M.*

HOW TO GET HERE: *From San Francisco, take Highway 101 South through San Jose to Route 152 West. Follow the signs to Watsonville. About a mile and a half west of Gilroy, on the left, is Goldsmith Seed. Continue a few miles down Hecker Pass Road to the winery, which is on the left.*

CHAPTER **6** Santa Cruz County

AREA OVERVIEW
Santa Cruz County begins beyond San Mateo and Santa Clara counties and stretches inland from the coast. The city of Santa Cruz is the major workplace and playground for the county, with its beaches and boardwalk. City attractions are spelled out in our first edition. In this book, we add some places in the surrounding county that merit your attention. Route 17 south of San Jose takes you over the mountains on a winding, sometimes treacherous road. Route 1 follows the ocean and is slower, but who's in a hurry?

ANTIQUE ROSES
①
The best way to describe the roses at this unusual garden is to tell you a story about tomatoes. Several years ago my wife, Catherine, started growing tomatoes in our backyard. When we bit into the first ripe one, we both said, "This is what a tomato is supposed to taste like." Now we can eat only homegrown or specialty farm tomatoes; the commercial ones have absolutely no taste.

So what does this have to do with roses? Well, when Patricia Wiley took me into her garden of antique roses and told me to sniff a rose of Castille, it was a similar revelation: This is what a rose is supposed to smell like. Patricia ex-

Santa Cruz

Santa Cruz

Watsonville

plained that we are so used to hybrids that have been bred for various purposes that we are often left without the pleasure of the pure aroma of a historic rose.

Roses of Yesterday and Today is basically a large mail-order business, selling bushes by mail all over the world. In a fairly small but attractive garden outside their offices, they have what is in effect a living showroom of their products. It's a veritable library of roses, with about 400 varieties on hand, some with histories traced back to the Roman Empire. Each is marked with a brief history, but if Patricia or one of her colleagues is available, it's useful to have a guide give additional information.

You can smell for yourself the afore-mentioned rose of Castille, believed to have been the inspiration for the creation of perfume. The Romans used to float rose petals in their baths for the fragrance; some now forgotten soul noticed that the flower left a film on the water, which led to extracting the oils from the rose for bottling. Another interesting rose is the eglantine, mentioned by Shakespeare in *A Midsummer's Night Dream*. It smells like an apple. You'll also see roses that don't look like roses, but don't be fooled. They are roses all right.

The best times to visit are May, June, and August, though the gardens are open all year.

ROSES OF YESTERDAY AND TODAY, *802 Brown's Valley Road, Watsonville. Phone: (408) 724-3537. Open 9 A.M. to 3 P.M., Monday through Saturday.*

HOW TO GET HERE: *From San Francisco, follow Highway 101 or Route 280 South to San Jose. Exit onto Route 17 to Santa Cruz. At Santa Cruz, follow Route 1 southbound. After Capitola, exit onto Freedom Boulevard and continue for 2½ miles. Turn left on Haymes Road. Go another 2½ miles to Brown's Valley Road. Turn left and continue about 3 miles to number 802.*

BEGONIA HEAVEN
②

Most of the year, Antonelli Brothers is your normal, garden-variety nursery—a friendly place to buy mulch, terra cotta planters, and a raft or two of pansies to decorate the yard. But June to September, stand back. The begonias are in bloom. From floor to ceiling the place is a riot of red, pink, white, yellow, and orange. Begonias will be hanging from the rafters in baskets and growing in pots by the rows in the main building and out back in greenhouses. You may want to bring along a pair of sunglasses—these flowers can knock your eyes out. Begonias are probably one of those things you don't think about much (even though the word is fun to say). These tuberous plants are natives of the mountain regions of South and Central America. So when they arrived in the western United States at the turn of the century, they felt right at home in the cool coastal climate around Santa Cruz.

By 1935 the Pacific Coast Hybrid was a world-famous begonia, and at least four Santa Cruz growers were in competition to produce the biggest and best blooms. The old "double-camellia type" with 4- to 6-inch blooms gave way to the new, improved "double-rose form" with flowers 12 inches across. The 5-inch carnation type went the way of the horse and buggy, replaced by the "giant doubled ruffled" and its dinner plate–sized flowers. The four original Antonelli brothers—John, Patrick, Peter, and Allie—developed at least four begonias: the double ruffled picotee, named after the lacy edges on lingerie; the hanging-basket picotee; minibegonias; and last but not least, double-ruffled hanging baskets.

Today, Antonelli Brothers is the only one of the original competitors who still has a showroom open to the public. It's run by the children and assorted relatives of the founders. Visitors are welcome to browse around and enjoy the annual display during the nursery's regular business hours.

In addition to the flowers and the human members of the Antonelli family, you'll also meet various furry and four-legged Antonellis, including Angelina the cat and Baron, an adorable golden retriever who walks around carrying a sign in his mouth that tells his name, his age, and the fact that he is not for sale (there have been lots of offers). In cages you can see a flock of ringneck doves and a rat named Willy that most people assume is a hamster.

If the begonias catch your fancy, you may want to participate in the annual Begonia Festival, sponsored by the nearby town of Capitola. Each September the begonia is celebrated with such activities as flower-laden floats in a parade down Soquel Creek, barbecues, fishing derbies, and sand sculpture contests on Capitola Beach. You can ask at Antonelli's about this year's festivities.

Bargain hunters: Note that in September, Antonelli's sells their begonias at half price. When the bloom is finished and the plant goes dormant, just cut the plant back and store it until next summer. Since begonias are perennials, they will come back year after year, if stored properly. Such a deal!

ANTONELLI BROTHERS NURSERY AND BEGONIA GARDENS, 2545 Capitola Road, Santa Cruz. Phone: (408) 475-5222. Open daily, 9 A.M. to 4:30 P.M. in the winter, 9 A.M. to 6 P.M. in the summer. (Begonias bloom in summer and fall and are at their best in August and September.) Admission: Free.

HOW TO GET HERE: From San Francisco, take Route 101 or 280 South to Route 17 and continue to Santa Cruz. If you have plenty of time and want to drive the coastal route, take Route 92 from 101 or 280 to Half Moon Bay and then turn left and follow Route 1 to Santa Cruz. At Santa Cruz, follow Route 1 South to the 41st Avenue exit. Follow 41st Avenue south (to the right) to Capitola Road and turn right. Stay on Capitola Avenue until you come to Antonelli's, on the right side of the road.

GLAUM EGG MACHINE

Surely you have been in the situation when you ran out of milk or ice and were saved by one of those vending machines. Well, we know of only one machine like this. Out of eggs? Here's an adventure for you, as well as a celebration of California ingenuity. Take two crisp dollar bills and place them in the vending machine at the Glaum Egg Ranch in Aptos. The money disappears into the machine, then you hear a clucking noise, and out comes a tray of freshly laid eggs!

This machine was the invention of Marvin Glaum, an egg rancher who is also a busy man. Each day his hens lay about 72,000 eggs, which he sells mostly to distributors who package and sell them all over the Bay Area.

He was glad that people wanted to stop by and pick up some eggs directly from the source, but the interruptions sometimes interfered with his work. His solution was the world's first clucking egg-vending machine. Visitors get a kick out of it, and Marvin gets to tend his chickens uninterrupted.

The eggs are the jumbo-sized variety; the number of eggs $2 will buy is determined by the day's market value. The added bonus is that the drive to the ranch takes you into some beautiful country.

GLAUM EGG VENDING MACHINE, *Glaum Egg Ranch, 3100 Valencia Road, Aptos. Phone: (408) 688-3898. Open 24 hours a day. Two dollars buys as many eggs as the day's market price allows.*

HOW TO GET HERE: *From San Francisco, take Highway 101 South or Route 280 South to San Jose. Exit to Route 17 South to Santa Cruz. At Santa Cruz, continue on Route 1 South toward Watsonville. Take the Freedom Avenue exit, and go left over the highway overpass. Go past Aptos High School; turn left on Valencia. The egg machine is ½ mile down the road.*

COVERED BRIDGE

The sight of a covered bridge on a country road may be common in New England, but it is a rare surprise in California. And when that covered bridge also happens to be the the tallest in the United States and the only one made of redwood, it's a landmark.

It certainly is important to the folks of Felton. Their bridge cost about $5,000 to build in 1892, and over the past few years they've spent more than $300,000 to fix it up. To preserve their investment, no cars are allowed to cross on it, but you can walk over it, take pictures of it, or simply admire its quaint beauty.

The plaque outside the entrance to the bridge will tell you a bit of its history. Once it was the sole connection between Felton and the lands on the other side of the creek (today there's a busy highway leading to the other side).

When you admire the imposing structure with its huge redwood beams and long floor planks, think of all the flapjacks that were consumed to get it to look the way it does today. Most of the money raised for restoration came from pancake breakfasts sponsored by the local fire department.

FELTON BRIDGE, *off Graham Hill Road, as you enter Felton from Route 17. If you are on Route 9, turn right at the intersection of Graham Hill Road and look for the signs leading to the bridge.*

One of the unusual things about the Santa Cruz coast is that it is farmed all the way to the ocean. As you drive along Route 1, you'll see brussels sprouts and artichokes growing in the fields on both sides of the road. This is comparatively low-maintenance farming, in contrast to the old days, when dairy ranches were a major part of the county's economy. Fortunately, a taste of this 1880s farm life has been preserved, and it recently opened its gates to the public as Wilder Ranch State Park. It is located just a few minutes south of Davenport, a few miles north of the busy city of Santa Cruz.

WILDER RANCH
(5)

It took 10 years to get this park set up, and the attention to detail has paid off. Billed as a "cultural preserve," the Wilder Ranch is practically a self-contained village, surrounded by 35 acres of farmland. The Wilders were known for producing the sweetest and best butter around and for being an upstanding and innovative family. One of the many docent volunteers dressed in period costumes will tell you all about the Wilders and the various aspects of farm life in the late nineteenth century.

The tour is arranged so that you first stop at a little visitors' center, where you get an introduction to the place and switch your pace back to that of a century ago. Then you can stroll to the area that interests you most.

One innovative spot is the dairy barn, which housed more than 200 cows in the Wilders' day. They built it over a creek, which provided natural air conditioning for the livestock. They also built doors in strategic locations, taking advantage of the ocean breezes so that the barn wouldn't smell like, well, a barn.

The horse barn is built with classical arches and a decorative weather vane. You can see the blacksmith shop, complete with smithy and apprentice at work, farm animals, and an old stucco-covered adobe, said to be the oldest remnant from the Mexican rancho days in the county.

The yellow Victorian family home is the center for the social part of the visit. Here you can walk from room to room and experience the more genteel aspects of life on the ranch. A docent will probably be working in the kitchen, churning butter or preparing breads and beverages. Another docent acts as the gossipy next-door neighbor, telling stories about what everybody was doing back then.

You may notice the two-car garage built quite far from the house. The Wilders were among the first in the county to buy "horseless carriages"; they kept them far from the home, just in case the new-fangled things exploded.

There is much to see and do here. It is amazing to think that this almost became a commercial and housing development. Public opposition blocked that, and the state acquired the property in 1975. Now the "cultural preserve" is here for all to enjoy.

Wilder Ranch is located in the area hardest hit by the earthquake of October 1989. Though there was some damage, park officials expect the ranch to be in operation by spring 1990.

WILDER RANCH STATE PARK, *Route 1, Santa Cruz. Phone: (408) 423-0746. Open daily, 10 A.M. to 4 P.M. There is a $3 parking fee; admission is free.*

HOW TO GET HERE: *From San Francisco, take Highway 101 or Route 280 South to San Jose. Exit Route 17 to Santa Cruz. At Santa Cruz, head north 2 miles on Route 1. The ranch is on your left.*

WHALE AND JUICE WATCHING
6

The town of Davenport was once a bustling whaling center. Named for a ship captain, Davenport had more than its share of bars and rooming houses to serve an industry of roughnecks. Eventually the whalers depleted their own resources, packed their harpoons, and went elsewhere. They were replaced by a generation of folks repelled by the slaughter of whales; with this new population, Davenport evolved into a charming, bucolic, coastside town. Now instead of being the site of slaughter, it's one of the prime whale-watching spots on the coast. Visitors from all over gather in a lovely tree-lined park right off Route 1 to watch the whale migrations in spring and fall. It's a very informal process with no visitors' center or admission fees. You simply pull into the parking area on the ocean side of the road, walk up the hill, and look out to sea. Even though you are only minutes from Route 1, the high bluff transports you to another world, perhaps one inhabited by a passing family of whales.

Just down the road, on the ocean side, is one of the area's New Age businesses that has become a familiar name throughout northern California, the Odwalla Juice Company. In case you're wondering what in the world an odwalla is, it's not the latest exotic California fruit. The company is named after a piece of music by the avant-garde jazz group Art Ensemble of Chicago. I can't vouch for the piece of music, but I can say that this is some of the best juice I've ever had. The apple juice tastes just like an apple; blended confections like strawberry creme and tropical mango are like dessert—rich and thick and creamy but with nothing guilt-inducing like sugar or cream added.

Odwalla got going about 10 years ago when Greg Stiltonpohl started making juice in his backyard and selling it in the ideal marketplace, the health-conscious Santa Cruz area. Eventually the company grew to a million-dollar-a-year business and is now Davenport's second largest employer (with about 80 employees)—only Lone Star Cement, which you'll notice on the highway, is bigger. Fruits and vegetables are pressed and squeezed and blended, then shipped out in refrigerated trucks to stores all over the Bay Area.

Visits inside the plant are available only by prior arrangement. Here you'll see enormous juicers and pressers pulverizing carrots, apples, cranberries, oranges, lemons, limes, grapes, coconuts, and whatever else is in season. The colors and smells are dramatic.

You'll also see an unusually casual company in a lovely and (dare I say it?) very California environment. There's lots of wood and glass and New Age music being played. It's the sort of workplace where staff members take turns preparing a hot lunch for the rest of the crew to share. Whatever they are doing, it works. It's also the kind of place that is so laid back that they haven't quite formalized their tour policy. Be sure to call before you pop in.

ODWALLA JUICE COMPANY, *Route 1, Davenport. Phone: (408) 425-4557. Tours by appointment only.*

HOW TO GET HERE: *From San Francisco, take Route 1 South all the way to Davenport; this is the slow, scenic route. Or take Highway 101 or Route 280 South to Route 92 to Half Moon Bay, then continue on Route 1 to Davenport.*

Even though most people come to Santa Cruz in the summer when the boardwalk is open and the beach is hopping, there is at least one special fall and winter attraction, and it's right on the coast at Natural Bridges State Park. That's where the Monarch butterflies flock to spend the winter. On clear days you can see a sky full of these colorful and amazing creatures. They arrive in October and stay until February.

The park is an easy and pleasant place to enjoy the spectacle and learn some amazing butterfly facts. For example, butterflies can travel at the amazing speed of 30 mph—not bad for a creature only two or three inches big. Like the swallows to Capistrano, the butterflies return to this spot every year. Considering that their life span is only about nine months, it's mystifying how this could be. Is this information genetically encoded and passed onto the next generation of caterpillars? Inquiring minds want to know.

This park, and the town of Pacific Grove to the south, have ideal climates for the Monarchs. The temperature is just right, their main source of food—eucalyptus—is to be found in abundance, and there's protection from the wind and elements.

Here at Natural Bridges is a lovely path that takes you into the area of heaviest concentration. A large wooden platform surrounded by trees is provided so you can stand and watch the clusters of butterflies, though one of the more popular practices is to lie down and enjoy the view.

NATURAL BRIDGES

There is more to do at Natural Bridges than just butterfly watch. There is a good beach with lots of tidepools, a variety of resident sea birds, and students from University of California–Santa Cruz (UCSC) making notes and sketches, or simply skipping class. The name of the park comes from the large arch of rock out in the ocean. Once there were three of these geologic bridges, but storms and erosion had their way with two of them. The name Natural Bridges stuck, and so did the nickname Fallen Arches.

NATURAL BRIDGES STATE PARK, *on West Cliff Drive, Santa Cruz. Phone: (408) 423-4609. Monarch butterfly season is October through February.*

HOW TO GET HERE: *From San Francisco, take Route 1 South all the way to Davenport; this is the slow, scenic route. Or take Highway 101 or Route 280 South to Route 92 to Half Moon Bay, then continue on Route 1 to Santa Cruz. Once in town, look for signs to Natural Bridges State Park.*

BIG BASIN REDWOODS STATE PARK ⑧

Bay Area population boomed in the 1850s. The nearby Santa Cruz Mountains provided lumber for fences and houses. Eventually conservationists like John Muir started saying, "Hey, we'd better look to the future," and restrictions were imposed on blind and thoughtless uses of the land. While Muir's efforts evolved into the National Parks System, a lesser-known conservationist named Andrew P. Hill helped start the California State Parks System.

Hill was a San Jose–based artist and photographer. As the legend goes, a local newspaper assigned him to photograph a redwood grove in the Big Basin area of the Santa Cruz Mountains. This grove was one of the last virgin redwood forests left. Amazed by the beauty of the place, Hill was snapping away when suddenly goons employed by the local lumber mill chased him off the property. Hill was outraged that anyone could consider such a wonder of nature a personal possession, so he formed the Sempervirens Club, named after the *Sequoia sempervirens* tree. This group convinced the lumberman to sell his property to the state and convinced the state to create a public park. Thus the California State Parks and Recreation Service was born, and in 1902 Big Basin Redwoods became the first state park.

Over the years the Sempervirens Club has evolved into the Sempervirens Fund, an organization that assists the state in reforestation efforts, public education, and fund-raising for further land acquisition around Big Basin. Thanks to the efforts of this organization, Big Basin is a marvelous place to enjoy the natural wonders of northern California. Within the park are lots of animals (including deer); lush canyons; sparse, chaparral-covered slopes; several waterfalls with streams rushing downhill to a creek that empties into the Pacific Ocean; and, of course, the main attraction, the redwood trees, some of them thousands of years old.

There are more than 80 miles of hiking trails, ranging from an easy ½-mile loop through some of the more impressive trees to an intimidating, 35-mile sky-line-to-sea route. Near the coast, off Route 1, is a visitors' center called Rancho del Oso. It used to be the ranch of Herbert Hoover's brother Theodore; now it is a nature education center offering interpretive talks and guided walks. Big Basin is much less crowded than Muir Woods; you'll always be able to find places where you will not see another soul. Though there is much to do, you don't have to do anything at all but find a nice place to sit and listen. This is a park of re-creation rather than recreation.

Although the park is close to San Francisco in terms of miles, it takes nearly 2 hours to get here because the roads are hilly and winding. If you realize the time factor in advance, you can use the drive as a way to cool down from city pressures and relax into nature.

BIG BASIN REDWOODS STATE PARK, *Santa Cruz Mountains. Phone: (408) 338-6132; Sempervirens Fund can be contacted at (415) 968-4509. For camping reservations, call (800) 444-7275. Park hours: 6 A.M. to 10 P.M. daily. Day use fee: $3 per vehicle and $1 per dog. Overnight camping: $10 a night (up to 8 people).*

HOW TO GET HERE: *From San Francisco, take Highway 101 South to Route 280 South to Route 84. Continue past Woodside to Skyline Boulevard (Highway 35 South). After about 10 miles take Route 9; turn right (west) and continue for about 5 miles to Route 236. Turn right and follow the road to park headquarters.*

East Bay

The Bay Bridge, which links San Francisco to Oakland, Berkeley, and the other communities of the East Bay, has always played the ugly duckling to the more famous bridge to the west, the Golden Gate. In October 1989, the Bay Bridge made headlines twice. The first time was during the World Series, when the San Francisco Giants and the Oakland Athletics faced off against each other in what was dubbed "the Bay Bridge World Series." Then, at the start of the third game of the series, an earthquake rocked the Bay Area and once again the eyes of the world saw the Bay Bridge, this time because a section of the upper deck had collapsed onto the lower.

If all goes according to plan, the Bay Bridge, with its glittering nighttime necklace of lights, will once again serve as a link between San Francisco and the East Bay by the time you read this.

Even though the East Bay is not a major tourist destination, there are wonderful places to visit and great surprises to be found in the counties of Alameda, Contra Costa, Solano, and Yolo. The latter two are often combined under the heading "Yolano," and we will follow that custom here.

Travel times to East Bay destinations will greatly depend on the traffic on the Bay Bridge, which is unpredictable. Under ideal conditions, you can drive from

San Francisco to Oakland or Berkeley in about 30 minutes, to Walnut Creek in 50 minutes, to Vallejo in about 50 minutes, and to Woodland in Yolo County in about 90 minutes.

CHAPTER **7** Alameda County

AREA OVERVIEW

Alameda offers the most contrasts of any county in the Bay Area. There are the major cities of Oakland and Berkeley in the north, Hayward and Fremont in the south, and in the east, the booming suburbs of Dublin and Pleasanton with their gleaming new industrial parks and roadside hotels. In between all these population centers are miles of untouched land, thousands of acres of protected parks, and even some hidden lakes.

As you'd expect, the major action is near the main roads, Routes 80 and 24 up to Berkeley, Routes 880 and 580 through Oakland and Hayward, Routes 580 and 680 through Pleasanton and Livermore. But away from these busy highways, you'll find one of the earliest wine countries in northern California, the state's first major film community, the highest concentration of Ph.D.'s in the world, a Hindu shrine, and many more surprises.

PORT OF OAKLAND TOUR
①

Every Thursday during the summer, you and 399 other people can climb aboard a Red & White Fleet boat for a free ride on the Bay. This is a public relations gesture from the Port of Oakland, which manages one of the busiest ports in the nation (plus the Oakland Airport).

The trip begins at Jack London Square, near the historic Heinhold's First and Last Saloon, said to be Jack London's old hangout; there's also a replica of London's Yukon cabin nearby. Have a look inside before or after your 90-minute boat ride.

Guides keep up a steady patter as you glide along. You'll be told about the 13 million tons of cargo that is moved out of the port each year and how Oakland's port grew to be the largest container port on the West Coast (much to the chagrin of San Francisco across the way). You'll see tugboats at work, guiding huge ships in and out of the Bay, and you'll pass the medical ship *Mercy*, which has as many beds as three good-sized hospitals and is poised and ready for an emergency call.

This ride also offers views you'd never get from a car. You'll see new perspectives of Treasure Island and Yerba Buena Island, the underside of the Bay

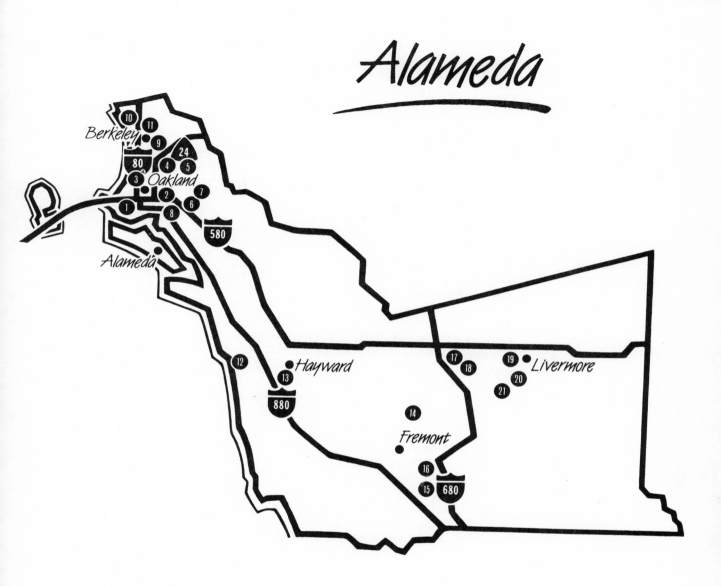

Alameda

Bridge, and the harbors of San Francisco and Oakland. You'll also see the Port of Oakland's giant computerized cranes in action, hoisting those 13 million tons of cargo. From the highway, these cranes look like monstrous mechanical horses from a George Lucas movie; from the Bay, looking up, they have the appearance of giant erector set sculptures.

PORT OF OAKLAND TOURS, *departing from the foot of Jack London Square, Oakland. Phone: (415) 839-7493. Rides available every Thursday from mid-May to late August. Boats depart twice daily, at 10 A.M. and 12:45 P.M. Always bring warm clothing, even on sunny days. Admission: Free.*

HOW TO GET HERE: *From San Francisco, take the Bay Bridge and continue on Route 880 to the Jack London Square exit. Follow the signs to the square, and enter at Embarcadero and Webster. You'll find ample parking.*

FORTUNE COOKIE FACTORY AND OAKLAND'S CHINATOWN ②

Have you ever wondered who in the world thinks up those fortunes that end your meal in most Chinese restaurants? In New York, I once got one that said, "Our tongue speaks for itself." Catherine topped that one evening in Berkeley when her cookie revealed the message, "Do not think of Charlton Heston today." If you're curious, or if you just want to see an unusual little factory that will take about 15 minutes of your time, visit Calvin Wong's Fortune Cookie Company, just a block or two from the main part of Oakland's Chinatown.

From the street it looks like another retail food operation, but in the back room you will see everything you need to grind out 80,000 fortune cookies a day to be shipped around the West Coast. There's the huge Mixmaster, constantly whipping up flour, sugar, and eggs for the simple dough. This formula is poured into individual baking devices, which are wonderful Rube Goldberg affairs. Gears and chains keep little baking pans revolving around a heated oven. A dollop of batter is dropped onto the lightly greased pan, a cover comes down on top of it, and in four minutes it goes around and through the oven and comes out baked and looking like a dollar-size pancake. Then a worker removes the soft cookie, slips a fortune in it, folds it, and sets it out to dry. All this is going on in about eight different stations with the radio blaring the Chinese Top 40.

Calvin will tell you how it all works and will explain that fortunes are bought in bulk from printing companies, although he does write his own special orders. Calvin has an X-rated edition, featuring not Confucius but Foo Ling U. He also has a "sassy" edition, as opposed to the more traditional fortunes in which good things will come to all. He'll also explain that the fortune cookie is an American invention, like chop suey, and comes as a surprise to Chinese people.

By the way, Oakland's Chinatown is worth a trip in itself, offering many of the same attractions as San Francisco's Chinatown but with less traffic. It is located primarily along the blocks between Harrison and Broadway and between

Seventh and Tenth streets. Here you can choose among several good restaurants (go for the places without the expensive neon marquees), and shop in exotic markets that carry everything from clay casseroles to Asian pasta to live catfish. To add an international flavor to your trip, you can visit Ratto's, a block east of Chinatown at Washington and Eighth, where you'll find every imaginable kind of dried bean, rice, spices, herbs, and pasta. They also serve an inexpensive Italian lunch and perform operatic selections on Friday nights. One block farther east at Clay and Ninth is the Housewives' Market, a longtime Oakland tradition, a lively marketplace of produce, meats, poultry, and noise.

FORTUNE COOKIE COMPANY, *221 Twelfth Street, Oakland. Phone: (415) 832-5552. Call for tours to make sure that an English-speaking guide is available. Tours cost 75 cents, which includes a package of cookies.*

RATTO'S, *821 Washington Street, Oakland. Phone: (415) 832-6503.*

HOUSEWIVES' MARKET, *Clay and Ninth streets, Oakland. Phone: (415) 444-4396.*

HOW TO GET HERE: *From San Francisco, take the Bay Bridge and follow Route 880 to Oakland. Exit on Jackson Street and go back under the freeway. Continue on Jackson to Twelfth Street and turn left. The Fortune Cookie Company will be on your left.*

EBONY MUSEUM
③

Even though the sign in front of the three-story Victorian in West Oakland says "Ebony Museum of Art, Inc.," this is also the home of artist Aissatoui Ayola Vernita, or as she prefers to be called, Vernita. Her museum is her lifetime's collection of art and cultural artifacts devoted to black culture, and it fills every nook and cranny of the house.

The third floor is a good place to start your tour. On this the top floor you'll see traditional tribal masks and pottery, plus some contemporary paintings and sculptures, including works by Vernita herself. The works of 16 African nations are represented on this floor.

Working your way down, the second floor is devoted to the subject of blacks in America. On the cheerful side, you will see Vernita's doll exhibit, a collection of some 600 toys, all proudly dark-skinned.

On the more sobering side you'll find the museum's most disturbing exhibit, which Vernita calls the "Stereotype Room." This is a collection of ads, posters, postcards, cups, ashtrays, and other items that depict blacks as "Uncle Tom" and "Aunt Jemima" stereotypes. Vernita has observed that many older black people cannot bear to look at the exhibit because it hurts too much, while the younger generation is fascinated to discover that such treatment existed. Vernita says she thinks it is important for all to be reminded of the degrading treatment of people of color, lest we forget and repeat the past.

The second floor also has a display gallery—which doubles as Vernita's living room—of changing exhibits by local artists. Last time I visited, she was showing her own creations of "soul food art." She had created jewelry and sculpture from chicken bones, collard greens, corncobs, pig knuckles, and other items that slave masters considered scraps (slave food). That blacks had the survival skills and ingenuity to create a cuisine from what others considered leftovers is a source of pride as far as Vernita is concerned. She hopes that blacks and others will find her art and jewelry inspirational.

Down on the first floor by the entrance is a gift shop stocked with Vernita's jewelry and African imports. There is no obligation to buy anything, but if you do, the admission fee to the museum is deducted from the price. There is no fee just to visit the gift shop.

EBONY MUSEUM OF ART, *1034 Fourteenth Street, Oakland. Phone: (415) 763-0141. Open 11 A.M. to 6 P.M. Tuesday through Saturday. Admission: $2 for adults, $1.50 for students.*

HOW TO GET HERE: *From San Francisco, take the Bay Bridge to Route 580 East. Exit onto Route 980 South toward downtown Oakland. Exit on Fourteenth Street and head east to number 1034.*

MORMON TEMPLE
④

Perhaps you've seen it from afar, a Land of Oz—like spire nestled high in the Oakland Hills. This is the Oakland Temple of the Church of Latter-Day Saints. Thousands of people visit each year, and only a minority are church members. The attraction? For one thing, many wish to take a closer look at the architectural splendor of the temple itself, though this is possible only from the outside (only church members are admitted inside the temple). For another, the gardens and terraces surrounding the temple are beautiful and provide one of the most spectacular views in the Bay Area. Last but not least, the genealogical library is open to the public. Here you will be shown how to trace your family's roots, free of charge. The catch is, you do most of the work.

When you arrive, you will be greeted by a guide who will tailor a tour to your time and interests. You will be shown the various panels depicting the life of Christ and, most important to the Mormons, the back panel, which represents Jesus after the Resurrection. You'll learn about the Mormon faith in general and about this temple in particular, including the facts that the spire rises 175 feet, that the temple was completed in 1964, and that it is but one of 41 worldwide that serve as regional centers for the Church of Latter-day Saints.

OAKLAND TEMPLE OF THE CHURCH OF JESUS CHRIST OF LATTER-DAY SAINTS, *4770 Lincoln Avenue, Oakland. Phone: (415) 531-1475. Grounds are open to the public daily, 9 A.M. to 9 P.M.; tours available during that time. Genealogical library is open Tuesday through Thursday, 9 A.M. to 9:30 P.M.; Friday, 9 A.M. to 5 P.M.; Saturday, noon to 5 P.M.*

HOW TO GET HERE: *From San Francisco, take the Bay Bridge and follow the signs toward Hayward. Take the Fruitvale Avenue exit. Go straight to Champion and turn left. Champion becomes Lincoln Avenue at the next stop sign. Continue on Lincoln; you can't miss it.*

JOAQUIN MILLER PARK
(5)

As long as you're in this neck of the Oakland woods, you might as well go across the freeway to get a different view of the Bay and the world in general. Joaquin Miller, for whom this 500-acre park was named, was an eccentric pioneer and all-around colorful character who came west from Indiana in 1852 and would become famous as the "poet of the Sierra." His artistic vision and Bohemian lifestyle made him about as far removed from the founding fathers of the Mormon Church as one could get. After his years as a newspaperman, lawyer, judge, convicted horse thief, and European traveler, Miller decided to live out his remaining years in the hills above Oakland. He had grand plans for building an artists' and writers' community, but this scheme never got off the ground. Instead, Miller's lasting contribution is what he put into the ground, literally: thousands and thousands of trees that today provide shade for the park. In fact, he is credited as being the one who thought up Arbor Day.

When Miller bought his 80-acre parcel in 1886, it was a bare hilltop. The giant redwoods had been logged to stumps. First he built his home and workplace, using poetic license to call it his "Abbey" on "The Hights." (No one knows why Miller chose that spelling instead of *heights*.) The structure still stands and is now a national historic landmark.

Miller also built numerous other structures that remain in the park. You can see the miniature stone castle that he named for Elizabeth and Robert Browning, and the Frémont Monument, which supposedly marks the spot where the explorer John C. Frémont first viewed the sunset over the Bay. There's also a funeral pyre that Miller built, intended to serve for his own farewell. However, Oakland officials had other ideas, and the "Indian-style" cremation the poet envisioned never took place.

In addition to these structures, the park offers many wooded hillsides and deep canyons with picnic sites, playing fields, trails, paths, and beautiful views. The Woodminster Amphitheater and the Cascades were built well after Miller's time. The 2,500-seat amphitheater was a WPA project completed just before the beginning of World War II; it comes alive each year with musical productions. The paintings and water display called the Cascades came from a fountain originally built for the 1939 World's Fair on Treasure Island.

There is much to see and do in this compact city park. Your first stop should be the ranger station and information center, where you can get a map and more details about the landmarks and points of interest. No need to be alarmed if you see work crews sawing away near the ranger station. Various agencies dispatch work crews to cut firewood from fallen trees; lots of people come here to fill up their cars with bargain firewood.

JOAQUIN MILLER PARK, *Joaquin Miller Road, Oakland. Phone: (415) 531-2205. Open during daylight hours daily.*

HOW TO GET HERE: *From San Francisco, take the Bay Bridge to Route 580 East, toward Stockton. Continue past downtown Oakland to Route 13. Exit north onto Route 13 and continue to the Joaquin Miller Road exit. Follow Joaquin Miller Road to the right, up the hill, and take the third left to the entrance. There will be signs along the divider in the road.*

OAKLAND ZOO ⑥

When most of us think of zoos in California, we don't get beyond the San Diego Zoo and its wonderful facility in Balboa Park. Perhaps because there is so much to do in the Bay Area, we tend to forget that there are fine zoos around here, too. One of the most enjoyable is the Oakland Zoo in Knowland Park, which is located on the eastern border of the city, just off Route 580.

This is a comparatively small zoo and thus is quite manageable; you can roam around at leisure and not get exhausted. The director, appropriately named Joel Parrot, says zoos should present animals as diplomats of their species, teaching humans about their lives. The zoo is designed to re-create conditions that approximate the native conditions of the animals. Large and small animals that would naturally share an environment are grouped together. In other words, hippopotamuses from Africa are displayed with small birds from the same region.

Also, most of the animals are not in cages; instead of those nasty old wire fences, natural barriers have been designed. For example, animals that are afraid of water are contained in areas surrounded by canals. Though it would appear as if the animals could easily hop out, these unobstructive barriers work just as well as the cages of yore while providing the animals with a more cheerful environment.

More than 300 animals are on hand, including lions and tigers and bears, and the only 9-foot African elephant that is completely show-trained. In addition, you and the kids can visit a separate petting yard.

If you don't get enough action at the zoo, Knowland Park is 525 acres of green lawn and rolling hills that includes a small amusement section and barbecue and picnic grounds. For an additional nominal fee you can take a miniature train ride through the zoo or a sky gondola ride above it.

OAKLAND ZOO, *in Knowland Park, Oakland. Phone: (415) 632-9525. Open 10 A.M. to 4 P.M. weekdays; 10 A.M. to 4:30 P.M. weekends. Admission: $2 per car into the park. Zoo is an additional $2 for adults, $1 for kids and senior citizens. No charge for the petting zoo.*

HOW TO GET HERE: *From San Francisco, take the Bay Bridge and follow Route 580 to Oakland. Continue toward Stockton and look for the Golf Links Road–98th Avenue exit. Exit there and follow the signs to the zoo.*

It's difficult to imagine a more ideal attraction for nostalgia buffs and prisoners of romance. The Dunsmuir House is one of the grand homes of the Bay Area, one of the few examples of colonial revival ever built here, and certainly the only one open to the public.

DUNSMUIR HOUSE AND GARDENS
⑦

This 37-room mansion surrounded by lush lawns and gardens was built in 1899 for the then grand sum of $350,000. Its history includes a spicy and tragic love story.

In the 1870s Alexander Dunsmuir, the scion of a British Columbian coal king, moved to San Francisco to handle his father's business interest there. He fell in love with a married woman named Josephine. His feelings were reciprocated, and she left her husband. Dunsmuir feared he would lose his inheritance if he married a divorced lady, so he and Josephine decided it was in their best interests to live together for 20 years instead (how that could be considered a more favorable arrangement during the Victorian era is beyond me, but that's what they did).

Finally, after the death of Dunsmuir's father, Alexander and Josephine got engaged. The opulent Dunsmuir House, nestled in the Oakland foothills, was the groom's wedding gift to his bride. Here's the tragic part: On their honeymoon, Alexander died of consumption. He never got to live in his dream house. He was 46. Josephine returned to Dunsmuir House and lived there for 18 months until her death in 1901.

Fortunately, the home's history gets happier after that. For more than 50 years Dunsmuir House was used as the summer home of the Hellman family (of Wells Fargo Bank fame). It was acquired by the city of Oakland in 1961 with plans to build a conference center on the property. This idea proved unfeasible, and the property and home fell into disrepair. In 1971 citizens formed a nonprofit organization to restore the house and grounds to their original condition and to develop the property as a cultural, horticultural, and historical center.

On a tour led by Victorian-clad docents, you will see the kind of life money could buy in the early twentieth century. Mahogany is used throughout, for exposed beams and finely carved columns. Parquet floors extend throughout the first floor and in the master bedroom—one of the nine bedrooms on the second floor. A 12-foot Tiffany dome rests above a central staircase. Beveled glass enhances the elegance.

An interesting aspect of this tour is that it includes a look at the servants' quarters. The spare and simply furnished workrooms and living quarters with bare light bulbs stand in stark contrast to the luxurious style of the owner's rooms—an American version of "Upstairs, Downstairs."

The exterior is as impressive as the interior. The huge white house, with its stately, columned portico, today sits on 40 acres. The original garden was designed by John McLaren, famous for his design of San Francisco's Golden Gate Park. The grounds feature a lovely lake with palm trees, a Victorian gazebo perfect for romantic handholding, and broad lawns for picnicking. History buffs might be interested in the old dairy barn and carriage house, which features six mahogany horse stalls.

Dunsmuir House is open to the public on Sundays, April 1 through the end of September; the annual Mother's Day celebration is a tradition for many Bay Area families. The house opens again at Christmastime and is decorated to the nines for the holidays. There are also several seasonal events, such as concerts. Watch for announcements, or call to see if one is upcoming.

DUNSMUIR HOUSE AND GARDENS, *2960 Peralta Oaks Court, Oakland. Phone: (415) 562-0329. Open Wednesdays and Sundays only, April through September, noon to 4 P.M.; also open several days around Christmas. Admission: $3.*

HOW TO GET HERE: *From San Francisco, take the Bay Bridge and continue on Route 580 East to the 106th Street exit. Turn left on 106th Street and go under the freeway. Make a right turn at the corner of Peralta Oaks Drive. Follow Peralta Oaks Drive until you come to Peralta Oaks Court. Make a left and follow it to the end.*

FLYING BOAT
(8)

In the historic North Terminal area of the Oakland Airport is a one-of-a-kind plane that has seen the likes of both Howard Hughes and Indiana Jones. It is the last of the flying boats, the *Seaflite 1*, and it's on display daily. Formerly called the *Halcyon*, the *Seaflite* was built by the British as a submarine detector in World War II. After the war, it was converted into a 39-passenger luxury ship, transporting well-heeled Londoners for a 4 ½-day voyage to Johannesburg and featuring a crew of seven to tend to every whim. The flying boat also made excursions to Australia, Hawaii, and Tahiti. After about 10 years of service, jet planes became the rage, and the great flying boat was put into mothballs.

Enter Howard Hughes, who had a secret plan to develop a sophisticated underwater detection system for the military. He bought the plane but didn't do much with it. Eventually the *Seaflite* fell into the hands of the Grant brothers, two airplane buffs who wanted to preserve this piece of history and to see if they could make this baby fly again. The Grants set up a nonprofit corporation to raise funds to restore the flying boat. The restoration process has been going on at the North Terminal of the Oakland Airport since 1987.

If you're thinking, hey, there are lots of airplanes that can land on water, what's the big deal? the distinction here is that this 1946 creation can take off and land only on water. It's also a romantic piece of nostalgia, a luxury plane complete with a table set for gracious dining. This plane had a cameo role in the film *Raiders of the Lost Ark*. Harrison Ford sat in the lush passenger section of the *Seaflite*, en route to his great adventure.

This attraction at the Oakland Airport has evolved through several interesting stages. It started as a curiosity, to visit on weekends, staffed by volunteers armed with hammers, paintbrushes, and enthusiasm. Now the place has its own full-fledged museum, managed by a professional and energetic promoter named Elliot Sacharow. An old storage shack has been converted into a two-story showcase collection of air history artifacts. Elliot says they have the world's largest collection of *China Clipper* artifacts in addition to the displays of model boats and seaplanes.

After you browse around the downstairs (caution: Elliot might try to sell you a souvenir!), you will be ushered upstairs to a video presentation. Finally, as the high point of the visit, ushers dressed in vintage flight attendant uniforms will escort you on a tour of the flying boat. These guides will tell you the colorful history of the ship and take you through all parts of the plane that have been restored.

The long-range plan is to bring the *Seaflite* back to airworthiness, so someday you may even get to take a ride on board. In the meantime, you can visit the flying boat on terra firma at the Oakland Airport. While you're in the neighborhood, you might also want to stop into the Western Aerospace Museum, located down the street on your way heading back to the airport's main terminal. It is a large old hangar that houses the mate of the plane Amelia Earhart flew on her fatal last journey (in fact, Earhart took off from here in 1939) and has many photos and historical artifacts on display. Last time I visited this was a fairly new exhibit, clearly a work in progress.

FLYING BOAT, *North Field, Oakland Airport. Phone: (415) 430-9050. Museum open 10 A.M. to 5 P.M. daily. Guided tours of the plane on Saturdays and Sundays. Admission: $5 adults, $3 children.*

WESTERN AEROSPACE MUSEUM, *Oakland Airport. Hours are irregular. Call first: (415) 638-7100.*

HOW TO GET HERE: *From San Francisco, take the Bay Bridge and continue on Route 880 to the Oakland Airport exit. Take the Hegenberger Road exit and continue to Earhart Drive. Turn right onto Earhart Drive. The Flying Boat is between hangars 9 and 10. The Aerospace Museum is also off Earhart Drive, opposite hangar 7.*

ARTSY EMERYVILLE
(9)

Not so long ago, Emeryville was just a quiet little town sandwiched between Berkeley and Oakland. It had two claims to fame. One was legalized gambling in one of several all-night poker clubs. The other was a collection of folk art in the town's mud flats. Other than that, there were some small homes and lots of big-rig trucks, rumbling to and from the loading docks in the big industrial warehouses in the southeast part of town.

Then the artists moved in. They converted old warehouses into cheap loft space for living and working. Artists need coffeehouses and inexpensive places to eat, so a couple of new eateries-cum-gallery places sprang up. Then the developers moved in across the road and set up an upscale, indoor public market, complete with specialty foods, flowers, fancy cookware, a wine merchant, butchers, bakers, and probably candlestick makers (the place is huge). There's even a jazz club and a 10-screen movie theater.

So now Emeryville still has the gambling, the remains of folk art in the mud flats, the little houses, and the loading docks, plus a lively arts community, nice cafés, and a public market worth spending part of an afternoon in, browsing, shopping, and snacking. The usual sad saga of such neighborhoods is that once the artists move in, fix them up, and make them fashionable, real estate prices go up and yuppies move in. This is not likely to happen in Emeryville. That's because artists have elected other artists to the city council. What's more, several of the main buildings in town are owned and operated as living and/or work spaces for artists. Emeryville was the first community in the Bay Area to pass legislation officially allowing this multiple use.

A drive down the streets can be an outside art tour. Alongside all the industrial buildings with loading docks you'll find elaborate postmodern structures, such as the one at Hollis and 64th Street. It used to be the rather drab home of the Jelly Belly jelly bean company; now it is a dramatic, multicolored office building with gleaming hubcaps forming a border over the entrance. Another interesting, historic-looking building is the former city hall, located across Stanford Street on Hollis; plans are to make it an art center.

Best time to visit the artists' section is during an "open-studio" day when the neighborhood's creative folks sweep their floors and open their doors to the public. You can meet up-and-coming painters, sculptors, and photographers, look at their work, discuss the process, and, if you're in the mood, strike a bargain agreeable to both parties. Open-studio days happen a couple of times a year; for information, call the Pro-Arts Council of the East Bay at (415) 763-7880.

Just about any day of the year you can visit such café galleries as Kathleen's Doyle Street Café (5515 Doyle Street; 547-3552) and Carrara (1290 Powell; 547-6763); these are places where you can have light meals, drink good coffee, and see the work by local artists hanging on the walls. Your waitress or waiter may also be the artist who painted the paintings.

ARTISTS' SECTION OF EMERYVILLE, *Powell and Hollis streets, Emeryville.*

PUBLIC MARKET AT EMERY BAY, *5800 Shellmound Street. Phone: (415) 420-1334. Open Monday through Saturday, 9 A.M. to 7 P.M.; Sunday, 9 A.M. to 5 P.M.*

HOW TO GET HERE: *From San Francisco, take the Bay Bridge to Route 80. Get in the right-hand lane and take the Powell Street exit. To reach the artists' section: From the off-ramp turn right, go past the Days Inn, go over a bridge, turn right at Hollis, and drive around until something looks interesting.*

To reach the public market: From the off-ramp turn right and immediately get into the left lane to turn left at the first stoplight, which will be Christie Avenue. Turn right at Shellmound Street; the entrance to the public market parking lot will be on your left just before the street takes a sharp curve to the right.

ADVENTURE PLAYGROUND

One of the most challenging and creative playgrounds in the Bay Area is to be found near the Berkeley Marina. Instead of swing sets, sandboxes, and other conventional trappings of city parks, here children are provided with hammers, nails, paint, and wood to build toys. Plus there are forts, ropes for swinging Tarzan-style, nets for climbing, and various odds and ends whose purpose is best left to a kid's imagination.

The Adventure Playground is a return to the old empty-lot concept. The idea for this type of playground began in Europe, where a playground designer observed children having a marvelous time using war debris as play equipment. With that kind of creativity in mind, the city of Berkeley set up the Adventure Playground in 1978. Materials are donated by local carpentry shops, lumberyards, and citizens who clean out their garages. All activities are supervised by adults, and kids seem to love being here. It seems to prove once again that all the expensive toys in the world can't beat the appeal of an old tire hanging from a tree.

Though the park is usually open only on weekends and holidays, school groups may make reservations during the week. A minimum of 15 children is required; learning-disabled or physically challenged group size is 8 minimum. Groups from outside Berkeley must pay a use fee.

ADVENTURE PLAYGROUND, *201 University Avenue, Berkeley. Phone: (415) 644-8623. Open during the school year on Saturdays and Sundays, 10 A.M. to 1*

P.M.; *open daily after June 25. Call for hours. Admission: Free.*

HOW TO GET HERE: *From San Francisco, take the Bay Bridge and follow Route 80 toward Sacramento. Immediately work your way into the right lane after you go under the overpass and exit at Powell Street. Turn left at the light and go back under the freeway. At the next light, turn right onto the service road that parallels the freeway. Turn right again, heading east, and continue until you come to a stop sign. This is the foot of University Avenue. Turn left for the Marina pier, and look on the left for the entrance to the playground.*

ACA FARMS
⑪

"Farms? In Berkeley?" is the slogan of a Bay Area dairy company, but it really suits Aca Farms, an organic-produce operation in the industrial section of West Berkeley. In this neighborhood of loading docks, freight trains, and plumbing supply houses, suddenly you come on rows of baby lettuces, stalks of corn, and tomatoes growing out of neat rows of raised beds. A closer look will reveal chickens, goats, pheasants, and pigs lolling around in cages and pens.

Aca Farms is the creation of José Barrera, who named his operation after his native Acapulco, Mexico. José was driving the loader for the giant soil and compost business next door, which had planted a few beds of vegetables to test out new soil formulas. José kept building more and more raised beds, which produced more and more beautiful herbs and vegetables. Local restaurants got wind of these goings-on and started buying this perfect, organically grown, freshly picked produce from him. Eventually local gardeners and home chefs started dropping by, and José had a successful enterprise on his hands. So successful, in fact, that he has been able to bring 30 members of his family to this country —parents, cousins, brothers—all working on the farm. The operation on Third Street is only about an acre or so of land; José has acquired other small parcels around town to keep up with the orders from snazzy eateries like Chez Panisse, Zuni Cafe, and China Moon.

One day a customer came by with a rabbit that she couldn't keep in her house anymore. One rabbit led to two, then three, and so on. Now there's a menagerie on hand, which provides great amusement for the kids while Mom and Pop pick out radicchio and edible flowers. (Watch out, parents—the animals are for sale!) Aca Farms is not only a great success story but a good place to purchase freshly picked produce and healthy plants to put in the garden. It's also a nice place just to look around.

ACA FARMS, 2222 *Third Street, Berkeley. Phone: (415) 849-9734. Open 9 A.M. to 4 P.M. Monday through Saturday; 10 A.M. to 3 P.M. Sunday. Hours can vary; be sure to call ahead.*

HOW TO GET HERE: *From San Francisco, take the Bay Bridge and head east on*

Route 80 toward Sacramento. Take the University Avenue exit and then turn right onto Sixth Street. Follow Sixth to Bancroft Way, turn right, and head for the Bay, and you will come to Aca Farms.

On your way from Hayward to the San Mateo Bridge, on your right you'll see a modern building just before the tollbooths. You won't be the first to think it's a restaurant. Many people pull in and expect to order lunch. However, they quickly find out that this is not a food chain operation but an operation that teaches about the food chain.

This is the Hayward Shoreline Interpretive Center, a small museum and park headquarters where you can get some information before venturing off into the surrounding 1,800 acres of bayland. Naturalists are on hand to help you understand the various displays that show who and what is living out there. They will also loan you free of charge a backpack filled with dip nets, bug boxes, maps, and binoculars, and you're ready to hit the trails, miles and miles of them.

To the uneducated eye, the Hayward shoreline looks like a barren mud flat. As it turns out, it is brimming with life, from pickleweed to clams and mussels to more than 140 species of birds. When you are ready to get your feet wet—literally—you can take a walk out into the marsh. Dip net and binoculars in hand, you can wander out through the channels of saltwater sloughs. You'll feel a million miles from the freeway.

This area has been described as a chemical desert. There is no fresh water at all, forcing animals and plants to find a way to live in a saltwater environment. As you might imagine, this is an ideal place for kids. During the week many school groups visit, and weekends are a popular time for families who wish to explore together. Since there are 8 miles of flat trails, the shoreline is perfect for bicycling (though sturdy mountain bikes are recommended due to potholes and the like). If you're interested in just plain aerobic walking, you can go for a long time without having to stop for a car or a light. Those interested in less strenuous activities can take advantage of the center's large observation platform; from here you can get a good view of the marsh.

No matter what time of year you visit, make sure you have waterproof boots and a warm jacket. It's almost always windy out on the marshland. Call ahead for a schedule of monthly nature programs.

HAYWARD SHORELINE INTERPRETIVE CENTER, *4901 Breakwater Avenue, Hayward. Phone: (415) 881-6751. Open 10 A.M. to 5 P.M., Tuesday through Sunday.*

HOW TO GET HERE: *From San Francisco, take Highway 101 South to the turn-off for the San Mateo Bridge. Cross the bridge, and after you pass the tollbooths, take the first exit to Clawiter Road. Go back over the freeway and turn left onto the service road. Then head back toward the tollbooths until you come to the center.*

HAYWARD JAPANESE GARDENS

One of the many benefits of the Asian influence on the Bay Area is the proliferation of Japanese gardens. These serenely beautiful public settings can be found not only in big cities (such as the Friendship Garden in Kelly Historical Park, San Jose) but also in suburban centers. But none is more beautiful or as instructive as the Japanese Garden of Hayward.

Situated behind a series of lovely Japanese-style buildings that house the city's senior center, the gardens offer an escape from the bustle of Hayward, an urban center not commonly associated with things of soulful beauty. It is located within walking distance of the Civic Center (some of the municipal buildings can be seen towering above trees in the garden—an interesting contrast).

Kimio Kimura is the landscape architect who created this environment. He learned the principles and traditions of Japanese gardening in his native Japan, then came to the United States in 1958 to attend the University of California at Berkeley. Here he learned the principles of American landscaping and California horticulture. The result is a blend of Japanese technique applied to plants that thrive in the west.

As you stroll through the gardens, you see tightly clipped and controlled pine, oak, and maple trees, most of them only 3 or 4 feet high. East-to-walk pathways lead to lovely sitting areas suspended over *koi*-filled ponds. Each turn delivers a new surprise, a sudden waterfall or a display of rock and gravel that simulates running water. Kimura's only request is that you walk slowly and view the garden as a series of several hundred little gardens. Each plant is groomed to look different from different angles. You can spend hours here if you wish.

Those interested in learning the principles of Japanese gardening may attend Kimura's free monthly seminars, held at 1 P.M. on the second Saturday of each month. Call for more information.

HAYWARD JAPANESE GARDEN, *Crescent Road, Hayward. Phone: (415) 881-6715. Open daily 10 A.M. to 4 P.M. Admission: Free.*

HOW TO GET HERE: *From San Francisco, take the Bay Bridge and follow Route 580 to the Foothill Boulevard South exit. Turn left on A Street and proceed two blocks to Ruby Street. Turn left, then left again on Crescent to the parking lot.*

SHINN HOUSE ⑭

I am constantly amazed by the way things can sneak up on a person on the backroads. You can find a treasure where you least expect it, a place to step off the busy modern streets and go back in time to a gentler, more gracious era.

Take the city of Fremont. At first glance, it could be any suburban community with wide, busy streets and a left-turn lane at every stoplight. It's a fairly new city. Until the 1950s there were actually five towns here, Centerville, Niles, Mission, Irvington, and Fremont. When they were consolidated, there was a danger of erasing the past and homogenizing the communities. The citizens realized that there is value in holding on to parts of that past, which brings us to the Shinn House, which is right off a busy modern thoroughfare.

This was one of California's first nurseries, a 300-acre ranch operated by the Shinn family, who moved from Texas in the 1850s. The Shinns were among the first to import rare trees from Asia and to appreciate the design of Japanese gardens. Through the years the ranch shrank as developers moved in, but the family held on to 4½ acres in the center of town. A surviving daughter-in-law turned it over to the city, which now maintains the property along with the volunteers of the Mission Peak Heritage Foundation.

There are two ways to enjoy the Shinn Historical Park. You can stay outside and simply enjoy the gardens, which are open daily. Within the 4½-acre park you will find grand lawns, colorful flowerbeds, and unusual fruit trees (including rare varieties of peaches and mandarin oranges) plus two formal Japanese areas with miniature plants and teahouses.

You can also go inside the Shinn family home, which has been restored and furnished in fine Victorian style and is open a few days each month. The house is a good example of middle-class Victorian life, as opposed to the opulence of the Dunsmuir Mansion. Still, this was an era of elegance, so there is a swooning couch in case the vapors in the air were too much for the lady of the house. Ask your guide about the ghost who is believed to still haunt the upstairs.

SHINN HOUSE, *Shinn Historical Park, Fremont. Phone: (415) 656-8404. Gardens open during daylight hours daily. House tours on the first Wednesday and third Sunday of each month from 1 to 3 P.M. Donation: $2 for adults. Special tours may be arranged in advance.*

HOW TO GET HERE: *From San Francisco, take the Bay Bridge to Route 880 South. At Fremont, take the Mowry Avenue exit and head east. Turn left on Peralta Boulevard; then make a quick right on Sidney Drive. Go left into the parking lot, past the Youth Science Center, through the main gate, and into the gardens. If the gate is locked, on days when the house is closed, there is a separate path that leads to the gardens. Park on the street nearby.*

They call a section of the Sunol Regional Wilderness Little Yosemite because it resembles its famous namesake. Once you get out on the trails and down by the Calaveras Creek, you feel like you're in a small-scale version of the great valley of the Sierra. Little Yosemite is just a part of one of the biggest open spaces in the East Bay. There are 17,000 acres to the adjoining Sunol, Ohlone, Del Valle, and Mission Peak wilderness areas with 31 miles of hiking and backpacking

LITTLE YOSEMITE

trails connecting the parks. This offers a great chance to feel like you have gone deep into the country though you're less than two hours from San Francisco.

This is not an attraction for a lot of planned activity. There is no museum, no campfire sing-alongs led by park rangers. This is a place for outdoorsy types who like to hike and get back in the woods, whether it's for day trips or one of the more challenging adventures involving backpacks and tents.

Part of the fun of visiting here is the enthusiasm of the naturalists who are on hand to teach the public about wildlife, plants, rock formations, birds, and how they all interact. They have a very practical and lighthearted approach to such necessities as dodging rattlesnakes and poison oak; their knowledge and good humor can help the skittish enjoy a back-to-nature experience without worrying about stepping in the wrong place or touching the wrong bush. Most important, they will help you see things you wouldn't ordinarily notice.

Many of the trails in the combined wilderness area are wheelchair accessible, and more than 60 campsites are available. This is also a popular spot for bicyclists. Park officials recommend that you drop by the visitors' center several days in advance of your planned visit to have someone help you map out a route based on your ability and interest and the current weather conditions.

The Little Yosemite area, which had been closed for many years because of vandalism, is now open for hiking. It resembles the great valley, surrounded by high peaks, but all on a much smaller scale. The reservoir, which is used by the San Francisco water department, is still off limits.

SUNOL REGIONAL WILDERNESS, *Geary Road, Sunol. Phone: (415) 862-2244. Park open from 7 A.M. to 8 P.M. during Daylight Savings Time; 7 A.M. to 7 P.M. the rest of the year. Visitors' center open Saturday, Sunday, and holidays, 11 A.M. to 4 P.M. Parking: $2, plus $1 per dog. Dogs must be leashed in developed areas. Picnic sites and barbecues are available along Alameda Creek. Overnight tenting sites are available by advance reservation. For camping reservations, call (415) 531-9043.*

HOW TO GET HERE: *From San Francisco, take the Bay Bridge to Route 580 East and follow it toward Stockton. Exit onto Route 680 South at Pleasanton. Follow Route 680 to the Calaveras Road exit. Turn left and continue on Calaveras Road for about 5 miles. Turn left onto Geary Road and follow the signs to the park.*

NILES CANYON RAILWAY ⑯

Back in the days when California meant Sacramento and San Francisco, the original transcontinental railroad made its final approach to the Bay Area by steaming through Niles Canyon. That line eventually became part of the Southern Pacific Railroad, and the trains rolled on for 110 years before the SP abandoned the route and Alameda County took over the land. The Pacific Locomotive Association brought the line back to life in 1988. It may be one of the shortest rail routes in the world, but it's also one of the most delightful.

First, you have to know something about the Pacific Locomotive Association, a rather austere name for a lighthearted club of railroad buffs. These folks would rather build track or toot a whistle than just about anything else. The club was founded by six friends who grew up around the railroads of the Peninsula. Right out of high school in 1961, they agreed to dedicate their energies to preserving an operating steam railroad from the era of the 1920s. They raised some money and bought their first engine for $750. Over the years they encountered many kindred spirits, and their association has grown to more than 300 members.

The PLA operated for several years in Richmond, with more than 10 steam locomotives, plus several other cars from the early days of railroading. Then they lost their lease and started looking for a new home. They landed in Niles Canyon, on the track originally built in 1869, the last leg of the transcontinental railroad's western route.

When I first visited the site to do a TV story about the group and their efforts, 2 miles of railroad track had been restored, by hand, by the volunteer members. The plan is to create a fully operating rolling museum, with all their historic train cars on display and a 9-mile ride from Niles to Pleasanton.

When you visit, you'll be able to see how far their plans have progressed. I should mention that when I last visited, they were not yet able to run their steam engines. Instead, they were using an old diesel car from the famous "Skunk Train" from Fort Bragg. The steam engines will presumably be rolling by the time you read this. When you do visit, if they're done with 5 miles of track, you'll get a 5-mile ride.

This is the ideal kind of place to take your kids or your parents or grandparents. It's for introducing new experiences of the way things used to be or inducing fond memories of the same. The club members love to talk about railroading and are glad to show off their collection.

NILES CANYON RAILWAY, *Sunol. Phone: (415) 682-3841. Trains depart from the platform at Kilkare Road and Main Street. Train rides are given between 10 A.M. and 4 P.M. on the first and third Sunday of each month. A $2 donation is requested to help pay for the group's efforts.*

HOW TO GET HERE: *From San Francisco, take the Bay Bridge to Route 580 East. At Pleasanton, exit onto Route 680 South. Take the Sunol exit, and go right. As you drive into the tiny town from the east on Main Street, you will see the temporary station on your right at the Kilkare Road junction.*

In the exclusive East Bay community of Blackhawk is an impressive antique and luxury car museum. We decided not to devote a full story to it, though, due to the rather exclusive admission price of $20 per person. Instead, we thought

SPECIALTY CAR SALES

you'd like to know about a place you can see a rather impressive collection of rare and antique cars for free.

Specialty Car Sales in the city of Pleasanton is like a gallery of vintage cars. Ben Gibson, who runs the place, takes collectors' cars on consignment and shows them off to prospective buyers. Like an art gallery, the display changes as quickly as the masterpieces sell, with rare, esoteric, and very expensive items sticking around for a while.

Last time I was there, I saw a 1925 MacFarland Roadster that could certainly find a home in a museum somewhere. It's not only the last of its kind in existence, it also has the claim to fame of having been built for and owned by the great heavyweight champion Jack Dempsey. You can drive it off the floor for a mere $295,000. I also saw a 1903 Thomas, glimmering in wood and brass and looking much like a horseless carriage, plus brands I had never heard of: Mitchells, Wilcoxes, Locomobiles, Speedwells.

Much display space is given to "muscle cars," those gas-guzzling but lovable speed demons of the 1950s and 1960s. Ben says these are the biggest attraction, bringing in as many as 500 weekend browsers who stare and reminisce. About 80 cars are on display at any given time. There are two showrooms, and in one corner you'll find some old jukeboxes and relics from the turn of the century to the 1940s. Ben has also set up a gift shop of sorts, selling such items as T-shirts, model trains, and toy trucks.

What car is most in demand? Ben says Cadillac convertibles from the 1950s and 1960s. He gets them frequently but sells them faster than Elvis could give them away.

SPECIALTY CAR SALES, *4321 First Street, Pleasanton. Phone: (415) 484-2262. Open 10 A.M. to 6 P.M. weekdays, 10 A.M. to 8 P.M. weekends. Admission: Free.*

HOW TO GET HERE: *From San Francisco, take the Bay Bridge to Route 580 East and continue toward Stockton. Turn south on Route 680 and take the first Pleasanton exit, which is Burnell Street. Head east toward town, continue past the fairgrounds, and at the second stoplight turn left onto First Street. Continue four blocks to number 4321. This is a very busy street, crowded with trucks zooming to the nearby gravel pits, so drive with caution.*

CHOCOLATE ADVENTURES IN CHEESE ⑱

The innovative chefs of Berkeley and San Francisco have spawned an entirely new classification of cooking called California cuisine, which has been imitated around the world. Still, who could have predicted Joan Pementel's unique creation? Chocolate cheese, or vice versa.

Joan has a shop that looks like a candy store. Inside you'll find normal-looking counters and display cases filled with chocolate treats. While you wait for service, you'll see a candymaker hard at work in back. What separates this place from your ordinary sweetshop is that everything is made with cheese. From the Edam Up Fudge to the Cheddi Rocky Road, traditional butter and milk have been replaced by curds and cultures.

It would be reasonable for you to ask, "But why?" and Joan will be happy to answer your question. For 23 years she managed the nearby Pleasanton Cheese Factory tasting room. After observing hundreds of visitors' likes and dislikes, she hit on the idea of combining chocolate with cheese. She experimented for a long time, came up with her own formula, and, with the help of her two sons, eventually opened her own business.

Realizing that customers tend to be skeptical at first, Joan offers free tastes; after that, most people are hooked, she says. With her Ann Richards hair and Carol Channing voice, Joan is a delightful and enthusiastic talker who can probably convince you to at least try the creations using Stilton and Limburger. The Cashew 'n' Bleu cheese creation is one of her most popular items, though she says that Americans tend to prefer the less adventurous cream cheese or cheddar-based confections. She sends much of her Stilton, Limburger, and bleu creations abroad to such stores as Harrod's in London; Europeans are apparently more appreciative of such items. Her other creations are apparently quite a hit at home, though. When I first encountered Chocolate Adventures, it was in a tiny closet of a shop. After about a year it moved into spiffy and roomier space down the street.

How does chocolate cheese taste? I liked it, though I must admit I avoided the exotic cheeses. The candies are reasonably priced, many at about 30 cents apiece. A note of caution, however. If the cheese chocolates are not going to be eaten right away they must be refrigerated. We left some sitting around in the "Backroads" office and sort of forgot about them. Several days later some poor, unsuspecting soul found what looked like an inviting box of chocolates and helped himself. It was a sour experience not soon forgotten.

CHOCOLATE ADVENTURES IN CHEESE, *830 Main Street, Pleasanton. Phone: (415) 846-3229. Open daily 9 A.M. to 6 P.M.*

HOW TO GET HERE: *From San Francisco, take the Bay Bridge to Route 580 East. Continue past the intersection of Route 680 and take the next exit for Hopyard Junction. Continue to downtown Pleasanton. The road will become Main Street.*

Hanging above the ladder truck and rescue squad of the city of Livermore's Fire Station #1 hangs what could be the most famous light bulb in the world. It's been the subject of many newspaper and magazine articles, television pieces (including "Bay Area Backroads" and Charles Kuralt's "On the Road"), and entries in *Ripley's Believe It or Not* and the *Guinness Book of World Records.*

WORLD'S MOST FAMOUS LIGHT BULB

Its claim to fame? It's the world's longest-burning light bulb. The tiny 3-candle-power globe has been on the job since 1901.

Battalion chief Jim Wright is the light bulb's historian. When he's not out dousing flames or rescuing kitties from treetops, he's collecting items for his scrapbook on the bulb. He'll tell you about the Shelby Electric Company, the manufacturer of this bulb; having produced such an efficient product, the company went out of business.

What keeps the bulb burning? Jim's theory is that it's the combination of heavy filament, low output, hand-blown glass, and sturdy construction. This is one tough bulb. Jim says that before the light's notoriety, he and the boys used it for Frisbee target practice. Now that it's a celebrity, the bulb has been moved to a higher corner of the firehouse, safe from flying recreational objects.

LIVERMORE LIGHT BULB, *at Firehouse Station #1, 4550 East Avenue, Livermore. Phone: (415) 373-5450. Open for drop-in inspection.*

HOW TO GET HERE: *From San Francisco, take the Bay Bridge and follow Route 580 East toward Stockton. At Livermore, exit at Livermore Avenue and head into town. Turn left on East Avenue, which is just past Fourth Street. Continue for about 2 miles to the firehouse.*

GOAT'S MILK ICE CREAM

OK, you don't have to taste it, but you really should take the time to visit the folks who make it at the Jimbarski Dairy Farm in Livermore. The ice cream is their way of showing you that fresh goat's milk can be very tasty. Jim and Barbara Muszalski are the heads of the household, and they don't seem to take anything too seriously, including their names. The farm moniker was created by blending their first names with the last syllable of their last name. They claim to have the only Polish goats in the county.

Jim, Barbara, and their daughter Jamie are genuine capriculturists. In other words, they are devoted to goats. They raise prize breeders on their hillside ranch outside of town and always have at least 50 goats of various ages on hand to show visitors. What makes their story so amazing is how it all came about.

Not many years ago the family lived in a beautiful suburban home with a black-bottom swimming pool in upscale Los Altos. To keep daughter Jamie from turning into one of those pouty Molly Ringwald–type teenagers, they forced her to enroll in a 4-H club. Jamie soon fell in love with baby goats, and in no time the suburban home backyard was filled with nine pregnant nanny goats. After enough complaints from the neighbors, they decided to buy a place where they could have as many goats as their hearts desired. Now mother and daughter run the farm during the day while Dad still commutes to Silicon Valley for a day job. They are so isolated that the goats can make noise all day and Jamie can practice with her rock band at night. And in case you're wondering, Jim and Barbara love the band and like to sit in on practices.

Now, about those goats. There are six varieties of goats at the farm, and these enthusiastic capriculturists will gladly tell you all about them. The Nubians are the ones with the floppy ears, the La Manchas have tiny buds of ears and no horns, and so on. They are all incredibly friendly because they were bottle-fed as kids and just love people. Barbara and Jamie feel that goats are among the most misunderstood animals. They emphasize that although they are friendlier than most livestock, they are still livestock and can't be allowed to run loose, like the family dog. You can go up to the fence and pet them, but be sure to employ caution because they are much like children in that they will put anything in their mouths. While I was talking to Barbara, one was lunching on the sleeve of her jacket.

On a tour, you'll be shown baby goats being fed. You can watch milking, and if there's not too big a crowd, you can try to do the milking yourself. You'll also be taken back where the bucks are kept, and Jamie will show you that not all billy goats are bad actors. She is a living endorsement of 4-H clubs, at least until she plugs in her guitar at night.

And for the finale, be prepared to taste ice cream made with goat's milk. Face up to it, the "Jimbarskis" are so enthusiastic and winning that you will not be able to refuse the offer. Fortunately, they prove their point. Fresh goat's milk has none of that taste we associate with goat cheese. The ice cream tastes like ice cream. I had the chocolate.

JIMBARSKI GOAT FARM, *10077 Tesla Road, Livermore. Phone: (415) 449-1879. Open most weekends during the day, other times by appointment. Call before visiting.*

HOW TO GET HERE: *From San Francisco, cross the Bay Bridge and take Route 580 East toward Stockton. Exit at the Livermore Avenue exit and follow Livermore to the right through town. Eventually the street name will change to Tesla Road. Continue past the Wente Brothers winery and head out into the country. Look for 10077 Tesla Road on the right side. Turn up the driveway and head up the hill. Watch for the "Goat Crossing" sign.*

I am often asked how much we keep coming up with new places on "Backroads." Much credit is due to the relentless research efforts on the part of the staff of the TV show, but occasionally tips come from surprising places. For example, during a book-signing event for the first edition of this book, a friendly woman writer approached me and asked if I had ever been to the Orchid Ranch in Livermore. I confessed I had never heard of it, and she told me that her brother in New

ORCHID RANCHING

Jersey is an orchid grower and he makes special visits west just to visit this place. So off we went to Livermore.

The Orchid Ranch is a cooperative venture of three separate orchid companies, each specializing in a different kind of Orchidaceae. Here you'll encounter 35,000 square feet of greenhouse space filled with Phalaenopsis, Laelia, and other exotic-sounding and -looking flora. In contrast to the famous Acres of Orchids of South San Francisco, this is a small, intimate operation; when you visit, you talk directly to the grower, not to a retail clerk. The atmosphere is very low-key; you can wander around at your leisure.

If you're like me, you don't know much about orchids. I always thought they were fragile, hothouse creatures, but no, I learned that orchids grow in all climates and are rather sturdy. Other surprising orchid facts: They are the second most prevalent plant family on the earth, second only to grass; there are 30,000 different types; and the houseplant varieties do not like soil—their roots need lots of air, so they thrive in material like tree bark.

Each of the three operations takes on the personality of the operators. Maynard Michael runs Orinda Orchids; he and his wife are chemists, and they experiment to create hybrids and can engage you in a sophisticated and scientific discussion of their Phalaenopsis.

The Tonkins are a friendly but quiet couple who started out as hobbyists and became experts. They grow Paphiopedilum, the type of orchid that has a little pouch in front; like them, their section is quiet and serene, more like someone's private garden than a retail outlet. If your timing is right, you'll catch them in the act of pollinating each flower with a toothpick. Frank Fordyce is probably the most loquacious; he used to work at Acres of Orchids, so he's used to dealing with the public en masse. He grows several types and has prepared elaborate signs so that you can wander along and read about each variety. In his section you'll find the most familiar-looking orchids, called Cattleya, or "prom orchids." All three growers are experts in their fields and are often asked to judge orchid competitions.

Within the greenhouses, almost every color to be found in nature can be seen, though certain times of the year are better for blooms than others. Winter and spring are considered the best times for a visit, not only to see the flowers but also because the Livermore Valley can get very hot in the summer and early autumn; though the temperature is regulated within the greenhouse, it can be as hot as 80 degrees inside, which is no respite from the 90-degree-plus outside.

ORCHID RANCH, *1330 Isabel Avenue, Livermore. Phone: (415) 447-7171. All three growers are open during regular business hours on weekends; times vary on weekdays, so be sure to call ahead.*

HOW TO GET HERE: *From San Francisco, take the Bay Bridge to Highway 580*

East toward Stockton. At Livermore, take the Portola Avenue exit. After you pass Frontage Road, take an immediate right turn onto North Murietta. Go about a mile or so to Isabel and turn left. Follow this road about another mile, and look for the ranch on the left.

CHAPTER **8** Contra Costa County

I hope the good residents of Contra Costa County will take it as no insult when I describe their region as the Bay Area's version of southern California. First of all, the weather is definitely warmer than in San Francisco or Oakland. Beyond that, there is a San Fernando Valley look and feel to the area that tells you this may be the California of the future. Wide boulevards connect more shopping malls than Main Streets, girls and boys are blonder, cars are everywhere, and driving long distances to get somewhere is routine.

Contra Costa is the newest of the area's boom communities, and it's still growing with astonishingly speed. Yet this is where John Muir settled down and did much of his writing, and this is where you can still find a remote island, like East Brother Island, to spend the weekend.

Walnut Creek and Concord are the major cities, connected to the rest of the Bay Area by routes 24, 4, and 680. The eastern part of the county is much less populated, which makes for interesting backroads destinations. For the citizens, though, it makes for a feeling of being ignored, to the point that there is always a movement afoot to secede and form a separate county.

Most Bay Area residents don't know much about San Pablo. They may know San Pablo Avenue, a major thoroughfare that links several East Bay communities including Oakland, Emeryville, Berkeley, Albany, El Cerrito, and Richmond. But the little town of San Pablo is probably unfamiliar. Being surrounded by the city of Richmond doesn't help. But this 2.9-square-mile city of 23,000 residents is worth a visit, particularly if you can meet Ann Roberts.

Ann is the driving spirit behind the San Pablo Historical and Museum Society, and she will show you around the Alvarado Adobe and the Blume House Museum. Both are part of a rather remarkable complex called Alvarado Square, which contains not only the museums but city hall, the police station, and community offices. The sprawling Spanish-style complex is built on the site of the original home of Governor Juan Bautista Alvarado, who grew up as a brother to his contemporary, General Vallejo, and ended up his bitter rival. Ann and other volunteers have researched the lives of the Alvarados and have decorated rooms to match the period in a re-created adobe home. The displays here tell a story of all of California and its early development.

Beyond the displays, Ann is a walking encyclopedia. A former librarian, she describes herself as one who lives to make order out of chaos. She says she has survived with 3-by-5-inch cards but now has developed a new technology that is more effective in keeping track of information: 4-by-6-inch cards. One lesson we learn over and over is that it's not just the buildings or displays that make a destination interesting; you might also meet the most fascinating people.

The Blume House Museum is reached through the Alvarado Square Courtyard, a lovely landmark landscaped by Lawrence Halperin, a visionary who has been behind some of the nation's most attractive urban projects. The Blume House Museum itself is what Ann calls a "folk Victorian" home. It used to sit high on a nearby hill until the Chevron people decided to use that location to build the Hilltop Mall shopping center. The historical society convinced the oil folks to pick up the house and move it to Alvarado Square. Now it sits as an example of middle-class farm life at the turn of the century.

Don't be surprised if you happen to see a troop of decorous militiamen in the courtyard. They are La Guardia Civil de Rancho San Pablo, a local group of Hispanic-Americans who dress in costumes of the early Hispanic soldiers. They are led by a local restaurateur, Marco Gonzalez, who is trying to show that there were Hispanic heroes in early American history.

You might also note the marker in front of the Alvarado Adobe. It says that San Pablo Avenue was once part of the Lincoln Highway, the first transcontinental road. Unfortunately, San Pablo Avenue is now lined with discount stores, auto parts shops, and so much generic urban clutter that it would be easy to drive by Alvarado Square or the city of San Pablo without knowing they exist. That would be a pity.

ALVARADO ADOBE AND BLUME HOUSE MUSEUM, *1 Alvarado Square, San Pablo. Phone: (415) 236-7373. Museum open Sundays, 1 to 5 P.M. Tours available at other times by calling Ann Roberts at (415) 222-3519.*

HOW TO GET HERE: *From San Francisco, take the Bay Bridge and head toward Sacramento on Route 80. Exit on San Pablo Dam Road, and turn left, heading toward the ocean. At San Pablo Avenue, turn right and continue for about a mile to Church Lane. The adobe and Alvarado Square are on the left.*

POINT PINOLE
② In his wonderful book *The East Bay Out* (Heyday Books, 1974), Malcolm Margolin writes about the wonders of Point Pinole by relating a conversation he had with a friend: "What . . . you've never been to Point Pinole? You've been to Paris,

Contra Costa

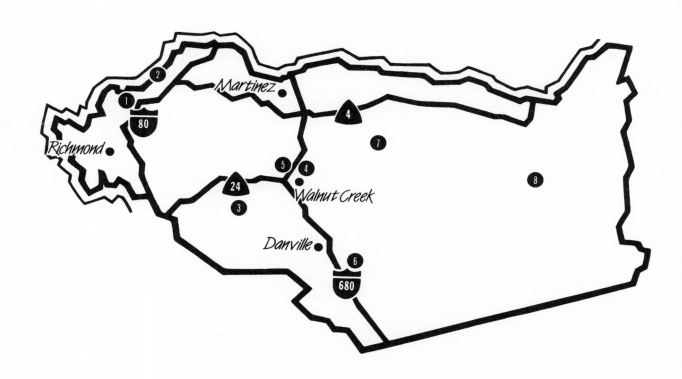

Richmond

2

1

80

Martinez

4

7

5

4

Walnut Creek

24

3

Danville

6

680

8

but you haven't seen the Point? Incredible." After reading that, I had to go and was not disappointed, although it's about as far from Paris, physically and spiritually, as you can get.

Point Pinole is a vast expanse of wilderness not far from the busy cities of Richmond and San Pablo. I know this statement can become a cliché, but it's like being in another world. Now an East Bay Regional Park, it offers miles of trails for walking, biking, pushing a baby carriage, skating—just about everything but driving. You must park your car in the lot at the entrance and then either stroll in or ride the shuttle bus that is operated by the park. This is a particularly good destination for those who travel in wheelchairs. One area is specifically designed for wheelchair access, and specially equipped buses in the parking lot take people and their wheelchairs into the park.

You should also know that this is a very large park with 2,100 acres to roam. There are spectacular bay views, a million-dollar fishing pier, beaches (although swimming is discouraged), marshes, wildlife, and one of the most unusual histories of any park.

This used to be a dynamite factory, dating back to the Civil War days. It was located in as remote a spot as possible, back when the thought of condos and industrial parks was science fiction. At Point Pinole, as late as the 1950s, the Atlas Powder Works, and before that the Giant Powder Works, made dynamite, nitroglycerine, and other explosives here. The remains of bunkers that were built to test the explosives are still around. The paths leading to them were once for a narrow-gauge train that ran between the buildings. That track, by the way, is now at Disneyland, shuttling folks around the park.

When the plant finally went out of business, the land that had been protected from development because of the explosive nature of the plant came up for grabs. Fortunately, some concerned citizens stepped in, and now it is protected forever as a park. As Malcolm Margolin says, there is something very hopeful in the fact that a former dynamite factory can become the site of a peaceful, beautiful shoreline park.

You can be your own explorer at the park and seek out your own activity. It could be wandering through the remains of huge bunkers that were used to test dynamite or strolling or rolling along the edge of the bay. Whatever it is, you will feel totally removed from the rest of civilization. It literally is a step back in time. The only exception is the new fishing pier, which juts out into San Francisco Bay and from which you can see seven counties on a clear day.

POINT PINOLE REGIONAL PARK, *Richmond. Phone: (415) 531-9300. Open 7 A.M. to 7 P.M. daily. Parking fee: $2.*

HOW TO GET HERE: *From San Francisco, take the Bay Bridge to Route 80 North. Exit at Hilltop Drive in Richmond and head west, toward the bay. Turn right on San Pablo Avenue, then turn left in a few blocks onto Atlas Road. The entrance to the park is on the right, where Atlas Road becomes Giant Road.*

Perhaps you remember the old Bing Crosby movie *The Bells of St. Mary's*. Well, it was not filmed here on the campus of this beautiful college in the town of Moraga, but bells do chime on the hour. St. Mary's is the kind of campus we used to see in those innocent movies about college life. It's a peaceful little time warp only a few minutes from the bustling new towns of Contra Costa County. Unlike its neighbors, this place has deep Bay Area roots. St. Mary's was founded five years before UC Berkeley and was housed in both San Francisco and Oakland before relocating in 1928. That's when the Christian Brothers who run the school, decided to move from Oakland farther out into the country. They built a lovely campus—and a national reputation as an early football power, with its famous coach of the 1930s, Slip Madigan.

BELLS OF ST. MARY'S
③

Today St. Mary's is content to be out of the way and often ignored. Their athletic program is still successful, but they no longer fill giant arenas like San Francisco's Kezar Stadium. That's part of the charm of the place for a visitor. It's a school that doesn't want to get much bigger. The layout is inviting for study or just for strolling.

When the school was moved to Contra Costa County, it was thought that the community would grow around it. But the Depression postponed that development, and until the 1970s the college stood alone in front of a beautiful hillside. Even today most of the suburban growth has gone in other directions, and there is a remote quality to the campus.

As you drive up and park, you might think you are in Mexico or at least Santa Barbara. The white stucco buildings with red tile roofs have a definite Spanish flavor, as do the many courtyards and porticoes. A tall tower, yes, with bells of St. Mary's that play on the hour until 9 P.M., looms over the campus. It was modeled after a cathedral in Cuernavaca, Mexico. In the chapel below the tower, the inspiration and design are from a cathedral in Sicily.

St. Mary's is a place to wander around and lose yourself. You can sit and read or chat in any of the courtyards or just stroll around the grounds. There is even an art gallery on the premises, which is open from Wednesday through Sunday afternoons and Thursday evening until 8 P.M.

With all this beauty, do you know what was the college's biggest claim to fame? This is where a famous *Life* magazine photograph was taken, showing how many students could be jammed into a phone booth. Don't look for the booth. It was brought in just for the photo session.

ST. MARY'S COLLEGE, *Moraga Road, Moraga. Phone: (415) 376-4411. Open for visitors during daylight hours.*

HOW TO GET HERE: *From San Francisco, take the Bay Bridge and follow the sign to Route 24 and Walnut Creek. After you go through the Caldecott Tunnel, look for the Orinda–Moraga Way exit. Head east (right) on Moraga Way and continue for about 5 miles to the end. Turn left on Moraga Road and look for the entrance to the campus on the right.*

BORGES RANCH

You would be hard-pressed to find any walnuts or even many creeks in the Contra Costa boomtown of Walnut Creek. It is the home of glistening office buildings, housing developments, shopping centers, and industrial parks. So it comes as a genuine surprise to find that only a few minutes away from downtown, the Old West is still alive. We can thank the citizens of Walnut Creek for that.

In the mid-1970s the voters decided to make sure that part of the past was saved forever from development. That included the old Borges Ranch, which at the time was a rundown bunch of shacks on 1,400 acres of rolling farmland. Ron and Marni White were hired to live on the property and take charge of restoring it to its turn-of-the-century reality. With the help of countless volunteers, including many schoolchildren, they did a remarkable job.

Today the ranch stands as a living monument to the old days. The old buildings are spruced up, with animals in the barn, a working blacksmith shop, functioning outhouses, old-fashioned water pumps—just about everything as it was except for a few modern conveniences like telephone and electricity. And it's a working ranch, where the Whites tend 300 head of cattle and a variety of other farm animals and grow their own produce.

As employees of a city-owned facility, Ron and Marni spend a lot of their time with local school groups. They dress up in the fashions of the time and stay in character as they re-create an era. Ron assumes the role of Rattlesnake Jim and weaves quite a tale. Don't get the idea that it's just for kids, though. Ron says their slogan is "For wide-eyed kids and those who remember." The adults remember tools and implements that their parents or grandparents may have used. The kids get wide-eyed over the darnedest things. Marni says they are most fascinated by the outhouse. While her husband is the ranger for the entire ranch and the adjacent Shell Ridge Open Space, she specializes in interpreting history.

There are still some members of the original Borges family around, too. The ranch now leases grazing land to them, and a few times a year they run roundups and other programs, which might include such activities as sheepshearing or horseshoeing.

Borges Ranch is run as a hands-on operation. The Whites want you to get all the sights and smells and feel of life on a farm. If you haven't done that in a while, you should know that you're even encouraged to get dirty. Don't worry, it all washes off.

BORGES RANCH, *Borges Ranch Road, Walnut Creek. Phone: (415) 934-6990. Tours Saturdays at 10 A.M. and 1 P.M.; at other times by appointment. Admission: Free.*

HOW TO GET HERE: *From San Francisco, take the Bay Bridge and follow the signs to Route 24 and Walnut Creek. Exit at Ygnacio Valley Road and head east through Walnut Creek at Oak Grove Road. Turn right (south) and continue as Oak Grove turns into Castle Rock Road. About a mile later, turn onto Borges Ranch Road and continue to the ranger station.*

Let's face it. Outside of the Borges Ranch, it's hard to find anything really old in Walnut Creek. This bustling suburb is all new. In fact, if you come here only once in a while, the town seems different each time. That's why places like Borges Ranch and the Shadelands Ranch Historical Museum are so important.

SHADELANDS

Whereas Borges Ranch is out in the country, Shadelands is right in the thick of things. Shadelands was the home of Hiram Penniman, an Illinois farmer who became one of the pioneers of Walnut Creek. In those days he had 250 acres of land, mostly planted with fruit and nut trees. Now the ranch has been pared down to 2.7 acres. But even though Shadelands is surrounded by modern office buildings and busy thoroughfares, it's still possible to get an idea of what life must have been like when this was undeveloped countryside at the turn of the century.

From the outside, Shadelands reminds me of the American dream home, the kind Judge Hardy owned in the Mickey Rooney movies, or if you're of a different generation, the kind Ferris Bueller's grandparents would have inhabited. The white frame house is set back from the road by a large front lawn. Inside, the rooms are decorated circa 1903, complete with the dining room table set for dinner.

For my money, the most interesting historic pieces are in the parlor. One is a beautiful Swiss music box that the tour guides have nicknamed Stella. Stella plays huge metal disks, each about three times the size of a modern vinyl record album (remember those?). Shadelands has quite a collection of these disks, and if you ask nicely, your guide might play a request.

Another parlor piece that caught my fancy was the vacuum cleaner, a nearly useless object that stands as a testimonial to the powers of some traveling salesman. This contraption looks like a giant bellows, and when you push on the large handles, it's supposed to create suction to pick stuff up off the rug. I'm not convinced it ever sucked up a speck, but apparently salesmen convinced housewives that the exercise involved would be good for the development of their bosoms.

A good time to visit is during one of the two special events held annually. At Christmas the house is decorated for the holidays, and in April there's a Tulip Tea open house. The rest of the time, Shadelands Ranch welcomes visitors on Wednesdays and Sundays.

SHADELANDS RANCH HISTORICAL MUSEUM, *2660 Ygnacio Valley Road, Walnut Creek. Phone: (415) 935-7871. Open Wednesdays and Sundays, Admission: $2; seniors, $1.*

HOW TO GET HERE: *From San Francisco, take the Bay Bridge and follow the signs to Walnut Creek. Take Route 24 to Route 680 North and then exit onto Ygnacio Valley Road. Head east (right) on Ygnacio Valley to Via Monte. Make a U-turn and double back to the entrance of the museum.*

FOSSILS AND FIRE TRAILS (6)

Catherine and I make many appearances around the Bay Area, talking to groups about our books, the TV show, and the backroads in general. During the question-and-answer periods, we are always asked to recommend places for people with specials needs or interests. Fortunately, the Bay Area is so diverse that we've always been able to come up with places for everyone. But we thought we were stumped when someone asked for a place where she could hike *and* hunt fossils. Fortunately, we remembered Las Trampas Park.

This is one of the the East Bay Regional Park District's newest and least-known places, and it's so low-key that it doesn't even have a visitors' center. Ranger Richard Clinnick roams around in a truck that doubles as his office and triples as a quasi-museum loaded with fossils, the tusks from prehistoric elephants, and other ancient memorabilia found on the grounds.

Clinnick says they've found signs of three-toed horses, camels, rhinoceroses, and other animals usually associated with Africa here in the East Bay. Hikers and fossil hunters have also found evidence of ancient plants and seashells that seem to indicate that this canyon was once part of the ocean.

If you're looking for fossils, apparently it's simply a matter of hiking the 3,000-acre park, being patient, and keeping your eyes peeled. However, you are not allowed to take them home. All finds should be turned over to the park supervisor, who will in turn send them to the University of California to be studied. In other words, the pleasure is in the hunt.

Of course, you don't need to be a fossil fancier to enjoy a visit to Las Trampas. During one of my last visits I met up with a delightful man named Jerry Olmstead, who was in the process of making the first trail map of the park. This process involved his walking the entire park, accompanied by his faithful dog, and making copious notes and measurements. Jerry taught me the art of "rambling," which is infinitely more appealing to me than "hiking" ("hiking" sounds like work). The basic idea is that you are never in a hurry, you never feel like you are working; you simply ramble at a comfortable pace, experiencing the sights and sounds and smells. Jerry's map ought to be ready by now at most East Bay Regional Park offices.

Las Trampas really is an ideal place to ramble with no particular destination in mind. To explore the terrain, you have two choices: taking the meadow route, where trees and creeks offer shade and relief from the heat, plus the sight of many birds and animals, or the ridges, which are stark rock formations with no protection from the sun or wind from which the views are spectacular. The ridge trails can lead to many surprises, including some miniature caves.

LAS TRAMPAS REGIONAL PARK, *Bollinger Canyon Road, San Ramon. Phone: East Bay Regional Park District, (415) 531-9300; chief ranger, (415) 837-3145. Open during daylight hours. Admission: Free.*

HOW TO GET HERE: *From San Francisco, take the Bay Bridge and follow the signs to Route 24 and Walnut Creek. From Route 24, exit to Route 680 South and continue to the Crow Canyon Road exit. Head right (west) on Crow Canyon Road to Bollinger Canyon Road. Turn right and follow the entrance to the park.*

On the backside of Mount Diablo is the little community of Clayton, a place that not only has a town museum but *is* a museum, for all practical purposes. Back in the 1850s Clayton was a thriving mining town with hotels, bars, wineries, and bawdy houses. By the turn of the century the mines were spent and the boomtown was deserted. What was left was a picturesque little village with Wild West–looking buildings and raised wood plank sidewalks. In 1964 Clayton was incorporated into the sprawling metropolis of Concord.

In recent years the town has been making a comeback, or losing its special identity, depending on your point of view. A 1500-unit residential development was built here, bringing new life and tax revenue into the community and taking away acres of open space. Restaurants were built to look like the old wooden buildings. It's a cute place to visit and takes just a few minutes to drive around the entire town, past the 130-years-of-continuous-service post office and the Clayton Club, which has been the town watering hole since 1858. The buildings and environs have a genuine Old West look; a movie crew could set up cameras and roll for a western without too much fuss.

One of the main attractions in town is the aforementioned town museum. Now, town museums are a staple here on the backroads, and when you visit a lot of them, you will begin to notice that many of the artifacts are similar. What

HISTORIC CLAYTON

attracts me are the stories, which are always different. The story about the naming of Clayton is a good one, told to me by Connie Rehr, the museum's curator.

Apparently, Joel Clayton and his buddy, Charlie Rhine, were the area's first landowners. They had ambitions to create a town by mining the riches of Mount Diablo and exploiting the immigrants arriving in droves from England and Wales. They flipped a coin to determine whether their kingdom would be called Clayton or Rhineville. Clayton, obviously, won the toss.

Clayton became a rip-roaring town, notorious for having the state's highest murder rate. And though copper, coal, and mercury were extracted from the Devil Mountain, processing the materials proved unprofitable. Most of the population not killed in barroom brawls moved elsewhere; those who stayed turned to agriculture and winemaking, until Prohibition put an end to the latter. Not much happened in Clayton until it was incorporated into Concord and the Clayton Historical Society founded a town museum in Joel Clayton's old house. The museum itself is a pair of buildings furnished in the style of the late 1800s, with antique farm machinery, mining gear, and the obligatory photographs on display. The old Clayton jail is also on the site.

CLAYTON HISTORICAL SOCIETY MUSEUM, *6101 Main Street (also called Clayton Road), Clayton. Phone: (415) 672-0240; Phone for appointments: (415) 672-4786. Open Wednesday and Sunday, 2 P.M. to 4 P.M. or by appointment. Admission: Free.*

HOW TO GET HERE: *From San Francisco, take the Bay Bridge and follow the signs for Route 24 toward Walnut Creek. Exit on Ygnacio Valley Road and head east for about 8 miles. Turn right at the light on Clayton Road; follow it about 3 miles to the south. The town and museum are on Clayton Road, which is called Main Street when you reach the town.*

PICK-IT-YOURSELF IN BRENTWOOD (8)

If you love fresh fruits and vegetables and want to have the fun of picking them yourself right off the tree, vine, or stem, plan a trip out to Brentwood and environs. More than 30 farmers in this eastern part of Contra Costa County have banded together to produce a Harvest Time guide, which lists the various farms and the best time you can visit for the kinds of produce you want.

Advice is given about what and how to pick, and such amenities as picnic tables, rest rooms, and sometimes old farm equipment for the kids to climb around on are provided. When it's time to pick fruits and nuts off trees, sturdy ladders are set up in the fields. Even though there is a bit of work involved, the folks roaming around the perfect aisles of trees and rows of plants seem to be having a grand old time. After all, we just have to pick the stuff; the farmer has to plow, plant, water, and weed all year.

The pick-it-yourself season begins in late May, usually with berries, followed by cherries, nectarines, apricots, peaches, and plums. The vegetables usually start getting good around July. Here you can get tomatoes that really taste like tomatoes and sweet corn that can make a Hoosier like me happy. Walnuts and almonds are available into the fall and early winter months.

Plan to arrive in Brentwood in the early morning (most farms open about 8 or 9 A.M.) or late afternoon (most stay open until 4:30 or 5 P.M.). This is one of the hottest regions in the Bay Area, and you will want to avoid working in the heat of the day. Also be sure to wear comfortable clothing and shoes that you don't mind getting scuffed and dirty. Most farms provide containers, but it wouldn't hurt to bring your own.

For those who do not feel like getting their hands dirty, most farms have produce stands with already picked items. Harvest Time farms are well marked along the main road, Route 4, but a Harvest Time map is a highly recommended guide. You can pick one up at the participating farms or from the Brentwood Chamber of Commerce, located on Oak Street in the center of town. Or you can send away for one by enclosing a self-addressed, stamped envelope to Harvest Time, P.O. Box O, Brentwood, CA 94513.

PICK-IT-YOURSELF FARMS, *Route 4 and vicinity, Brentwood.*

HOW TO GET HERE: *From San Francisco, take the Bay Bridge and follow the signs to Walnut Creek via Route 24. Continue on Route 24 past Walnut Creek to the Route 242 turnoff toward Antioch. This road will take you to Route 4 toward Stockton. Stay on Route 4, following the signs to Brentwood. It's about an hour and a quarter drive from San Francisco in ideal traffic conditions.*

CHAPTER **9** "Yolano" County

Before you go searching, there is no such place as Yolano County. The name comes from an association of farmers who banded together to entice visitors to visit their farms in Yolo and Solano counties. These adjoining counties cover a lot of space and border the Central Valley, which produces much of the food for the United States.

Solano County includes the cities of Vallejo, Fairfield, and Benicia. Each has a long military history, and the Mare Island Naval Base is still located in Vallejo and the Travis Air Force Base is still in Fairfield. Benicia's military history goes back to Civil War days. Much of Solano is reached by Interstate 80 as it leads to

AREA OVERVIEW

Sacramento and eventually all across the country. Vallejo is less than an hour's drive from San Francisco; Fairfield and Benicia will take a bit longer.

Yolo County is much less populated, and its major city, Woodland, is in the northern part of the county. This is farm country with a national impact, because of the importance of the agricultural school at the University of California at Davis. Most Yolo destinations are about 90 minutes from the Bay Bridge.

In these counties, the hills of the Bay Area disappear and the terrain flattens out. Driving along some of the farm trails, you might think you are on the plains of the Midwest.

VALLEJO NAVAL AND HISTORICAL MUSEUM ①

Vallejo is one of those cities that gets passed by, thanks to the California freeway system. Plenty of folks go to see Marine World on the outskirts of town, but few venture into the downtown or waterfront area. Pity, they are missing a lot. For one, there's the harbor, which has recently been beautified with parks and walkways. There are many lovely Victorian buildings to see in the old section of town. And there's one of the most impressive town museums in the Bay Area.

Most local museums are headquartered in old homes, where they try to jam a series of collections into every available nook and cranny. The Vallejo Naval and Historical Museum has 25,000 square feet of space in what used to be the city hall. It is spacious and allows for elaborate changing displays as well as permanent exhibits.

A word or two about the name. The city of Vallejo has been married to the navy and nearby Mare Island since the mid-1800s. The town grew because of the naval industry. So the histories are basically one and the same.

Even the museum director, Jane Fedderly, is a former naval officer. She acknowledges that some people are intimidated by the *museum* descriptive. "I hate to tell people where I work," she told me, "because they think it's one old fossil dealing with other old fossils." In fact, neither could be further from the truth. Jane is lively and imaginative and a great storyteller, and her spirit carries throughout the museum.

During our visit, there was a World War II exhibit, using modern multimedia techniques to show Vallejo's and California's involvement in the war. That was downstairs, on the floor devoted to changing exhibits. Upstairs, you enter a different world. You realize that as you ascend the grand stairway, which takes you past the prow of a ship. As you walk up the steps and past the prow, the murals that fill the walls give you the feeling of taking a trip through the sea. At the top of the stairs is one of the most popular attractions, a periscope from a submarine that now gives you a 360-degree view of Vallejo.

The entire upstairs is devoted to naval history, with models of some 20 ships,

Yolano
(Yolo & Solano)

505

113

Woodland

7

6

5

80

4

3

2 Fairfield

12

12

37

1

Vallejo

RioVista

plus weapons, uniforms, documents, photos, and whatever else you would expect to find in a naval museum.

VALLEJO NAVAL AND HISTORICAL MUSEUM, *734 Marin Street, Vallejo. Phone: (707) 643-0077. Open 10 A.M. to 4:30 P.M. Tuesday through Friday, 1 to 4:30 P.M. Saturdays. Admission: Adults, $1; children and seniors, 50 cents; members of the military, free.*

HOW TO GET HERE: *From San Francisco, take the Bay Bridge to Route 80 and continue toward Sacramento. After crossing the Carquinez Bridge, look for the Georgia Street exit to Vallejo. Follow Georgia Street all the way into downtown Vallejo until you come to Marin Street. Turn right on Marin for two blocks to Capitol. Museum is on the corner.*

THE FISHMAN
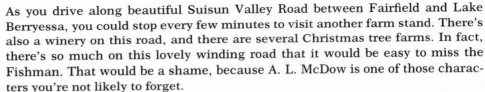

As you drive along beautiful Suisun Valley Road between Fairfield and Lake Berryessa, you could stop every few minutes to visit another farm stand. There's also a winery on this road, and there are several Christmas tree farms. In fact, there's so much on this lovely winding road that it would be easy to miss the Fishman. That would be a shame, because A. L. McDow is one of those characters you're not likely to forget.

A. L., who likes to be called the "Fishman," has a home up on the hill, overlooking the road. A native of Oklahoma, he was raised on catfish and fish stories. When he retired and moved to California, he realized that lots of fisherfolk would be passing by his house after a weekend of angling. So he devised a business that guarantees that no one would return home empty-handed and embarrassed.

The Fishman dug a pond and started raising catfish. Soon he had several ponds, including one down by the road, all stocked with whiskered fishies. Then he built a little "store" off the road, put in tanks with the largest catfish plus crayfish and *koi*, and installed coolers with ice-cream bars and soda pop. The hook baited, he sat back and waited.

As predicted, cars stopped and customers asked to buy the biggest fish in the tank. He'd offer to clean them for cooking and most would say, "No, just put a hook in its mouth . . ." And they'd go home happy, able to show the neighbors their "catch."

The Fishman's place also functions as a retail fish market for anyone who wants to buy fresh fillets. You can also fish in his ponds, paying only for what you catch. You can take your time and swap fish stories with A. L., who, by the way, claims that no one has ever topped him. With his wonderful drawl, he'll tell you the one about the 80 pounder that took him three poles to pull in. Can you top that?

If you decide to simply buy some fish to take home for supper, A. L. will take care of all the unpleasant tasks for you. He says his favorite method of preparing catfish is to coat it with cornmeal and fry it in a skillet, but they are good on the barbecue grill, too.

When we last met, A. L. had expansion plans. By the time you read this he may have rest rooms, picnic areas, and maybe even a little sheltered rest area for folks eager to escape the hot sun.

THE FISHMAN, *Suisun Valley Road, near Fairfield. Phone: (707) 426-1480. Open Tuesday through Sunday, 7 A.M. to dark.*

HOW TO GET HERE: *From San Francisco, take the Bay Bridge and follow Route 80 toward Fairfield to the Suisun Valley Road exit. Go under the freeway and continue on Suisun Valley Road, heading west, for about 5 miles. The Fishman is on the right side of the road. Look for the signs.*

GRIZZLY ISLAND

Before you take the long drive to Grizzly Island, you should know that this is not a park, and there are no grizzly bears here. The California Department of Fish and Game runs the program at this unique and beautiful marshland, and they make it clear that the place does not cater to the whims of people. The goal is to provide a good environment for wildlife. There is no visitors' center, no interpretive museum, just the marshland, the animals, and you're on your own.

If that hasn't discouraged you, then this is your kind of place. Grizzly Island is what much of the Bay Area used to look like. It is 55,000 acres of flatland with interconnecting sloughs and levees, sprinkled with an occasional eucalyptus grove. Its beauty is subtle, without the drama of dense forests or lush hillsides; it is peaceful and wild.

The major activity for humans is to drive around the place or to park the car and walk. If you are quiet and have patience, you'll probably see a jackrabbit hopping from bush to bush or an owl high in a tree. The most visible residents are the tule elk; starting with a population of 7 in 1976, the head count is now close to 200 and growing. This is one of the few wild refuges left for these original inhabitants of Suisun Marsh.

By the way, if you do happen to get close to the elks or animals, be advised to keep your distance. These are wild animals and are easily frightened.

Fall and winter are special times on Grizzly Island. Thousands of migratory birds take up temporary residence. Some 200 species have been spotted. Fall is also a good time for hiking since under normal conditions the area is fairly dry.

The value of this marshland should come to mind as you wander around. Suisun Marsh constitutes 13 percent of the total wetlands left in California; only 5 percent of the state's original wetlands remain. In other words, this area is very critical for the preservation of our wildlife.

Fishing and hunting are allowed during the appropriate seasons. For safety reasons, hikers are requested to avoid the area during the waterfowl season, which is from October through January, on Wednesdays, Saturdays, and Sundays, the days when hunting is allowed.

Visitors are urged to stop by the headquarters office on their way in; office hours are 8 A.M. to 4:30 P.M. Maps, bird lists, and other forms of information are available.

GRIZZLY ISLAND HEADQUARTERS BUILDING, *2548 Grizzly Island Road, Grizzly Island. Phone: (707) 425-3828. Open all year. Be sure to call ahead to find out if it is a hunting day.*

HOW TO GET HERE: *From San Francisco, take the Bay Bridge and continue on Route 80 toward Sacramento. At Fairfield, look for the exit onto Route 12 and Suisun City. Go east (right) on Route 12 for about a mile; turn right on Grizzly Island Road. Follow it for quite a while as it winds through much of the marsh and takes you to the headquarters.*

VACAVILLE MUSEUM

Vacaville is a surprising town. It looks like it should be out in the middle of rural farmland, not surrounded by new and bustling suburbs and busy Interstate 80. Once upon a time, the land around Vacaville was one of the richest fruit-producing areas in the United States. Fortunes were made here, which led to neighborhoods with some beautiful and stately streets with names like Buck Avenue, where the town historical museum is located.

The Bucks made big bucks, here and in Marin County. A sister in the family created the Buck Foundation in Marin; another Buck decided that Vacaville should have a museum, so she donated the land and a considerable sum of money to build one, right next door to her own house. Consequently, the town museum fits right into the residential neighborhood and is as lavish as the rest of the buildings on the block.

From the outside, the town museum looks like an ornate private home, with large white columns gracing the façade of a red brick manor that sits well back from the road. The entrance looks more like a hotel lobby than a museum foyer. A huge crystal chandelier hangs from what appears to be a 20-foot ceiling; a grand piano sits in the bay window, of floor-to-ceiling glass. Museum director Ruth Begell tells me that people usually expect a town museum to be an old building that needs new plumbing. They are clearly surprised and delighted here.

This first-class treatment continues throughout the museum. Exhibits are nicely lit and attractively arranged, and they are not only informative but also entertaining. Because the museum is fortunate enough to have such things as climate control and excellent security, Ruth can acquire items for display that other, less endowed town museums cannot. For example, during my first visit, there was a wonderful exhibit on John Muir, which included his original journals, photographs, and personal artifacts.

On permament display are vestiges of the town's history, from colorful fruit-packing labels and ads to farming tools and personal items. The first donation to the museum was somebody's collection of 200 flatirons. Not long after, another resident donated 100 pieces of antique lingerie. The museum has such a large collection that not all items are on display at all times. These are well cataloged by a volunteer staff of researchers headquartered upstairs, and you can make an appointment to visit.

VACAVILLE MUSEUM, *213 Buck Avenue, Vacaville. Phone: (707) 447-4513. Open Wednesday through Sunday, 1 to 4:30 P.M. Admission: Adults, $1; children, 50 cents. On Wednesdays admission is free.*

HOW TO GET HERE: *From San Francisco, take the Bay Bridge to Interstate 80 and continue toward Sacramento. When you pass Fairfield, begin looking for the Alamo Drive exit in Vacaville. Exit on Alamo Drive and loop back over the highway. Continue west on Alamo Drive for about a mile until you reach a four-way stop. Turn right on Buck Avenue. Continue to number 213. A long driveway leads to the parking area in back.*

POPCORN KING OF SOLANO VALLEY

I can't think of anyone who doesn't like popcorn, can you? I know people who can't watch a movie without it, and some dieters claim it's a filling, low-calorie, high-fiber dinner.

What you may not know is that popcorn is a crop, different from eating corn, and there are popcorn farmers like Jess Jones. He started growing popcorn for good ol' Orville Redenbacher (yes, Virginia, there really is an Orville Redenbacher), then became good enough at it to start his own brand, complete with his own picture on the label.

Jess has about 600 acres of farmland, some located right around the farm, other acres scattered around Solano Valley. As you will see, popcorn looks like midget regular corn: The ears are smaller and more compact, and the stalks are not as high as an elephant's eye. If you hold an ear in your hand, you will notice that the kernels are hard on the cob, not soft like sweet corn. Jess grows five different types of popcorn, including a black corn that he packages for a nearby winery as part of a gift pack. The connection is not totally arbitrary. It seems that in terms of subtleties, the popcorn industry can rival the wine industry. Take, for example, the shape. The "flower"-shaped popped kernel is good for eating as is; the "mushroom" shape is for candy-coating. Jess describes air-popped corn as "leathery"; the self-proclaimed "popcorn king" prefers his made with oil or butter; it improves the flavor and texture, he says. Jess really likes to eat the stuff. He takes some along on camping and hunting trips, and he says he becomes very popular (no pun intended) when he goes into a bar, whips out a popper, and makes enough for everybody.

Farming is never a glamorous business, as a visit to Jess Jones's popcorn farm will reveal. This is a real roll-up-your-shirtsleeves operation. Though visitors are welcome, this is a working farm with no official tour guides or visitors' center per se. In fact, it's a good idea to call ahead to make sure they're not neck-deep in harvest or a rush-order panic so that someone—probably Jess's wife, Mary Ellen—will be available to show you around. In spring the fields can look lush and green; but if you arrive after the harvest, the fields will look pretty bleak and the surroundings will seem very dry and dusty.

No matter what time of year you visit, you can observe the operation of an authentic popcorn farm. You will see the silos where the corn is stored until it is ready for processing and the large barn where kernels are stripped and placed in a bin to dry; your tour guide may show you the meter that registers the moisture left in the corn—a critical factor in determining whether the corn is ready or too pooped to pop.

You can also see the family house, where you will find the highly scientific test lab and tasting room—the Jones family kitchen. Here the Joneses set up a couple of regular old store-bought poppers—one that uses air, another that uses oil—to be sure that certain batches are OK. They know they've got a good batch when not a single kernel remains unpopped.

As for tips for the home popper, storage is very important; keep the lid on tightly to prevent moisture from escaping or invading. If you have some popcorn that's been sitting around a long time and it seems too dry, Jess says to put about a tablespoon of water per pound of corn into a tightly sealed container, shake it to distribute the moisture, then let it sit for a day or so. That ought to take care of it.

JESS JONES FARMS, *7179 Rio Dixon Road, Dixon. Phone: (916) 678-3839. Call ahead to arrange a time to visit. There is no charge, and you can purchase containers of popcorn right off the conveyor belt.*

HOW TO GET HERE: *From San Francisco, cross the Bay Bridge and follow Route 80 toward Sacramento. Take the Midway-Lewis exit and turn right (east) on Midway Road. Continue about 1½ miles (you will cross some railroad tracks; even though the main highway seems to continue around a bend to the left, you continue straight across the tracks). At the stop sign at Highway 113 (Rio Dixon Road), turn right and continue about ½ mile. On your right will be a sign pointing down a gravel road to the farm.*

A fascinating free show is held at least three times a week just off Route 80 in the farm town of Dixon. Appropriately enough, it's right behind the Cattlemen's Restaurant at the Dixon Livestock Auction. This is a genuine slice of Americana held inside a large barn with grandstand seats and a stage for the auctioneer. Just like in the old Lucky Strike commercials, the auctioneer rattles away at speeds that only the insiders can understand, and the ritual of bidding and buying and selling unfolds every few minutes for about two hours.

You know you are in for an authentic experience when you leave your car in the lot and start walking toward the barn. The aroma of livestock greets you at first, then the sounds of animals, and then the crowd of farmers in their jeans and overalls, chatting amiably but getting ready to compete like gladiators for the animals they wish to acquire.

The auction process works something like this: Animals are led into a small ring just below the auctioneer. While he takes bids, two or three handlers keep the animal moving so that prospective bidders can see all angles. Unless you look very carefully, it appears that no one is bidding, but owner-auctioneer Jim Schene told me that the moves can be very subtle and the auctioneers get to know their customers. One buyer may simply wink or twitch; another may scratch his ear. One man shows up with a huge cigar in his mouth but never moves it unless he's bidding. It all gets very tricky since neighbors and friends may be sitting next to each other but also secretly bidding against each other.

Once a bid is over, the animal is weighed and the weight is flashed on a board. The ultimate price will be based on the weight of the animal. Then, in an imaginative touch of retailing, the details are shuttled in what Jim calls their "J. C. Penney," a device like all the old department stores used for sending money and receipts up to the cashier. At the auction, the shuttle goes to the office, where purchasers pay for their animals.

If you talk with the farmers in the grandstand, they can give you some idea of what they are looking for and why. Generally, those who are selling have run out of grass or hay to feed their cattle or sheep, and buyers are ones who still have plenty of feed around. The ultimate goal appears to be to add weight. Like the other stock market, it's a matter of buying low and then selling high. One farmer also advised me to sit still and make no false moves. Once he thought he was brushing the hair out of his eyes and was told that he had just bought a new calf. He said he was too embarrassed to refuse.

There's also a small café on the premises, where the farmers hang out and grab a burger or a piece of pie. On a cold winter's day, when the fog hangs in the valley, it's a good place to warm up. By the way, don't be concerned about just coming to watch. Jim Schene says he has regulars who come each week and never bid. They just enjoy the action.

LIVESTOCK AUCTION IN DIXON
(6)

During spring 1989, the auction house was the target of an arson fire that destroyed part of the barn. A group claiming to represent an animals' rights organization admitted setting the blaze, although at this writing nothing has been proved. In any event, the auctions continued, and Jim Schene was back in business within a week.

DIXON LIVESTOCK AUCTION, *Route 113, Dixon. Phone: (916) 678-9266. Hog and pig auction every Wednesday at 10 A.M. Cattle auction every Wednesday at 1 P.M. Sheep auction every other Tuesday at 10 A.M. during fall and winter; more regularly in spring and summer. Admission: Free.*

HOW TO GET HERE: *From San Francisco, take the Bay Bridge and follow Route 80 toward Sacramento. After Fairfield and Vacaville, look for the Route 113 exit. Head south, and the auction house is directly behind the Cattlemen's Restaurant.*

DAVIS FARMERS' MARKET ⑦

One of the happy developments of the late 1980s was the proliferation of farmers' markets throughout the Bay Area. Not only was this good for the small farmer who was being squeezed out of the marketplace by agribusiness, but it also reflected a growing interest in "real"—rather than processed and chemically ripened—foods. It also opened up new markets for exotic and ethnic fruits and vegetables, often grown by the area's recent immigrants.

One of the Bay Area's most enjoyable farmers' markets is in the city of Davis, in the rich Sacramento Valley. Several things make this particular market a pleasure to visit. For one thing, it's fairly small, with about 35 stalls on Wednesday afternoons, about 70 on Saturdays. It's also centrally located, in Davis's Central Park, so it's easy to find. The park setting is ideal for parents who bring their kids; the little ones can run around to burn off extra steam and be entertained by street musicians and clowns. Best of all for the grown-ups, the food is both wonderful and cheap.

These markets don't just happen. They require a lot of organization and planning, and Randy MacNear runs a tight and well-organized ship here in Davis. She recruits the farmers, locates their stalls in such a way that the customer strolls by an ever changing variety of products, and organizes special events throughout the year. For example, every Thanksgiving a special menu based on the bounty of this region is prepared and laid out on display for all to see, with copies of the menu printed and distributed so that folks can find the ingredients at the various stalls for their own holiday cooking.

This, like other farmers' markets, is a taster's paradise. You browse from stall to stall and snack along the way. Farmers will tell you how they grow their fruits and vegetables and the best ways for you to prepare the fruits of their labors. The ethnic mix here is truly impressive. You'll see Asian Indians in glittering scarves next to Chinese next to Mexicans next to fourth-generation Californians.

You are also sure to see and hear Alex, who walks around hawking his daughter's baked goods. Alex is the house Henny Youngman, and he's irrepressible. "This bread was brought over by my mother from the old country, and it's still fresh . . ." and on and on. The market wouldn't be the same without him.

DAVIS FARMERS' MARKET, *Central Park at Fourth and C streets, Davis. Phone: (916) 756-1695. Wednesdays 2 to 6 P.M. Saturdays 8 A.M. to noon. Admission: Free.*

HOW TO GET HERE: *From San Francisco, take the Bay Bridge to Route 80 and follow it toward Sacramento. Take the main Davis exit (not the first UC Davis exit), and continue back over the freeway and under the railroad crossing. Continue to E Street and follow it to Fourth. Turn left to C.*

Beyond the Bay

We in the San Francisco Bay Area have never been accused of being modest. With fierce pride we point to most of northern California as being our province. Long weekend trips to Yosemite or Lake Tahoe are considered commonplace and are highly recommended for visitors who want to see what this unique part of the world really has to offer.

The first *Backroads* edition offered just a few Beyond the Bay locations. The section has been expanded this time around. Highlights include the Central Valley, the part of northern California in and around the city of Sacramento; the Central Coast around Morro Bay and San Luis Obispo; Mount Shasta; Clear Lake; and last but not least, a *Backroads* drive to Los Angeles. Other popular Beyond the Bay destinations, such as Monterey, Carmel, and Yosemite, are to be found in the newly revised and updated edition of *Jerry Graham's Bay Area Backroads*.

With the possible exception of the Central Coast destinations, all of the areas require planning with reservations for hotel, motel, or campsite accommodations. Travel times are approximately 90 minutes to two hours to the Central Valley and the Gold Country, two and a half to three hours to Clear Lake, four hours to the Central Coast, and five hours to Mount Shasta.

CHAPTER 10 Central Valley

AREA OVERVIEW

The Central Valley is the farm belt of northern California, with the cities of Sacramento and Stockton as its major population centers. That population is certain to keep growing, as Sacramento continues to rank high on surveys as one of the best places to live and work in the United States. The area, though inland, is filled with waterways, from the Sacramento Delta to the active ports of Sacramento and Stockton. It's also an area of diverse cultures. You can find ancient Chinese towns in the Delta, Portuguese bullfighting in Manteca, Italian wineries and farms in Modesto. Perhaps the most American of all is graffiti night in Modesto, held the second weekend in June. Filmmaker George Lucas grew up in Modesto and did his early cruising there.

This region is overlooked by many visitors to the Bay Area, who thereby miss seeing the heartland of California. The state capital, Sacramento, is less than two hours from the Bay Bridge, and other portions of the valley are even closer. Routes 80 and 580 are the main thoroughfares. The best time to visit is in spring and fall, as summers can be extremely hot.

STATE RAILROAD MUSEUM

The largest interpretive railroad museum in the world is in the restored section of the state capital called Old Sacramento. With 2½ acres under one roof, this is an absolute must for anyone even remotely interested in trains and the role railroads played in the development of the United States. It is spectacular.

The whole thing started with a group of train buffs who began collecting old cars and memorabilia in 1937 in San Francisco. Over the years, as the collection grew, they tried unsuccessfully to find a home in the city. Thirty years later, the state decided to build a museum in Sacramento, which was the birthplace of railroading in California and the home of the local businessmen who became railroad barons and were known as the Big Four: Leland Stanford, Mark Hopkins, Charles Crocker, and Collis Huntington. The San Francisco group turned its collection over to the Department of Parks and Recreation, which now runs the museum. Even though it's a government-operated facility, this is California, and the influence of Disneyland and Hollywood is strong even here.

The entrance is a good example. After you pay your fee, you are ushered into a theater for a film orientation. The film is a good mood and scene setter, and without spoiling the finale, you should know that you will be primed to enter the museum proper afterwards. Then it's either a matter of roaming around on your own or stopping to talk with one of the "conductors," docents who conduct informational tours. You stroll from one glittering locomotive to another in the giant building, which resembles a fantasy railroad station. There are more than 20 authentically restored cars and more than 30 exhibits, ranging from phonograph records and games about railroading to a tribute to the 1,000 Chinese laborers who lost their lives building the road over the Sierras. There's also a separate miniature and model train exhibit with more than $100,000 worth of equipment.

The main attraction, of course, is the restored cars, which are so glitzy and dazzling that guides say people think they've "circused them up." But the fact is that everything is done to original design, even if it meant stripping 22 coats of paint off some cars to find the original colors. The cars are works of art, none more spectacular than the 1873 *Empire*, which ran freight on the Virginia and Truckee Railroad. It is displayed with floor and ceiling mirrors to show all its splendor. A close second in the dazzling category is Lucius Beebe's luxury coach, a private car that is decorated like a Victorian mansion. It's said that Governor Ronald Reagan's support for the museum followed his being wined and dined in that splendid coach.

Do talk with the conductors. They are all railroad buffs who can fill you in on details and direct your attention to such things as the white-walled wheels on some cars, which led to white-walls on automobiles, or the real gold leaf that adorns some of the locomotives. They can also answer just about any question having to do with railroading.

Although it's hard to pick favorites, the most popular exhibit is the moving Pullman car, a 90-ton car that is on a hydraulic rocker. Inside, the decor is strictly 1920s. When the train starts rocking, you would swear you are out on the rails.

In this age of jet travel and superhighways, it's easy to forget the role railroads played in the development of the United States such a short time ago. Here you can see how trains brought settlers and workers to the West and how refrigerator cars took fruit and vegetables to the East. You will also be reminded of a devotion to craftsmanship and style that were once a source of national pride.

CALIFORNIA STATE RAILROAD MUSEUM, *Second and I streets, Sacramento. Phone: (916) 445-4209 or (916) 448-4466. Open daily 10 A.M. to 5 P.M., except Thanksgiving, Christmas, and New Year's Day. Admission: Adults, $3; ages 6 to 17, $1; under 6, free. Steam train rides offered May through Labor Day, weekends and holidays only. Fee is an additional $3 for adults, $2 for ages 6 to 17. Plan to spend several hours here.*

HOW TO GET HERE: *From San Francisco, take the Bay Bridge and continue on Route 80 to Sacramento, which is about a 75-minute drive. In Sacramento, take the Route 5 North exit and quickly exit onto J Street. Follow J Street a short distance and turn left onto Fifth Street. Take Fifth for one block and turn left again on I street. Follow I to the museum, at the corner of Second.*

A SPECTACULAR STATE CAPITOL

Not every state capitol merits a mention in a guidebook of this type, but this building is truly special. The major reason is the six-year restoration that was completed in 1982. The tab was $68 million. That's a major production, even by Hollywood standards. Every Californian paid about $3 in taxes, which is less than the admission to most movie theaters these days, and it's easier to get in to see the capitol than it is to stand in line for a first-run film. The visitors' office on the basement level can give you a brochure for a self-guided tour, or you can take one of the tours offered daily.

If the building looks familiar, that's because it's modeled after the Capitol in Washington, D.C., complete with its own mall. The basic tour is of the working capitol, from the classic rotunda under the elaborate dome through the legislative chambers and past the familiar faces of assembly members and senators that we see in 30-second doses on the news. You'll ascend massive staircases built from California lumber. You'll see beautifully restored mosaic tile floors and murals that depict the state's history. It is all very impressive, like an ornate cathedral of government.

On the less traveled tour, you are taken into the six historic restored rooms that are furnished in the period of San Francisco's 1906 earthquake. Here you can see how Governor Pardee tried to direct the rescue efforts for the Bay Area, even though communications were difficult at best. There's even a replica of a telegram from President Teddy Roosevelt, saying that there were rumors of a disaster and offering federal help. The telegram arrived in Sacramento 12 hours after the quake. Everything is authentic in these rooms, from newspaper clippings to the obligatory spittoons.

There is one touch of subtle humor in the ceiling of one office. Since the re-creation of the 1906 earthquake crisis was done during the administration of Governor Jerry Brown, workmen left a memento of his crisis with the Mediterranean fruit fly. If you look closely, you will see a tiny medfly on one of the oranges painted on the ceiling.

It was the fear of earthquakes that led to the restoration. A study of the building's seismic safety showed that years of adding on had led to dangerous decay, and the building was crumbling. Fortunately, it was decided to restore the capitol, rather than starting over with a modern building. The best time to visit, by the way, is in the spring or fall when the extensive gardens outside the building are in bloom.

CALIFORNIA STATE CAPITOL, *Capitol Avenue and Sixteenth Street, Sacramento. Phone: (916) 324-0333. Tours are given hourly, 9 A.M. to 4 P.M. weekdays,*

10 A.M. to 4 P.M. weekends. Tours are free, but you must have a reservation. If you just want to drop in, you can stop at the Department of Parks and Recreation's tour office in Room B-27 of the capitol and sign up. Then you can browse through the small museum downstairs or enjoy the gardens until your appointment.

HOW TO GET HERE: *From San Francisco, take the Bay Bridge and continue on Route 80 to Sacramento. Take Business 80 to the Capitol exit and follow the signs.*

STANFORD HOUSE

In 1989, as part of its 150th birthday celebration, the city of Sacramento spruced itself up in fine style. Several state parks received face lifts, additions were built on the well-endowed Crocker Art Museum, and work progressed on restoring one of the city's finest homes, the former residence of Leland Stanford. The Stanford House was not only the headquarters of the state's eighth governor and cobuilder of the nation's first transcontinental railroad, but it was also the home in which Leland Stanford, Jr.—for whom Stanford University was founded—was born (after the youngster died, the parents founded the university in memoriam).

Now a state historic park, the Stanford House offers something rare: a chance to see a historic building *before* it is restored to its original splendor. This tour is the brainchild of Patricia Turse, who is likely to be your guide. As she will explain, the plans call for the house to be returned to its original splendor by the mid-1990s. As a history buff, Patricia had always been curious to see the process of restoring historic buildings and figured that others shared this interest. She has been very creative in putting together a tour that for now is mainly a walk through bare, dank rooms. Each room has a photo display of the way things looked when the Stanfords lived in it, so a visitor can really appreciate what goes into the detective work of restoration. It's like an archaeological dig or, more precisely, an architectural dig. The home had gone through many changes and uses: boarding school, orphanage, community center, and home for dependent adolescents.

Patricia will show you a cutaway section of a wall where you can see layer upon layer of paint—look though ultraviolet light to see the depth. You'll be shown hidden walls, covered fireplaces. As you watch all the layers of use being unpeeled, you are treated to a fascinating lesson in California history. She adds music and a reading to dramatize the ambiance of the grand ballroom as it was in the heyday of Stanford's parties.

The best part is that you will be able to visit again years from now and see what it looks like when it's finished! A child could be taken here as a first grader, then see it again as a sixth grader.

Another interesting aspect of the tour is that the photos on display of the original house were taken by the famous Eadweard Muybridge, the inventor of motion pictures. In 1878 Muybridge had been hired by Stanford to prove that horses lifted all four hooves off the ground when running; by shooting a quick succession of still photographs of a horse in motion, the idea for motion pictures (which is simply a series of 24 still photographs projected each second) was born. Muybridge became a family friend, and his photographs, probably intended as snapshots, are works of art. The historical content of the pictures—the furnishings, clothing, ambiance—is priceless for the historian; the artfulness of the photography will appeal to photography buffs.

STANFORD HOUSE STATE HISTORIC PARK, *802 N Street, Sacramento. Phone: (916) 324-0575. Tours offered at 12:15 P.M. Tuesday and Thursday, 12:15 and 1:30 P.M. Saturday. Be sure to call ahead for an appointment. Admission: Free.*

HOW TO GET HERE: *From San Francisco, take the Bay Bridge and follow Route 80 to Sacramento. Exit for Business 80 and then Route 5 North toward Redding. Take the J Street exit and follow J Street to Ninth Street. Turn right onto Sixteenth Street and continue to N Street. Turn right again to the Stanford House.*

JOHN SUTTER'S FORT

If not for John Sutter, there would not have been the 1849 Gold Rush, and without the Gold Rush, there would not be California as we know it. Sutter was a German-Swiss farmer who arrived in Mexican territory to build the New Switzerland, "New Helvetia." In the early and mid-1840s, Sutter recruited settlers from Europe and New England to come to his new settlement. Sutter's Fort became a famous refuge for pioneers, a friendly place where they could get free shelter and supplies. It was Sutter who dispatched the rescue team that saved 45 members of the ill-fated Donner party and brought them to safety at this fort; today one of the children's dolls is on display in the Sutter's Fort museum.

In 1847 Sutter contracted James W. Marshall to build a sawmill on the south fork of the American River, about 50 miles east of the fort. When Marshall was trying to deepen the tailrace of the mill, he accidently discovered gold, and the California Gold Rush was on.

The rest, as they say, is history. Sutter's Fort prospered for a while as a way station for transient miners and as a trading post for miners' supplies. However, as time went on, unscrupulous men began swindling Sutter out of his holdings; squatters took over much of his land, and the U.S. Supreme Court declared much of his land grant invalid. Sutter, the man who founded the first settlement, moved on. He and his wife settled in Pennsylvania, where he died penniless in 1880. (For the story of James Marshall, see the Marshall Historic Park in Coloma, page 163.)

Sutter left behind an entire town inside 2½-feet-thick adobe walls, with businesses that included a bakery, gristmill, and blanket factory, all of which can be seen in what is now the restored historic park.

Tours are offered in a variety of ways. You can walk around on your own carrying a device that looks like a small telephone. At each stop along your way, you will hear narration and explanations of the displays. Larger tours may arrange for a guide to handle the background information. One of the best times to visit is on a "living history" day, when folks dress up in costume and adapt the roles of people in the 1840s, including John Sutter. The actors stay in character to demonstrate the life of the settlement. And instead of using historic artifacts that need great protection, the parks people have created authentic replicas that visitors can handle. In other words, you can join in with the breadmaking, blacksmithing, and other chores.

For years the Sutter's Fort Historical Park had been in the shadow of glitzier places around Sacramento, like the Rail Museum and the state capitol. But for Sacramento's sesquicentennial celebration of 1989, the fort made such improvements as the hands-on demonstrations so that people won't skip it anymore. It's a significant building in California history and is worth a look, particularly when combined with a visit next door to the Indian Museum (see following story). It's also a successful attempt to give Sutter his due, as he died a misunderstood man.

SUTTER'S FORT STATE HISTORICAL PARK, 2701 L Street, Sacramento. Phone: (916) 445-4422. Park open 10 A.M. to 5 P.M. daily; closed on major holidays. Admission: Adults, $1; children, 50 cents; under 5, free; higher admission prices for special events.

HOW TO GET HERE: From San Francisco, cross the Bay Bridge and take Route 80 to Sacramento. Follow the signs to Business 80, which will require staying in the left lane when you get to Sacramento. As Route 50 splits off to the right, stay on Business 80 and then take the N Street exit. Look for the sign for Sutter's Fort at the exit. Go up two blocks to L Street and turn left. Continue to the fort, which is at Twenty-eighth and L.

INDIAN MUSEUM

If you want to understand California, you must know about the Indians, and this is a wonderful place to get your education. Here you will learn that the southern Indians were pretty much wiped out by Spanish missionaries, but the northern Indians thrived, and many are still around.

Elsie King-Gillespie is usually at the museum, and she can tell you just about anything you would like to know about Native Americans. Elsie is a third-generation Hupa and was one of the forces behind rehabilitating the museum in the 1980s. This project was accomplished by contacting the elders of many tribes, interviewing them, and asking for their best photos and collections.

The museum is set up so that if you wander through, you will get a full picture of the Indians of California. For me, the most incredible display is of tiny feather baskets, as small as a grain of sand. These were made by medicine women, who used them to capture evil spirits. The weavers go into a trance while making these baskets. Enlarged photographs accompany the display, and you can see that these are about the size of the eye of a needle.

Also of special interest is the display about Ishi, the state's last Indian who lived in the wild. His story is famous: After witnessing his parents' murder by surveyors, Ishi wandered into a northern California town. He was jailed; "Wild Indian Captured," the headlines said. Two UC Berkeley professors who had studied Indian lore heard about Ishi, befriended him, and brought him to San Francisco, where he lived for five years until dying of tuberculosis (which he apparently caught from his contact with Caucasians). The exhibit shows many photos of Ishi, the fur cape he wore in the wild, the suit and tie he was given in San Francisco. Four people who knew Ishi have come into the museum to tell Elsie of their remembrances, that he was a gentle and kind man who couldn't resist throwing stones at passing cable cars. His story is one of human tragedy, one that contradicts prejudices about the state's original inhabitants.

Elsie probably shows more kids the way it really was than any other guide in the state. She can also enhance the displays of beads and jewelry, religious and spiritual articles. The exhibits are all very well presented and explained.

CALIFORNIA INDIAN MUSEUM, *2612 K Street, Sacramento. Phone: (916) 324-7405. Open every day except major holidays from 10 A.M. to 5 P.M. Admission: Adults, $1; children, 50 cents.*

HOW TO GET HERE: *Since parking is at a premium, walk from Sutter's Fort (see previous entry). The museum is right behind the fort, part of the same park complex.*

FORD FEVER Where in the world would you expect to find the most complete collection of Fords? Dearborn, Michigan? Until recently, the answer would have been Deer Lodge, Montana. Fortunately for us in northern California, the answer is now Sacramento.

This is the collection—perhaps obsession is a better word—of a successful small-town banker named Edward Towe. He fell in love with Fords when he was a youngster in Montana and began collecting Model T's. As a moneymaking adult, he further indulged his passion to include the entire "alphabet series"— Model A's, Model T's, etc.—plus Thunderbirds, Fairlane Skyliners, and Falcons.

Eventually he opened a museum, but when he ran out of space in that building, it was time to face the fact that not many folks pass through Deer Lodge. So Towe conducted a nationwide search and decided that a huge warehouse in Sacramento, California, was the place to build a world-class Ford museum.

This is a long-term project, containing not only the collection of cars, but also dioramas and videotapes chronicling the history of the U.S. highway system, the role of public transportation, the growth of the oil industry, and similar subjects. When I visited the museum a few months after it opened in 1988, it was still in its beginning phase but was well worth the visit. The cars are set up chronologically, allowing the visitor to walk through decades of automotive and American history.

You'll see perfectly restored Model A's and T's, the cars that democratized the road (before Henry Ford developed the production line, cars were the playthings of the very wealthy). Also on display in the early automotive section are one of the world's five remaining model B's, circa 1904; a 1911 Phaeton; and several early trucks.

Most fun are the flops, such as the Edsel and the hardtop convertible, cars that seem to symbolize all that was silly and innocent in the 1950s, when Americans thought wealth and resources were infinite. The hardtop convertible, which was supposed to allow the driver the convenience of putting the top down without ever leaving the front seat, featured eight individual motors that allowed the trunk to open and the metal top to fold its way out of sight. Unfortunately for Ford, the tops tended to get stuck in the middle of the operation, leading to more than one disgruntled owner finding his way back to the dealership with the top suspended in midair.

Other cars of historical interest include the first Chevrolet Camaro and ex-Governor Jerry Brown's famous 1974 Plymouth, which he insisted on using in lieu of the traditional limousine.

One thing I can guarantee, no matter where you grew up, you will find at least one car on display that will trigger deep memories of your most impressionable years—a kind of Proust's madeleine on wheels. This place is a must stop for anyone fascinated by cars or Americana.

TOWE FORD MUSEUM, 2200 Front Street, Sacramento. Phone: (916) 442-6802. Open 10 A.M. to 6 P.M. daily. Admission: Adults, $4; high schoolers, $2; children kindergarten through eighth grade, $1. Senior discount available.

HOW TO GET HERE: From San Francisco, take the Bay Bridge and follow Route 80 to Sacramento. Look for the downtown Sacramento exit via Business 80. After exiting, cross the Tower Bridge, then take the first right onto Front Street. Follow Front for a few blocks, and the museum will be on the right.

SMITTY'S VINTAGE AIRCRAFT REPAIR

Much of the action in the Delta centers on water-related activities. So it comes as a bit of a shock to be driving along a levee road and happen upon Smitty's. All of a sudden, boats give way to vintage airplanes, the kind you'd expect to see Indiana Jones commandeering during a fast escape. The sight is so arresting that lots of folks have to stop to find out what's going on. Fortunately, they get to meet Loren Schmitt—aka "Smitty"—who's been running his repair shop here for more than 30 years.

Smitty is a mellow kind of guy who will lean up against a plane and complain that so many folks come by on the weekends that it's hard to get his work done, at the same time making it clear that he enjoys the distraction. Anyway, he and his crew of helpers and hecklers usually break a few times during the day to chat and to barbecue the latest catch from the Delta or devour a pie or two.

Like many of us, Smitty came upon his mission in life by accident. He was tinkering around on a friend's plane when he realized he had a knack for specialized service. The surprise is that he doesn't fly himself. He claims he was too busy to learn when he was younger. When I suggested that he was still a relatively young man, Smitty made it clear that fixing planes is just fine; flying them is for somebody else. His thrill comes when a plane he's worked on goes out onto the strip, starts right up, and then soars.

Flying buffs from all around bring their old-time planes here. This is one of the few places anywhere that specializes in simple flying machines, the kinds without fancy cabins, pressurized chambers, or computerized controls. Most of the planes are made mostly of wood and fabric.

On any given day, you'll find vintage aircraft in various states of assembly out on the landing strip and inside the shop. The day I visited, I happened upon a stockbroker from Sacramento who was doing some work of his own on a totally stripped frame of a plane that didn't seem much bigger than the models I remember from my childhood. Smitty roams around from project to project, handing out advice and giving hands-on help.

This is not the kind of place to build an entire trip around. A gratifying visit depends on how busy everyone is at the moment and how many interesting planes are on hand. But if you are driving around the Delta and want to take your chances on an interesting diversion, you might consider dropping by Smitty's. By the way, if you want to explore the Delta after your visit, continue on Route 160. It winds around for about 30 scenic miles.

SMITTY'S AIR REPAIR, *River Road, Clarksburg. Phone: (916) 744-1661.*

HOW TO GET HERE: *From Central Sacramento, take Route 5 South, 5 miles to the Meadowview Road–Pocket Road exit. Turn left (east) on Pocket Road, cross over the freeway, and then turn right on Freeport Boulevard, which is also Route 160. Go south for 2 miles to the town of Freeport. Cross the bridge and turn left on River Road. Continue for 1 mile and look for a small airfield on the right. That's Smitty's.*

In the story about the Warm Springs Fish Hatchery in Sonoma County in my first book, I explained that recent environmental protection laws have led to the creation of fish factories. Without going into the long process again, you should know that a similar operation exists outside Sacramento in a lovely setting along the American River. In this scenario, it was the Folsom Dam that interrupted the natural spawning process for salmon and steelhead, so the government has stepped in to help the fish reproduce. This is a large operation, with a goal of 4.5 million salmon births and 500,000 steelhead births annually.

Here at the fish hatchery, adult fish swim up an elaborate staircase built to replicate the natural process of swimming upstream from ocean to river. From September to January the salmon make their final climb—final because, as in the wild, they die after spawning. The steelhead have a much better deal with nature, spawning from January through March and surviving the ordeal.

If you are at all queasy, you will will want to stay away from the area where fish sperm and eggs are extracted and implanted. Better to wander around the many tanks where the babies are raised until they are big enough to be released into the Delta. Or you can simply admire the view of the river.

NIMBUS FISH HATCHERY, *American River, near Folsom. Phone: (916) 355-0666. Open 7 A.M. to 3 P.M. during the summer, 8 A.M. to 4 P.M. the rest of the year. Admission: Free.*

HOW TO GET HERE: *From Sacramento, take Route 50 toward Lake Tahoe. Exit at Hazel Avenue. Turn left on Hazel and cross over the freeway. Turn left on Nimbus Road and follow it a block or so to the hatchery parking lot.*

FOLSOM

As you drive east out of Sacramento, you will soon see signs urging you not to miss historic Folsom. I second the motion. This is a growing suburban community that has managed to preserve its Gold Rush–era charm. Located on a beautiful stretch of the American River, Folsom offers many nearby locations for camping and picnicking, as well as several within the city limits.

Folsom began as a boomtown when gold was discovered in the American River. After the Gold Rush, Folsom continued to prosper, due primarily to its navigable waterway, fertile agricultural land (fruit trees ripen earlier here than in most parts of the state), and proximity to the state capital. Today many towns and cities in America have restored and preserved the historic part of town. In the case of Folsom, the Old Town section *is* downtown. It looks today much as it did 100 years ago, with elevated sidewalks and a grassy medium separating the two directions of traffic along the main drag, Sutter Street. When planning a visit, it is wise to keep in mind that in summer, temperatures can exceed 100 degrees. Those susceptible to heat prostration might prefer to visit in spring or fall or on a dry winter's day.

The best place to begin a visit to Folsom is at the town History Museum at 823 Sutter Street, in the old Wells Fargo Building. Here you can pick up a map of points of interest around town, including the town's stately homes, the remains of the town's first sawmill, and "Emma's place," the town's original "house of convenience."

Just off Sutter Street is another point of interest. In the old Southern Pacific train station, the depot of the West's first railway, is the local Chamber of Commerce. If you continue out to the grounds, you will find a town within the town of Folsom. On a lucky day you'll meet Folsom Jim, who has been panning for gold in the area since 1932. Here next to the old train depot he has built barns, miners' cabins, a blacksmith's shop, a mock cemetery, and various exhibitions of historic artifacts. He will also show you how to pan for gold. Folsom Jim is one of the town's great characters and is worth seeking out.

Several blocks from the main downtown area is the Folsom Powerhouse, a place that reminds me of the set of a Hollywood science fiction movie made about 1929. This is National Historic Landmark 633, the site of the first commercial long-distance transmission of electrical power in California, a shipment of 22 miles to Sacramento. The equipment is amazing to look at, almost a work of art. The powerhouse is open for tours, staffed by volunteers who love to show off the impressive generators, turbines, and other pieces of equipment on display. These guides are convinced they can teach you everything you ever wanted to know about electricity in 15 minutes, more or less.

OLD TOWN FOLSOM, *a half hour's drive from downtown Sacramento.*

FOLSOM HISTORICAL SOCIETY, *Wells Fargo Building, 823 Sutter Street (near Wool), Folsom. Phone: (916) 985-2707. Open Wednesday through Sunday, 11 A.M. to 4 P.M. Admission: Free.*

FOLSOM JIM'S PLACE, *on the grounds outside the Chamber of Commerce, 200 Wool Street (near Sutter), Folsom. No set hours; call ahead to the Chamber of Commerce for an appointment. Admission: Free. Chamber of Commerce phone: (916) 985-2698. Open 9 A.M. to 5 P.M. Monday through Friday.*

FOLSOM POWERHOUSE, *7806 Folsom-Auburn Road (at Riley Street), Folsom. Phone: (916) 988-0205. Tours given Tuesday through Saturday, noon to 4:30 P.M. Call ahead for tour reservations. Admission: Free.*

HOW TO GET HERE: *From San Francisco, take the Bay Bridge and continue on Route 80 to Sacramento. Take the Route 50 turn, and about 20 minutes past Sacramento, take the Folsom Boulevard exit to "Historic Folsom." Follow the road into town, and turn right on Sutter Street.*

One of the very best reasons to visit Folsom is to stop at the Candy Store Gallery to meet Adeliza McHugh. Her place is located on the fringe of the Old Town section, an unusual location for an art gallery that turns up in such publications as *Connoisseur*. Just the fact that her tiny gallery is filled with wonderful works of modern art makes this is a must stop. Add to that Adeliza herself, a disarmingly sweet woman in her late seventies who greets you like a kindly grandmother welcoming someone about to marry into the family. She's hospitable and warm and at the same time sizes you up as you look at the art, some of which is pretty wild. As you evaluate a Roy De Forest drawing or a Robert Arneson sculpture, she will scold you a bit if she thinks you don't "get" it.

It is rare for name artists to exhibit their works in such a remote gallery; after all, who thinks to go to Folsom to spend several thousand dollars on a canvas? To her credit, Adeliza has inspired great loyalty from her artists. In the 1960s she brought along a young group of struggling artists who were teaching at the UC Davis campus and living around Sacramento. She encouraged and nurtured them and displayed their work when few others would. Then they became famous. When Adeliza started selling Roy De Forest's work, a drawing sold for about $150; now his work sells for $5,500 and up, and Adeliza often gets first dibs. Last time I visited the Candy Store, Adeliza had just sold an Arneson sculpture for $16,000, but she had mixed feelings. Of course she liked making the sale, but she also hated to part with the piece.

Other names that got big after they encountered Adeliza include Clayton Bailey, Gladys Nilsson, and Luis Cruz Azaceta. If these names don't ring a bell, let me assure you that an art background is not a prerequisite for an enjoyable visit to the gallery. It is a small, two-room house that really used to be a candy store. It is so small that no more than 20 works are on display at a time. There is no pressure to do anything but look. The artists are all contemporary, and most of them work in brilliant colors.

Best of all, Adeliza is a kick. She says location has not been a problem. "Just the other day, someone came in from Morocco," says Adeliza. "I said, 'Where the hell is Morocco?'" I know, your grandmother never talked like that, but Adeliza is no ordinary grandma. And this is no ordinary art gallery.

CANDY STORE GALLERY, *605 Sutter Street, Folsom. Phone: (916) 985-2927. Open 10 A.M. to 4:30 P.M. Wednesday through Sunday.*

HOW TO GET HERE: *From Old Town Folsom (see previous entry), go through the main section of shops and continue to 605 Sutter.*

If there is another town as small as Folsom that has a zoo of this caliber, well, you could knock me over with a peacock feather. And to make that easy for you, peacocks roam freely here; everyone seems to pick feathers and take them home as souvenirs. I'd also be surprised if you've ever been to a more charming or a more inspiring zoo.

It all started back in 1953 when a bear was left homeless by a fire in the nearby woods. The kindly director of the town park agreed to care for the bear, affectionately and appropriately called Smokey. Then a lost reindeer was turned in, and the town fathers decided that as long as they had two animals, they might as well start a zoo. But not just any zoo. This was to be a *misfit* zoo, a haven for animals nobody wants or needs. Some are disabled, some are abandoned pets; there's even a mountain lion that was left homeless when its dope-dealing master was sent to jail (he had been using the large cat as a very effective watchdog).

The population also includes Smokey's son, a huge elk, monkeys, a pack of wolves, skunks, bobcats, raccoons, coyotes, plus a small staff of workers, volunteers, and a continuing parade of kids and adults enjoying the place.

Much care has been taken to identify and name each animal and to treat it with the utmost consideration. Tours can be self-guided, with hand-printed signs on each cage telling first about the species and then about the personal history of the animal.

Director Terry Jenkins keeps it all together, working continually to add better cages and more space for her critters. She wants a visit here to be a learning experience for the animals on both sides of the cages. Humans are urged to learn that wild animals must not be used as pets and that animals are not disposable; they are living creatures, not just toys to have fun with for a while then throw away. Terry takes pride in the fact that the Folsom Zoo keeps animals until they die, unlike larger zoos, which keep only animals with minimal problems.

As for the animals, she wants them to learn that humans are not all bad and that they can be caring and helpful.

As you can tell, this is a nice place, the kind of destination where you feel better when you leave than when you came in. It's small and can be seen in about an hour, but you are welcome to linger as long as you like.

FOLSOM ZOO, *50 Natoma Street, Folsom. Phone: (916) 355-7200. Open Tuesday through Sunday 10 A.M. to 4 P.M.; closed Monday. Admission: Ages 13 and up, $1.50; ages 5 to 12, 50 cents; age 4 and under, free. Free admission on the first Tuesday of each month.*

HOW TO GET HERE: *From San Francisco, cross the Bay Bridge and take Route 80 beyond Sacramento to Route 50, and continue for another half hour or so to the Folsom exit. Follow Folsom Boulevard into town to Natoma Street. Turn right onto Natoma and continue through a residential section until you come to Stafford Street. Enter the parking lot, and follow the signs to the zoo.*

FOLSOM PRISON ARTS AND CRAFTS SHOP

I know, I know, visiting a state prison is probably not your idea of a good time. But this place is different. First of all, Johnny Cash made it famous. Second of all, it's a beautiful drive to get here. Last but not least, the prison gift shop is surprisingly appealing.

The arts and crafts store at Folsom State Correctional Facility sells items made by inmates. The proceeds from sales go to the inmate who made the item, with 25 percent skimmed off to go into a welfare fund to support prison programs. As you might expect, you'll find the obligatory paintings and charcoal sketches expressing male fantasies about women but also fine leather goods, jewelry, and woodwork. The shop is operated by inmates under the watchful eye of supervisors.

Another reason to visit is to see the prison's historical museum. Here you'll learn about the place, built in 1880 and nicknamed by its involuntary occupants "the end of the world." Here you'll see a video about the prison, historical artifacts, uniforms, and photos. The museum is staffed by the Retired Correctional Officers Association.

FOLSOM PRISON ARTS AND CRAFTS STORE, *Prison Road (off East Natoma Street), Folsom. Phone: (916) 985-2561, ext. 4491. Open 8 A.M. to 5 P.M. daily. The prison museum is open 10 A.M. to 4 P.M. Thursday through Monday. The $1 admission goes to cancer research.*

HOW TO GET HERE (FOR ONLY A BRIEF VISIT): *From the Folsom Zoo, continue on East Natoma, and look for signs to the prison on the left.*

GALT FLEA MARKET

There are several large flea markets in the Bay Area, in places like San Jose, Alameda, and Marin City. They're open on the weekends and have been practically taken over by pros who roam from market to market selling their goods. That lends a commercial air to the experience. But the flea market in Galt is the old-fashioned kind, where jus' folks clean out their attics and basements, rent a stall, and sell you their old stuff at prices you can't resist. The reason for this great flea market is the fact that town residents can get a booth for free; out-of-towners have to pay a fee to set up a table. The operation is run by the city government; the original idea was to cut down on the number of garage sales around town. Now it's a reason to visit the town.

The Galt flea market has a number of things going for it. For one thing, it's open during the week, on Wednesdays. For another, there is no admission charge.

Yes, you will see the occasional professional, with packaged jewelry and hardware displays, but mostly you'll see regular folks selling the most unusual variety of things. As you stroll around the 200-plus stalls, you can find everything from a ceramic swan to a live parakeet and from a bust of Nefertiti to a plastic King Kong. Last time I was there, a man had nothing but some lovely bamboo bar stools and his child's outgrown ice skates.

The most bizarre item I saw was a mailing list with about 10,000 names and addresses on peel-and-stick labels. The man who bought it would identify himself only as a merchant in the "adult" mail-order business. He was thrilled with his find. My guess is that Chuck Ranberg of Sacramento, California, may not be so thrilled (or maybe he will be).

For another experience entirely, you can visit the flea market on Tuesday, which is wholesale day. The parking lot will be dotted with license plates from around the West, the pros who roam from market to market looking for goods to turn around and sell. You do need a resale license to buy anything on Tuesday, but if you're simply curious, you can just wander around.

GALT FLEA MARKET, *across from City Hall, Galt. Phone: (209) 745-2437. Open Tuesday 8 A.M. to 8 P.M. for wholesale, Wednesday 7 A.M. to 4 P.M. for regular flea market. Admission: Free.*

HOW TO GET HERE: *From San Francisco, take the Bay Bridge and continue on Route 580 to Stockton. Exit at Peltier Drive and head east (right) to Route 99 North. Continue to Galt. Exit at the C Street central exit and head west (left) on C Street into town. At the bright green bank building, turn left onto Civic Drive, and look for the flea market across from City Hall.*

THE CHICKEN THAT WON THE WEST

The colonel from Kentucky may have made more from fried chicken than anyone ever thought possible, but Neil Pollard is nothing to cluck at. Not that the proprietor of the roadside attraction that bears his name is a mogul. It's just that the effort and imagination that went into building a town ought to bring Neil and his late father some kind of lasting fame.

You are first aware of Pollardville as you drive up or down Route 99 between Stockton and Lodi. This is the heart of the Central Valley, an area of huge farms, flat land, and wide-open spaces. Suddenly, in the sky, you'll see a likeness of a giant chicken perched on a huge metal pole. The chicken brings folks in to the large restaurant, which, as you might expect, specializes in fried chicken. Neil calls this "the chicken that won the West."

But it's what's behind the restaurant that is the attraction: an entire Western ghost town out in the middle of a big field. Actually, it's an entirely re-created ghost town that the Pollards put together piece by piece in the 1950s. The centerpiece is a hotel set that was used for the movie *The Big Country*. After the Pollards acquired that, they were off and running. They picked up some abandoned buildings from around the state and brought them onto the property, including a small brick jail from Jamestown and the post office from Mountain Ranch. All in all, more than 20 buildings line a dirt road.

Activities around Pollardville depend on Neil's mood and how well business is going in the restaurant. At various times there have been staged gunfights, Wild West days, and other events. At last visit, Neil was opening up some of the shops to local craftspeople.

In addition to the restaurant and the Wild West town, there is also a large and well-equipped theater on the property, housed in what looks like an old showboat. On weekends Neil presents the melodrama *The Drunkard*, during which customers can boo and hiss the villain while eating fried chicken, of course. The chicken, by the way, is good.

POLLARDVILLE, *Route 99 between Stockton and Lodi. Phone: (209) 931-0272. Restaurant open daily for lunch and dinner. Wild West town open daily, but shops operate only on the weekend. Dinner theater is presented on Friday and Saturday nights.*

HOW TO GET HERE: *From San Francisco, cross the Bay Bridge and take Route 580 East to Route 205, which leads to Interstate 5 North. Just past Stockton, turn east at the Eight Mile Drive exit. Follow Eight Mile Drive to Route 99. Go past the Route 99 turnoff and then turn right on Frontage Road. Follow it to the giant chicken.*

MICKE GROVE

Every summer, when the temperature hovers around the 100-degree mark, thousands of people in the San Joaquin Valley are thankful for William G. Micke. He was an early settler, a son of German immigrants who came west from Missouri to make his fortune in farming. As he watched the valley grow, he saw what "progress" could do to the land, so he bought some 65 wooded acres just to save them from the woodsman's ax and then donated them to the county. That was back around the turn of the century. Now the grove of valley oaks provides much needed shade and relief—a veritable oasis.

Micke Grove Park has become the most visited facility in all of San Joaquin County, but don't be concerned about crowds. There is so much to do here that you will not feel hemmed in. There is a zoo, a Japanese garden, a carnival ride area, a swimming pool, baseball fields, loads of picnic areas under the oaks, and the most extensive county historical museum I have ever seen. Taking up some 14 acres, this museum alone is worth the trip. It offers an entertaining, easy-to-understand display of how the San Joaquin Valley feeds the nation and much of the world.

The exhibits, which take up several halls, barns, and outdoor areas, include the largest collection of hand tools west of the Mississippi, nearly 4,000 of them, used by various craftsmen. There are more than 75 tractors, orange crates and apple carts, a model dairy, a weaving exhibit, a blacksmith's shop, a vineyard, a one-room schoolhouse, and special displays showing the various crops of the region, including dairy, grapes, tomatoes, nuts, hay, and grain.

Mike Bennett, the young director of the museum, is a grandson of one of the early farmers of the area. He feels that the San Joaquin Valley is the friendliest place in California and has designed the museum to be low-key and hospitable as well as authentic. Mike loves to watch grandparents bring kids and show them the tractors they used to use. He also tries to offer as many hands-on exhibits as possible. His proudest achievement is the Sunshine Trail, a garden designed for the visually impaired. You graze your way through the trail, tasting, touching, and smelling native California plants. It's a sensual treat.

MICKE GROVE PARK, *11793 North Micke Grove Road, Lodi. For park information, call (209) 953-8800; for museum information, call (209) 368-9154. The park is open during daylight hours all year round. The museum is open Wednesday through Sunday from 1 to 5 P.M. Special tours may be arranged for groups. Parking fee: $2 per car on weekdays; $3 per car on weekends; seniors free. Museum admission: Free.*

HOW TO GET HERE: *From San Francisco, take the Bay Bridge to Route 580 and continue east toward Stockton. Proceed on Route 205 and then take Interstate 5 North. Pass Stockton and exit at Eight Mile Road in Lodi. Head east about 6 miles, until you come to Micke Grove Road. Turn left and follow it into the park.*

WINDMILL MAN

Don Quixote is alive and well in Stockton, though this modern incarnation goes by the name of Frank Medina. He has a collection Señor Quixote never dreamed possible. Frank calls himself the "king of the windmills" and claims to have the world's largest collection. It's a boast you'll have to take at face value; he also claims he's the only man in his eighties to have all his original teeth. Both collections are to be seen on a drive down Waterloo Road in Stockton.

The windmills are visible from the road. They cover the front and side lawns, almost obscuring Frank's house. He's amassed over 500 of them from all over the world, and he's looking for more. Now a retired hay and cattle farmer, Frank has been fascinated by them since childhood, when a visit to Grandma's ranch was a real treat. There he had a windmill outside his bedroom window; the sound of it clanging was like a lullaby to the youngster. He decided he loved windmills so much that he would devote his life to collecting them. Even today, whenever he sees a windmill, he feels he's got to have it.

Every windmill in Frank's collection works. He personally checks on the equipment and makes sure each mill can pump water and make electricity. He has bought them intact and in parts, dispensing as much as $9,000 for a particularly desirable one. Almost all were manufactured by the Aeromotor Company of Chicago, which made what Frank calls the "Cadillac of windmills."

For years people have stopped, taken pictures, and asked Frank about this remarkable collection. Be forewarned, however, that shortly after our story on Frank appeared on television, we received a letter from a viewer saying that Frank wanted to charge this man $25 per photo for permission to step on his property and shoot. Clearly, Frank is an independent fellow who might decide to say or do just about anything. My guess is that if you approach Frank in the right way, you will be welcomed. He loves to talk and boast, vowing he can outclimb and outwork any youngster in his sixties. He will also gladly show you his teeth, which he swears have never been cursed by a cavity.

The windmills are in full view from the public road, and they are worth at least driving by.

FRANK'S WINDMILLS, 6553 Waterloo Road, Stockton. Phone: (209) 931-3523.

HOW TO GET HERE: *From San Francisco, cross the Bay Bridge and take Route 580 toward Stockton. Then continue on Route 205 to Interstate 5 North to the Route 4 exit. Take Route 4 East (right) to Route 99. Continue north to the exit for Route 88, which is also Waterloo Road. Turn right (east) until you come to the windmills, about 2 miles east of Route 99.*

CHAPTER **11** Gold Country

The great California Gold Rush has begun again. In the past few years, more and more giant corporations have begun mining the hills of the Gold Country in earnest. Only this time, they use highly sophisticated machinery and hire skilled labor. This is not a time for the Gold Rush fever that once brought individual prospectors from all over the world.

There will never be another time like the great rush of 1849. For a few short years in the area known as the Gold Country, boomtowns housed thousands upon thousands of people; saloons, hotels, and other businesses sprang up overnight to provide services. In fact, many who found fortunes during the Gold Rush were suppliers to the miners, companies like Levi Strauss, Studebaker, Armour, and Ghiradelli.

But the Gold Rush fever cooled rapidly, and most of the people who had arrived from points all over the globe headed to San Francisco or Sacramento to

AREA OVERVIEW

build new lives. Only a few stayed behind. The Gold Country was more or less abandoned. It wasn't until more than 100 years later that this important area of California would find its niche as a tourist attraction.

The main road connecting the counties of the mother lode is appropriately named Route 49, which leads you 317 miles from the southern tip of the Gold Country at Oakhurst to the northernmost town of Downieville.

I recommend that you concentrate on one of the three general areas: the Southern Mines, centered around Columbia; the Central Mother Lode, centered around Jackson; or the Northern Mines, centered around Nevada City. Each area has its own local historical museum and its own particular flavor.

To get to the Southern Mines, take Highway 580 out of Oakland to Highway 205 to Route 120 to Oakdale; then take Route 108 to Route 49, which you pick up a bit south of Jamestown.

To get to the Central Mother Lode, follow Route 80 from the Bay Bridge to Route 50 in Sacramento; then take Route 16, following the signs to Jackson, or continue on Route 50 to Placerville.

To get to the Northern Mines, take Route 80 from the Bay Bridge to Route 49 North at Auburn and continue to the towns of Grass Valley and Nevada City. In Auburn you'll wonder about some giant statues rising high above various points in the city. They were all created by a local dentist named Ken Fox who started building statues as a hobby. His 42-foot-high concrete-and-steel creations include gold miners, Amazon warriors, and Chinese laborers. Because of their size, the statues will probably outlast Dr. Fox's fillings.

Also of note, just south of Grass Valley, is the Empire Mine State Historic Park. This was the largest and richest of all the hard-rock gold mines in the state and operated for more than 100 years. A tour of the mine and its many buildings and passages is offered by park personnel. A highlight is a visit to the home of the owner of the mine, William Bourne, whom we met earlier as the owner of Greystone in the Napa Valley.

In terms of distance from San Francisco, most areas of the Gold Country can be reached in 2½ to 3 hours. The roads that take you there are all good and fast. Route 49 is slow and requires that you take your time.

Keep in mind that night life is close to nonexistent in the Gold Country, and great restaurants are few and far between, but good food is available if you are selective.

For general information about traveling in the Gold Country, contact the Golden Chain Council of the Mother Lode, P.O. Box 1246, Auburn, CA 95603. Phone: (916) 885-5616.

In our first book, we suggested around a dozen stops in the Gold Country. Here are some more places of special interest, arranged south to north along Route 49.

Driving from the Bay Area, the first southern Gold Country town you'll hit is Jamestown, which is an ideal place to get into the spirit of things. On Main Street, head straight to Ralph Stock's Gold Country Prospecting Company. The place is easy to find; it's the only shop on Main Street with a dummy hanging from a noose out front. Ralph himself is easy to recognize, too. He's the guy with a twinkle in his eye and on his gold chain, watch, and bracelet. He even has a poodle named Twinkle who loves to dive for gold nuggets in the trough outside Ralph's shop.

Ralph's Gold Country Prospecting Company is a place to learn how to pan for gold. Ralph is part promoter, part teacher, and he's good at both. Some call him the P. T. Barnum of the area, but basically he's a guy who likes to have a good time and is able to tailor an expedition to fit your budget, from lavish helicopter tours into remote spots to a simple two-hour adventure for the family on foot.

At the shop, which is filled with artifacts that Ralph has found while in search of gold, he'll give a brief lesson on how to look for gold. The trick, according to Ralph, is to learn to see the gold "move." Then he'll take you to a nearby creek and let you get your feet wet, literally. Ralph says that twice as much gold is pulled out of the area today as during the 1850s. The major difference now is that most of it is extracted by giant corporations. Still, there are a few hardy prospectors who come in and try to strike it rich. These private prospectors must think highly of Ralph and his staff; wherever Ralph takes customers to pan, they're not far behind.

Even if you don't find a million dollars, and you won't, there is something enjoyable about getting out into the stream with a pan and sticking your mitts in the mud. When we were shooting a television story here, our associate producer, Vicky Collins, gave me a start when I saw something glittering under a handful of dirt. It turned out to be her wedding ring, but still, it was a quick insight into gold fever.

If you don't have the time to head for the creek, you can pay a dollar to pan in the box in front of the former livery stable, one of the town's original buildings, that is Ralph's headquarters. Take the time to stroll around Jamestown's Main Street. It is an interesting amalgam of a historic Old West town, with its boardwalks and hotels, and a growing tourist attraction.

GOLD COUNTRY PROSPECTING COMPANY, *18172 Main Street, Jamestown. Phone: (209) 984-GOLD. Open daily. Admission: Free to look around the former livery stable; prices for excursions vary according to elaborateness. Bring boots.*

HOW TO GET HERE: *From San Francisco, take the Bay Bridge to Route 580. Continue toward Stockton via Routes 205 and 5. From Route 5, exit onto Route 120 and take it to Oakdale. Then take Route 108 to Jamestown. Exit for historic Main Street and continue to number 18172.*

RAILTOWN 1897

Though Jamestown's Main Street has been in many movies, the old Sierra Railway Depot has seen lots more Hollywood action, on both big and little screens. *High Noon,* "The Virginian," "Dodge City," "The Lone Ranger," and "Petticoat Junction" are but a few of the movies and television shows shot here at the roundhouse and on the spacious grounds surrounding it.

Don't get the idea that this is an artificial place built for tourists and television producers. This is the real enchilada, the place where diesel locomotives connected the mines and lumber mills of the southern Mother Lode with the rest of the world. Hollywood discovered the place in 1956, and since then nearly 200 feature films, television shows, and commercials have been filmed here. For many years the railway did operate as a commercial tourist attraction. Then the state of California acquired the property in 1982 and opened the 26-acre park in 1983.

This is a must see for anyone even remotely interested in trains; in fact, Railtown reminds you of a giant real-life Lionel train set. A tour begins with a video presentation about the history of California railroading and this place in particular. From here a guide takes you on a 50-minute walk into the complex of century-old buildings, which includes blacksmith's and carpenter's shops and the stars of the show: a wide variety of steam locomotives and antique passenger cars, plus all the tools and equipment necessary to maintain them.

In contrast to the slick and shiny Rail Museum in Sacramento, Railtown 1897 is a grimy, greasy, lively working display. In the back of the giant roundhouse (the only historic roundhouse open to the public in the United States), the railroad cars can be powered out onto a giant revolving platform. The sight of steam pouring out of these mammoth machines and the sound of the whistles blowing creates lifelong memories.

The tour also includes a movie memorabilia room. Every time a film or TV crew uses this location, they leave behind a memento, so this part of the tour is a movie buff's paradise.

Between April and October you can take an hour-long train ride in 70- and 80-year-old passenger cars. The excursion covers 8 miles of oak-covered Sierra foothills and offers sights, sounds, and smells you can't get from the highway. Trains run four times a day.

A lovely way to end a visit is with a picnic lunch under shady oak trees in the park. Picnic tables and barbecues are provided.

RAILTOWN 1897 STATE HISTORIC PARK, *Fifth Avenue, Jamestown. Phone: (209) 984-3953. Roundhouse open all year; trains run April through October. Hours and train schedule vary thoughout the year, so be sure to call ahead. Admission: Roundhouse tour only, $2 for adults, $1.25 for children; train ride only, $7.95 for adults, $3.95 for children; roundhouse tour and train ride, $8.75 for adults, $4.25 for children.*

HOW TO GET HERE: *From San Francisco, follow the directions to Jamestown, but stay on Route 108 past Main Street. Take the next right to Railtown. There will be a sign on Route 108.*

The Gold Country is not a pilgrimage site for gourmets. In the Southern Mines area I've found only one restaurant—Hemingway's in Sonora—that compares favorably to modern cuisine establishments close to San Francisco.

However, there is one dish that is worth a trip to the Gold Country, and that's the "mile-high apple pie" at Sonka's Apple Ranch, just outside the town of Sonora. This dish has become so popular that nearly every freezer in the greater Southern Mines area contains at least one Sonka pie. What's more, the ranch itself has developed into a miniature county fair.

The Sonka family worked the land here for 100 years, until 1984. The ranch was then purchased by a real estate man named Hal Bomgardner. He and his wife added some promotional touches to the place and soon had a busy attraction on their hands. When one visitor marveled that the pies—which stand about 8 or 9 inches tall—seemed a mile high, a slogan was born, and soon signs on the highway advertised the home of the mile-high apple pie.

I can tell you from personal experience that these pies are wonderful. You can watch them being made. For health code reasons, you stand behind a plate glass window in the gift shop. You will be spellbound as the ladies turn pie making into a spectacle. See the miles of apples piled into the pie tins, covered with pastry crust, and whisked into the ovens! They also make other pastries, including mile-high strawberry pie (in season, of course), plus a variety of jams and jellies—it's all so darn wholesome.

The usual routine for the visitor is to walk around the gift shop for a while, to watch the pies being made, then to order a slice of pie hot from the oven. You can eat it while seated at one of the many picnic tables located between the ranch house and the gift shop. Then if the season is right, you can watch apples being picked, sorted, and crushed for cider. If you're in the company of children, on weekends they can take a 12-minute miniature train ride through the or-

MILE-HIGH APPLE PIE

chards and beyond. It's owned by a county deputy sheriff who needed someplace to put his 12-gauge railroad. The folks at the ranch welcomed him, and now he comes out on weekends and gives rides for a dollar.

All year round you can walk though the barn and meet a variety of animals, including mules, geese, and cows, all of them with incredibly cute names. If you bring Mom and a flag, you will have a real Americana experience.

SONKA'S APPLE RANCH, *Cherokee Road, Sonora. Phone: (209) 928-4689. Ranch open daily all year. Peak apple season is late summer through autumn.*

HOW TO GET HERE: *From San Francisco, follow the directions to Jamestown via Routes 580, 205, 140, and 108. After Jamestown, stay on Route 108 as you approach Sonora, but bypass the center of town. Turn right on Tuolumne Road (you will see a sign for Sonka's) and go about 5 miles toward Tuolumne City. Turn left on Cherokee Road, and the ranch will be about a mile up the road. There will be plenty of signs.*

COLUMBIA Walking down the main street of Columbia (which you must do; no cars are allowed) is a way to literally step back in time. The era you step back into is the 1850s, when this was the richest mining town in the world. The state Parks Department runs it now and has restored it in great detail. Many of the original shops adorn Main Street, its wood-and-brick sidewalks patched together just like in the Gold Rush days. As soon as you abandon your car in the parking lot, you will be greeted by the sights and sounds of a nineteenth-century mining town: strolling fiddlers, horse-drawn carriages, unshaven prospectors, even a stagecoach.

To make the idea of a visit even more inviting, the state also operates two hotels, the City and the Fallon, one at each end of town. These are beautifully restored buildings, decorated with antiques and authentically re-created Victorian wallpaper. One concession to modern times is that each room has its own sink and flushing commode; the bow to authenticity is that guests must go down the hall to shower. Students from nearby Columbia College help operate the hotels and the city's famous restaurant.

A great way to get your bearings in town is to take the stagecoach ride. It departs from the Wells Fargo Express Stop (no, not an automatic cash machine, but a real Pony Express stop) in the center of town. This 15-minute ride takes you around town in an authentic horse-drawn stagecoach just like we've seen in a million westerns. There's even a surprise event that takes place during the ride, but I won't spoil it for you.

One of the town's most popular attractions, for reasons that become obvious, is Nelson's Columbia Candy Kitchen. Four generations of Nelsons have worked in this large store and kitchen, and they still make candy the old-fashioned way, using antique equipment and techniques you won't see anywhere else.

A wonderful way to pass the time is to watch Michael Nelson at work, which is usually in the morning and early afternoon. Health codes prohibit you from actually going inside the kitchen, but you can watch through the giant windows. Working with huge copper pots, antique cast-iron melting vats, and marble cooling slabs, candy is made from scratch. Christmas draws a crowd to see the process of making candy canes, involving taffy pulled on a huge hook. The Nelsons also make old-fashioned candies that are nearly impossible to find elsewhere, such as horehound cough drops, made from the herb found in their own pasture.

One of the town characters who is hard to miss is Phineas, who dresses like an old-time prospector. He claims he went into a mine in 1855 and when he emerged it was the 1980s. His Rip Van Winkle act is brought off so convincingly that crowds gather to hear his stories. Children really enjoy hearing about "the way it used to be" and his nineteenth-century perspective of the late twentieth. Phineas also leads tours and teaches how to pan for gold.

As you continue your tour around Columbia, you will see that the town claims to have several firsts, including the first barbershop in California. There's also the first school in California, perched on a hill above town and restored thanks to the many 25-cent contributions of visiting schoolchildren. The schoolhouse was originally located near the town cemetery, possibly as a subtle lesson in discipline.

All the shops along Main Street are named as they were in the Gold Rush days. Though the butcher shop is set up as an exhibit, the dry goods stores are open for business, selling old-fashioned bonnets, jewelry, dinnerware, and souvenir items; you can also see a live demonstration at the blacksmith's place (one of the first in California). Uniformed park rangers are on hand around town to answer any questions you might have about Columbia. They know their history and can also give you tips about other places to visit in the area.

COLUMBIA STATE HISTORIC PARK, *Columbia. Ranger's station phone: (209) 532-4301. Stagecoach rides are offered frequently throughout the day; schedule varies seasonally. Phone: (209) 785-2244. Shetland pony rides are also available. Stagecoach rides cost $3 for adults, $1.50 for children. Columbia Candy Kitchen is on the main street in Columbia State Historic Park. Phone: (209) 532-7886. Hours vary throughout the year.*

HOW TO GET HERE: *From San Francisco, take the Bay Bridge and continue on Route 580 toward Stockton. This becomes Route 205; take this to Route 5 North. Exit from 5 North onto Route 120 and stay on 120 to Oakdale. Then take Route 108 to Sonora. At Sonora take Route 49 to Columbia.*

MARK TWAIN'S CABIN

As you drive up Route 49 from Columbia to Angels Camp, you'll pass a sign pointing to Mark Twain's cabin. It's worth a detour to see where the great writer lived during his days in the Gold Country. It will just take a few minutes.

This spare cabin makes Abe Lincoln's beginnings look palatial. It's just a timber cabin—a shack, really—without much room for anything but a desk and a place to sleep. You can't actually go inside; there's a fence around the cabin to preserve it. But you can peek inside to see the little writing desk. It may give you a fresh perspective next time you complain about the slowness of your word processor.

It was here that Twain wrote his famous story "The Celebrated Jumping Frog of Calaveras County." It's located on Jackass Hill, so named because the braying of the large number of the aforementioned animal living on this hill could be heard for miles. Today the main sound is that of dogs barking, as this is a rural community with a very large and vocal canine population.

By the way, a frog-jumping contest is still held each spring at the nearby Calaveras County Fairgrounds.

MARK TWAIN'S CABIN, *Jackass Hill. Gates are open during daylight hours.*

HOW TO GET HERE: *From San Francisco, take the Bay Bridge and continue on Route 580 toward Stockton. This becomes Route 205; take this to Route 5 North. Exit from 5 North onto Route 120 and stay on 120 to Oakdale. Then take Route 108 to Sonora. At Sonora take Route 49 North to Columbia toward Angels Camp. Look for the highway marker on the right side of the road, about 15 minutes beyond Columbia.*

STEVENOT WINERY

Few places in California do not have their own wine industry, and the Gold Country is no exception. Historically, the Gold Country was one of the first wine regions in California. Prohibition took the wind out of its sails, and it has taken quite a while to get up to speed again.

One of the most picturesque and successful of the current generation of wineries is outside the town of Murphys. The Shaw family lived on this property in the early days. Farmer Shaw tended his crops in front of the farmhouse and his gold mine in back. He also built the first swimming pool in the area.

In the 1930s the swimming pool was open to the public for a nickel a day. That's how the current owner, Barden Stevenot, first came to know the property. His parents brought him here to swim when he was a child, and he made a secret vow that he would buy the place someday. His day came in the 1960s, when the ranch came up for sale and Stevenot was doing pretty well for himself in the family mining business.

The idea to establish a winery came as an afterthought. Most of the grapes are grown on the property, and today Stevenot wines are winning awards and are served in the finer restaurants in the Gold Country.

Several things make this winery worth a visit. First of all, the natural surroundings are beautiful, especially in spring, when the wildflowers are in bloom. There is a small cultivated garden with picnic tables overlooking the vineyards —an ideal setting for an outdoor lunch. The tasting room is unique, unlike any other I've visited. Farmer Shaw built it around the turn of the century, styled after the grass-roofed huts he had seen during a visit to Alaska. The story that goes with the place is that he had also picked up the habits of hard drinking and carousing at all hours, and Mrs. Shaw didn't want him in the main house. So in a sense this was Shaw's private tasting room. It's a remarkable structure, with grass growing on the roof and rough-hewn wooden timbers inside, providing a cool escape from the summer heat.

Unfortunately, the ranch house and swimming pool are not open to the public (it's Barden Stevenot's private residence). But you can see antique farm equipment strewn casually around the property like sculpture and Indian artifacts that have been found on the property. Tours of the winemaking operation are given occasionally, so if you want to see that, be sure to call ahead.

STEVENOT WINERY, *2690 San Domingo Road, Murphys. Phone: (209) 728-3436. Tasting room open daily, 10 A.M. to 4:30 P.M. Admission: Free.*

HOW TO GET HERE: *From San Francisco, take the Bay Bridge and continue on Route 580 toward Stockton. This becomes Route 205; take this to Route 5 North. Exit from 5 North onto Route 120 to Oakdale. Then take Route 108 to Sonora. At Sonora take Route 49 North to Angels Camp. Turn right on Murphys Grade Road and follow it for 8 miles. Across from the Murphys Hotel, turn left on Sheep Ranch Road and follow it 2 miles to the winery.*

WHERE THE GOLD RUSH BEGAN

In 1848 California was mostly wilderness. The area had only recently become part of the United States, the spoils of the Mexican-American War. A wealthy farmer named John Sutter needed lumber for new construction in the Sacramento Valley (see John Sutter's Fort in Chapter 10). He dispatched a workman named James Marshall to build a sawmill in the mountains near the American River. On January 24, 1848, Marshall noticed some shiny golden flakes in the water near the mill, and the world changed.

Within a year, California's non-Indian population boomed from 14,000 to more than 100,000, and that original wave of "forty-niners" was soon followed by more fortune-hunters. Word of "gold in them thar hills" attracted refugees from around the globe, and not for the last time in history would California be the place people came to make their dreams come true.

That is the gist of the story you will hear when you visit the Marshall Gold Discovery Site in the town of Coloma. Like Columbia, the old boomtown is the park. They are different, however, and you should see both. For one thing, Coloma is bigger and more spread out in a traditional parklike setting. Whereas the main appeal in Columbia is the liveliness of the town's main street with its cute shops and wandering singers, Coloma is more, well, educational. The main attractions here are purely historical: the self-guided tour of a miner's cabin, the old schoolhouse, the blacksmith shop, the Chinese community store, and last but not least, the mill and monument to John Marshall.

The mill is a very impressive scale replica of Sutter's mill, which had been abandoned after the Gold Rush. Some of the original timbers were recovered from the river and are on display. Occasionally (most frequently during the summer months) the mill is put into action—an impressive sight, to say the least. You can call ahead to find out if the mill will be running at the time of your visit.

From the mill you can walk down to the place where John Marshall found the gold; then you can cross the river to an area that has been set up for recreational panning. On weekends volunteers are on hand to demonstrate the technique. Last time I was there, my guide was a young printing supplies salesman who liked getting decked out in "sourdough" duds and transforming himself into "Rattlesnake Jim."

A visit here would not be complete without going to the Marshall monument and gravesite. This statue of Marshall is perhaps the only positive thing to have come his way as a result of his discovery. As you will learn when you visit the park, Marshall was hounded by those who believed he had "special powers," and when he said he had no secrets, he was threatened and ridiculed. He lived out his days as a blacksmith and a regular customer of the area's saloons, squeezing out an income by signing his name. Now his bronze-coated statue towers above his grave, high on a hill, facing the place where he found such stuff as dreams are made of.

The park has many picnic sites, so plan to spend some time here.

JAMES MARSHALL GOLD DISCOVERY SITE, *State Historic Park, Coloma. Phone: (916) 622-3470. Open 10 A.M. to 5 P.M. daily except major holidays. Admission: Free. Wheelchair accessible.*

HOW TO GET HERE: *From San Francisco, take the Bay Bridge to Route 80 to Sacramento. At Sacramento, follow Route 50 to Placerville and exit onto Route 49 heading north. Route 49 goes right to Coloma. Follow signs to the park.*

LOLA MONTEZ'S BATHTUB Grass Valley is a lively Gold Rush village in the Northern Mother Lode. The town has a mining museum (located on Allison Ranch Road, at the end of Mill Street), a state park where you can peek into the shaft and administration offices of one of California's richest mines, and 367 miles of tunnels running beneath its streets. Along two of the main drags, Main and Mill streets, you'll see architectural and decorative remnants of the Gold Rush: gas lamps, brick façades, and little houses where Gold Rush families lived.

On Mill Street you'll find the Nevada County Chamber of Commerce, and it's worth a visit for several reasons. For one thing, you can pick up a walking map for a self-guided tour of the town; for another, you can get all sorts of information about attractions and antique shopping in the area. Best of all, the house that is used for the Chamber's offices has an interesting past.

On the front porch you'll see an old wooden bathtub, now used as a flower planter. This, my friends, is no ordinary bathtub. This is Lola Montez's bathtub. In fact, the house used to be Lola's.

Lola Montez is one of the most fascinating characters of the California Gold Rush, and certainly the most glamorous. As one Chamber of Commerce person said with a giggle, "Her bathtub was the only clean thing about her." She was one of the legendary beauties of her time. Her international romances and liaisons made headlines and fodder for gossip; the stories make Liz Taylor and Joan Collins look like nuns.

She was born Maria Dolores Eliza Rosanna Gilbert, in Ireland, in 1818; she grew up in India (her stepfather was a general in the East India Army). When the lovely Maria was a teenager, her mother betrothed her to an old geezer, a justice of the supreme court of India. She rebelled by eloping with a young lieutenant. Eventually she ran away from him and fled to Europe, where she reinvented herself. In Spain she changed her name to Lola Montez, learned to dance like a señorita, and told everyone she was the daughter of a famous matador. Lolo became infamous for her erotic "spider dance," which involved layers of tinted chiffon creating an illusion of a web and movement of total abandon. With her thick black hair, voluptuous bosom, pinched waist, and white shoulders, Lola was the "It" girl of her time.

Her dazzling beauty, her charm, her fame, and her dancing gave her access to society and the royal courts of Europe. Newspapers reported her affairs with various minor princes, the composer Franz Liszt, and King Ludwig I of Bavaria, who built her a beautiful home, bestowed upon her the title Countess of Landsfeld, and consulted her on matters of state.

Eventually she came to America and, after several more affairs, ended up in the mining town of Grass Valley. Here Lola built a modest home and decorated it lavishly. She tended a garden and raised animals, including a goat, a sheep, a horse, a dog, a bear cub, and a mountain lion. Lola's days did not end well. She became a Bible-thumper and self-destructively repented for her sins, living out her final days in New York City, her health, beauty, and money gone. She died in January 1861.

Today as you step past the gate of the little fence that surrounds Lola's house, imagine the international beauty tending the garden and her animals. With any luck, you'll run into Carol Peters, who grew up in Grass Valley, fascinated by the legendary Lola. Carol now works for the Nevada County Chamber of Commerce and owns a little beaded handbag that purportedly once belonged to the Madonna of the Gold Rush. And most important, Carol tells the entire story of Lola and her misadventures with the flair of an accomplished comedian. What's more, she does it without pausing for a breath.

LOLA MONTEZ HOUSE AND NEVADA COUNTY CHAMBER OF COMMERCE, *248 Mill Street, Grass Valley. Phone: (916) 273-4667. Open 8:30 A.M. to 5 P.M. Monday through Friday; 10 A.M. to 3 P.M. Saturday.*

HOW TO GET HERE: *From San Francisco, take Interstate 80 from the Bay Bridge to Route 49 North at Auburn and continue to the towns of Grass Valley and Nevada City. Once in the town of Grass Valley, follow the blue signs for "Tourist Information."*

CHAPTER **12** Eastern Sierra

AREA OVERVIEW

In our first book, we wrote about what there is to see and do in Yosemite National Park, which can be beautiful and uncrowded in the spring, fall, and winter and uncomfortably jammed with tourists in the summer. If the crowds get to be too much for you in Yosemite, keep going. You can take either Tioga Pass (Route 120) through the national park or the Sonora Pass (Route 108). Here you will be in *real* backroads country. This side of the Sierra has its own beauty and attractions; the ride will take you through incredible scenery. Just be sure to check road conditions before you go. Both passes are sometimes closed during winter and early spring.

As soon as you start coming down from the crest of the mountains, the scenery changes dramatically. Lush and dense on the western slopes, it becomes dry and sparse on the eastern side. The attractions follow suit. Most visitors stop to take a look at the ghost town of Bodie and the prehistoric and vanishing Mono Lake to the north or the Mammoth Lakes ski area to the south. Route 395 cuts through the high valley between the mountain ranges and provides easy north-south access. Several small lakes all along the valley are popular with boaters and fishermen.

To the north, the town of Bridgeport offers decent, if modest accommodations and is an easy jumping-off point for Bodie. Bridgeport is a pretty little town with an 1880 Victorian courthouse and a clock tower that plays "Twilight Time" at 6 P.M. You can walk through the entire town, which features several restaurants, sporting supply stores, plus a place I didn't get a chance to visit called the Lady Bug shop. Now *there's* an idea for a franchise. . . .

Bodie State Historic Park lies about 30 minutes outside Bridgeport. It's an adventure just getting there; the state decided that to maintain the authenticity of the decaying ghost town, the last 3 miles outside town should be a dirt road. The journey does get one in the mood for the experience of walking through what is perhaps the most impressive ghost town in the West.

BEST LITTLE GHOST TOWN IN THE WEST

It's as though time froze in the 1880s. More then 120 abandoned buildings have been left alone—not restored. Many contain the clothes, tools, and personal effects that were left behind when the Gold Rush here dried up as quickly as it began. This is not a one-street ghost town but an entire village with several streets and a very eerie quality that makes the visitor marvel at what went on just a century ago. What's remarkable is that what you see is only the 5 percent that remains of this once thriving Wild West town. Fires and natural disasters destroyed most of the buildings until the state Parks Department moved in and decided to maintain the town in a state of "arrested decay." It should be noted that mines are active again on the hillside above Bodie, causing concern for the preservation of the delicate ghost town.

In its day, Bodie was known as the baddest bad town in the West. Fully 65 saloons operated at full steam; so did legions of ladies of the night. Violence and murder were daily occurrences. The atmosphere was best expressed in the diary of a young pioneer girl who moved to town with her father. She wrote, "Goodbye God, I'm going to Bodie."

You should be advised that since this is not just a tourist version of a ghost town, there are no commercial facilities in the park. Prepare to eat and drink elsewhere. Also, even though the park is open all year, Bodie is one of the coldest places in the United States and often the only way in is by cross-country skis or snowmobile. Summer and early fall are the best times to visit. Rangers are plentiful and helpful, and there are a museum and a visitors' center where you can get a map and enough information for a self-guided tour.

BODIE STATE HISTORIC PARK, *Bodie. Phone: (619) 647-6445. Open 9 A.M. to 5 P.M. in summer, 9 A.M. to 4 P.M. the rest of the year. Parking fee: $3.*

HOW TO GET HERE: *From San Francisco, take the Bay Bridge and head east on Route 580. This becomes Route 205. Take this to Route 5 North. Exit from 5*

North onto Route 120 to Oakdale. Then take Route 108 all the way over the Tioga Pass and down to Interstate 395. Turn right and head south, past Bridgeport about 8 miles, then turn left on Route 270 heading east. Follow this road which will become Bodie Road, to the park.

MONO LAKE   Mono Lake is believed to be a million years old. It features some of the most unusual outer space–like scenery you'll find on earth. It's also the focus of a major environmental movement trying to save it from shrinking away to nothing. The problem is that for more than 50 years the Los Angeles water district has been diverting water from the rivers and streams that feed the lake, and by now the water level of Mono has fallen more than 40 feet. This has also led to increased salinity of the already salty lake, and there are fears that that will upset the delicate balance of wildlife.

One of the great attractions here—and the main source of the lake's alien appearance—are the giant tufas, or limestone formations, which stick out of the water like stalagmites. Volcanic islands in the lake have become breeding grounds for sea gulls and are migratory stops for a number of birds, many of which feed on the millions of brine shrimp that live in Mono Lake. Though the lake is in danger of drying up and blowing away, it is one of the world's great natural and scenic wonders.

There is much to do here: hike, swim, take a naturalist-guided tour. Exotic events, such as moonlight tours, are fun and beautifully eerie. And if you want to try taking a dip, Mono is said to be even saltier than Utah's Great Salt Lake, so it is unlikely that you will even need to tread water.

The most accessible part of Mono Lake is the South Tufa area, where you'll find ample parking plus well-labeled exhibits describing the various phenomena of the area.

MONO LAKE TUFA STATE RESERVE, *Mono Lake. Ranger's station phone: (619) 647-6525.*

HOW TO GET HERE: *From Bodie (see previous entry), head south on Route 395 and watch for the signs to the South Tufa area. Turn left and head for the parking lot.*

MAMMOTH LAKES   The Mammoth Lakes ski area is a bustling destination for folks from southern California. There seems to be an unwritten agreement in the winter that the northern California skiers will head for Tahoe and the southern Californians will go to Mammoth. The town is loaded with hotels, motels, and restaurants, and the many lakes provide recreation and beauty.

Near the town of Mammoth Lakes is a worthwhile attraction. Hot Creek Geological Site is a place where hot springs bubble up into pools that form as the creek winds its way through the rocky valley. This site gives you a good idea of how much activity there is underground. Don't be surprised if you feel the earth move. This is earthquake country, and ever changing geological forces are always at work here. A series of placards describe the various geologic events going on around you and identify the abundant wildlife, which includes horned owls and bald eagles. The park has a visitors' center, helpful rangers, and many hiking trails.

Most folks go for the waters, and you will indeed see bathers soaking in the various ponds. Be advised that the water is extremely hot and that sudden temperature changes can cause burns.

FOREST SERVICE FOR MAMMOTH LAKES AND HOT CREEK VISITORS' CENTER, *just outside Mammoth. Phone: (619) 934-2505. Open daily sunrise to sunset.*

HOW TO GET HERE: *From Bodie or Mono Lake (see directions to Best Little Ghost Town in the West), head south on Route 395 toward Mammoth Lakes. Look on the left for a sign to the Hot Creek State Park. (If you get to the turnoff for the town of Mammoth Lakes, you've gone too far.)*

CHAPTER **13** Lake Tahoe

AREA OVERVIEW

In the first book, we gave a lengthy description of Lake Tahoe and all it offers. In this book, we add several more places to visit.

Bay Area residents are likely to go to the lake for a variety of reasons, the least of which is the water. Tahoe is a major ski destination, a haven for gamblers and seekers of old-fashioned nightclubs, and both a swinging singles scene and a secluded mountain getaway. For the rest of us, there is always the spectacle of the lake, indescribably dazzling as you approach from the mountains and warm enough to swim in once it heats up in the summer.

Lake Tahoe itself is 22.5 miles long and 12 miles wide. It covers some 70 miles of shoreline in California and Nevada. It's the second deepest lake in the country, after Crater Lake in Oregon: Tahoe's maximum depth is 1,645 feet. In the summer the lake's temperature averages 68 degrees. In the winter, despite the huge snows above, the lake never freezes, cooling only to about 50 degrees. Finally, if you want an idea of how much water is in the lake, Tahoe could supply everyone in the United States with 50 gallons of water a day for five years.

Most of the action is on the south shore of the lake. If you do not wish to be alone, this is the spot for you. This is where you'll find plenty of franchised restaurants and souvenir shops. The town of Stateline is the home of most of the casinos, and the main road on the south side can get very crowded. You can get away and head into beautiful country from the south shore if you head out Route 88 toward the Kirkwood ski area and the town of Markleeville.

The north shore and the Nevada side of the lake above Stateline offer more seclusion and a less hectic scene. If this interests you, look for accommodations in the communities of Tahoe City or Carnelian Bay. Compared to the south side, they are low-key, and it's an easy drive in any direction to a wilderness trail or state park.

To the north, off Route 80, is the Donner summit with its state park facilities, lake, and monument to the famous Donner party. There's also an interesting ski museum at Boreal Ridge. Nearby is the town of Truckee, which used to be a funky little Old West town and is fast becoming filled with shops and restaurants. Note the huge rock that hangs above the town on a hillside. Legend has it that this large rock used to rest in perfect balance on a smaller stone and that it would move at the slightest touch. Nervous town fathers cemented it down many years ago and enclosed it in a fenced-in gazebo. Still, the rocking stone adds a bit of local color to Truckee.

There are many motels and hotels and even some nice bed and breakfasts in the Tahoe area. It's also relatively easy to get a cabin or a condo that comes complete with a modern kitchen and comfortable furnishings. Some of the condo complexes even offer maid service, pools, and hot tubs.

For those interested in gambling, all the casinos are on the Nevada side of the lake, and they range from opulent (like Harrah's and Caesar's Tahoe) to funky (like the parlors you'll find along the road on the North Shore).

There are several ways to get here. You can fly into Reno or South Lake Tahoe. At the airports you can rent a car or take a bus or a train (some hotels offer transportation).

For toll-free information on accommodations available, phone the Tahoe North Visitors and Convention Bureau, (800) 822-5959 from California or (800) 824-8557 from out of state, or the Tahoe South Visitors Bureau, (800) 822-5922 from California or (800) 824-5150 from out of state. For information on Emerald Bay, phone (916) 525-7277.

SKI MUSEUM, *Boreal Ridge. Phone: (916) 426-3313. Open every day. Winter hours: 11 A.M. to 5 P.M. Tuesday through Sunday; summer hours: 11 A.M. to 5 P.M. Wednesday through Sunday. Admission: Free.*

HOW TO GET HERE: *To get to the north shore from San Francisco, take the Bay Bridge to Route 80 North all the way to the Truckee exit. You can stop at Truckee, or you can take Route 89 South to Tahoe City. To get to the south shore from San Francisco, take the Bay Bridge to Route 80 but exit near Sacramento onto Route 50. Then take Route 50 all the way into South Lake Tahoe.*

When visiting Lake Tahoe, you will want to take a drive out along the south-western shore to Emerald Bay; with its intensely greenish-blue waters, some say it's the most beautiful inland harbor in the world. The drive offers the best views in the entire area. If you visit in the summer, allow enough time for a tour of Vikingsholm, a 38-room mansion open for tours led by state Parks Department personnel. If you visit in the winter, chances are the road will be closed by heavy snow. Built in 1929 and patterned after a ninth-century Norse fortress, Vikings-holm is the kind of place that simply couldn't be built today. It is said to be the finest example of Scandinavian architecture in this country and is filled with Norwegian furnishings and weavings.

Vikingsholm was the summer home of Lora Josephine Knight, the heiress to several fortunes, including Diamond Match and Union Pacific. Emerald Bay reminded her of a Norwegian fjord she once visited, and she decided it would be nice to have her own Viking castle. The three-story fortress is built of wood, mortar, and rock and features a sod roof and round rooms, the kind Viking kings used to sleep in for protection (round so that they could be surrounded by body-guards while in bed).

Inside are hand-hewn and carved woodwork, stone fireplaces, and a living room graced by beams meticulously crafted into the shape of dragons. Tradition-ally, only men could enter rooms that contained these dragon beams; but since this place was built by a woman, no doubt females did enter the dragon's lair.

In 1929 a place like this could be built on Lake Tahoe for $500,000; today, even Donald Trump would think twice about financing such a project.

Getting here is not easy. From the parking lot, visitors must trek down a fairly steep one-mile trail. Walkers can take a 4-mile hike from nearby Bliss State Park. Boaters can tie up below at the dock. For the less adventurous, the parking lot leads to an overlook where you can simply admire beautiful Emerald Bay and see from a distance Knight's teahouse, perched atop the only island in the bay. On former days when tea was served, servants would line the steep trail to help the guests up to the top to the one-room stone cottage. Visitors with access to a boat and good hiking shoes might like to visit the abandoned teahouse.

VIKINGSHOLM, *17 miles south of Tahoe City. Phone: (916) 541-6860 (Vikings-holm) or (916) 525-7277 (nearby Bliss State Park). Open in summer months only, 10 A.M. to 4 P.M. daily. Admission: Adults, $1; children and seniors, 50 cents.*

HOW TO GET HERE: *From North Lake Tahoe, follow Route 89 South and look for the entrance to Vikingsholm on the left. From South Lake Tahoe, head north on Route 89 and look for the entrance on the right. A steep 1-mile trail leads down from the parking area. Walkers can hike in on a 4-mile trail from Bliss State Park. Boaters can tie up below at the dock.*

CHAPEL OF LOVE   Remember the hit song "Chapel of Love" by the Dixie Cups? It's always on the top 10 list around the lake. That's because of the myriad of places in business to perform quick and easy marriage ceremonies. If you're in the South Tahoe area and run out of things to do, you could (1) get married or (2) watch somebody else get married. Most chapels allow spectators, as long as the bride and groom agree, and you don't even have to bring a gift.

Probably the busiest of these establishments is the Chapel of Love, aka Love's Lake Tahoe Wedding Chapel, located in Stateline, Nevada. It once held the Guinness record for most ceremonies in one day (168, to be exact, a number that has since been surpassed by a place in Las Vegas). The chapel was originally owned by one Reverend Love (thus the Chapel of Love) but has since been purchased by Dan Rawls, a robust, friendly Texan previously in the insurance and real estate game. Dan decided to return to his roots, which included four years in a religious school, and got his credentials to be a minister to matrimony.

Reverend Dan the Marryin' Man is what Dan likes to be called. He has a flair for the dramatic. His phone number is (800) MARRY US. His office walls are covered with photos of the celebrities who have tied the knot at the Chapel of Love, including country singers Glen Campbell, Charlie Daniels, and Lacy J. Dalton; in fact, it was Loretta Lynn who gave Dan his nickname after one of her crew got hitched.

There are two chapels within Reverend Dan's complex, each outfitted with elaborate video equipment, discreetly hidden from view and capable of producing such nifty special effects as multiple images of the happy couple revolving around the edges of the screen. Every ceremony is recorded, and afterward the couple decides whether to shell out $100 for a video of their nuptials. Like most of the wedding places in the area, the Chapel of Love carries an assortment of items like garters, flowers, and spare witnesses, if needed. Rings and gowns must be acquired elsewhere.

Clearly, this is not an attraction for everyone. It probably appeals most to those of us with a taste for quirky Americana and to philosophers who ponder the symbiotic relationship between gambling casinos and marriage parlors. (Was it Kirkegaard who said that life was just one big crap shoot?)

If you're thinking about getting married, remember that the ceremony is just a ceremony; the legal stuff needs to be done before a county clerk in Carson City, about an hour away.

LOVE'S LAKE TAHOE WEDDING CHAPEL, *Highway 50 at Kingsbury Grade Road, Stateline, Nevada. Phone: (800) MARRY US. Open Monday through Thursday, 9 A.M. to 10 P.M.; Friday and Saturday, 9 A.M. to 11 P.M.; Sunday, 9 A.M. to 6 P.M. All major credit cards accepted.*

HOW TO GET HERE: *From the main street of South Lake Tahoe, Route 50, head for Nevada and cross the state line. Pass the main casinos on the right, and look for Kingsbury Grade Road. Turn right and enter the chapel's driveway.*

Many visitors come to Tahoe to strike it rich and end up taking a bath. Folks come to remote Alpine County to take a bath on purpose. This least populous county in California does not have a school or a bank, but it does have Grover Hot Springs State Park, located just outside the town of Markleeville. The park's main attraction is the large public hot pool, kept between 102 and 104 degrees all year. It's a perfect place to soak your tired muscles after skiing or your tired psyche after taking a beating at the casinos.

GROVER HOT SPRINGS

The natural hot springs in this area predate civilization, having been caused by glaciers or earthquakes, depending on which geologist you ask. The water bubbles continuously from an artesian lake at 150 degrees and is cooled, treated (to remove the sulfur smell), and piped into the bath, which looks like an ordinary, concrete public swimming pool. Actually there are two pools, side by side. The usual procedure is to soak in the smaller, hotter pool until you can't stand it, then take a deep breath and dive into the cool pool, kept at about 70 degrees. When the outside temperature is zero, you really feel the extremes.

There are changing rooms on the premises, plus lots of state park grounds to wander, including a switchback trail leading 2,000 feet up steep mountainside to Burnside Lake, Nordic Track trails, and snowshoeing. If you're willing to get here early in the morning, particularly during midweek, you'll also find peace and quiet; chances are you and your companions will be the only ones here. However, late in the day during holidays and weekends, you can bet you'll have to wait in line to get into the pool.

It takes nearly an hour to drive from South Lake Tahoe to Grover Hot Springs, but the trip itself can be a pleasure. As you drive down Route 88, you quickly leave behind the hustle of the casinos and wedding chapels and find yourself in beautiful alpine forests. You can see why the folks in Alpine County are rather pleased about inhabiting the least populous spot in the state.

GROVER HOT SPRINGS STATE PARK, *Markleeville. Phone: (916) 694-2248. Open daily 9 A.M. to 9 P.M. year round. Park admission: Free. Admission to the baths: Adults $3; ages 17 and under, $2. Closed for a few weeks in September for maintenance.*

HOW TO GET HERE: *From South Lake Tahoe, follow Route 50 West toward Sacramento. Turn left on Route 88. Continue south to Woodfords, then turn left toward Markleeville. Watch for the right turn onto Hot Springs Road. That will take you into the park.*

FISH PEEP SHOW　One of the big surprises around South Lake Tahoe is a small park and demonstration project run by the U.S. Forest Service. It's right off Route 89 north of town, and you might easily miss it on the trip between the northern and southern sections of the lake. Once you park your car and stroll into the tree-shaded park, you'll feel a hundred miles away from the busy strip of motels and casinos.

The Stream Profile Chamber is a simple but fascinating concept. It's a place where you can literally look fish in the eye. From an underground viewing chamber, you look through an aquarium-style glass wall and watch all the action in a mountain stream. The Forest Service diverts fish from Taylor Creek into the simulated stream environment. In spring and summer you will see lots of rainbow trout. In September you can watch the Kokanee salmon spawn; you will notice that the males turn a bright red during this act of intimacy (see, we're not so different from the fishees, are we?). Occasionally a sucker gets past the ranger and into the chamber, but, as one Forest Service employee quipped, in the Tahoe area, there's still one born every minute.

This is the sort of destination that doesn't take a lot of time. The best way to enjoy your brief stay here is to stroll on the Rainbow Trail along the creek and look at the stream from above. Then head through the tunnel into the underground chamber to look at the fishes eye to eye. The visitors' center also provides information on the history of Lake Tahoe and of the Sierra. This is a good place to pick up pamphlets for exploring the various sections of the Tahoe forest.

STREAM PROFILE CHAMBER, *off Route 89, South Lake Tahoe. Phone: (916) 573-2600. Open daily 8 A.M. to 6 P.M., June through Labor Day.*

HOW TO GET HERE: *From South Lake Tahoe, take Route 89 North for about 7 miles and look for the entrance on the right.*

SNOW LAB　Most of the places in this book are easy to visit. You simply drive up to a parking lot and are greeted by someone, without much more effort on your part.

A visit to the Snow Lab is another matter entirely. It requires about a ¼-mile trek up a hill through the snow to a remote laboratory that would seem entirely unrelated to your life. However, you will learn here that scientists find out all sorts of things from the considerable snowfall in the Sierra, not the least of which is California's water quality and drought possibilities. If you are at all fascinated by high-tech equipment and how scientists do their work, this might be your kind of adventure.

The Snow Lab is the only hydrology research lab in the country, a part of the Pacific Southwest Forest and Range Experiment Station headquartered in Berkeley. The state Department of Water Resources, PG&E, and other agencies use the information gathered here. Biologists, geologists, and hydrologists employ electronic and manual methods of measuring every snowfall. From these tests they can predict what the spring runoff will be. When I visited in January after two years of drought, Jim Bergman, the hydrologist in charge, told me that the current snowfall and snow patterns indicated that the drought would ease. He emphasized that this was not a weather forecast but a report based on existing information in the snowpack. Though other sources predicted that the drought would worsen, Bergman turned out to be right; the drought did ease.

Profiling snow for water content is just one of the lab's functions. Scientists here also analyze other patterns, such as signs of acid rain and other pollution. The good news is that so far, Western snowfall remains relatively clean and healthy.

All sorts of exotic towers and complicated measuring devices are on hand at the lab site. Jim (or whoever is around at the time) will show you how things work and on occasion will take visitors out to a remote site where they measure new snowfall.

As you can see, this is the kind of destination that you plan when you find yourself in Tahoe with plenty of time on your hands, not to mention an interest in things scientific. The location is a bonus, for the lab is situated in beautiful woods, not far from the Boreal Ridge and Royal Gorge ski areas.

SNOW LAB, *Soda Springs. Phone: (916) 587-4838. Tours by appointment during the snow season.*

HOW TO GET HERE: *From San Francisco, take the Bay Bridge and follow Interstate 80 North to Lake Tahoe and the Soda Springs exit. Go back under the freeway and bear left at the Exxon station. Follow the main road, which is old U.S. 40, past the Soda Springs Store on your right. Continue for about ½ mile until you see the Snow Lab sign on the left, plus two redwood garages. Park here and walk up the road. Special arrangements can be made for groups and those needing assistance up the hill.*

VIRGINIA CITY

Finding your way to various Gold Rush towns can be quite confusing. To get to Nevada City, you have to go to northern California; to get to Virginia City, you have to go to Nevada. When you finally arrive, you will be entertained by a mixture of pure hokum and authentic history. Don't let the silly stuff—like the Bucket of Blood saloon and the Gunfighters' Hall of Fame—throw you off: Virginia City was once an important part of the territory.

You may remember Virginia City from the burning map shown each week on "Bonanza" (even though the Ponderosa was supposed to be located near here, the TV show was filmed elsewhere; ah, Hollywood). In 1875 Virginia City, famed as the site of the biggest silver and gold strike in the West, was the largest settlement west of the Mississippi. The fortunes of the Hearsts and the Sutros began here; Mark Twain and Bret Harte wrote for the local newspaper. The millions pulled out of the mines here were used to help finance the Union forces in the Civil War. With all that wealth, all types of people were drawn to Virginia City. Apparently you could get or do anything, as long as you had the cash to pay for it.

Perhaps that explains the honky-tonk atmosphere that lingers on, on Virginia City's main street today. The miners left by the 1890s, but the town has made several comebacks and now exists as a tourist attraction. Along the way on the one-hour-and-then-some drive from Lake Tahoe, you might think nothing could possibly inhabit these barren Nevada hills. You turn a corner and suddenly this boomtown looms in the distance.

The main road takes you right onto the main drag, which is C Street. Park your car and simply start walking in either direction. The street is an old-fashioned boardwalk, and you'll find a variety of tourist attractions, including the aforementioned Bucket of Blood saloon and Gunfighters' Hall of Fame, a re-created jail, gambling parlors, a fortuneteller, gift shops, ice-cream and candy parlors, and several museums claiming to have the desk where Mark Twain wrote his stories.

The building that housed the famous *Territorial Enterprise* newspaper is on C Street, and it's worth a visit. On the street level is yet another gift shop, but downstairs you'll find a museum with many relics from the days of the Comstock lode. The owner, John Shafer, has a good explanation for the tourist strip along C Street. "Virginia City was always a 'body' town," he says. "Opium dens and red-light districts were commonplace. We are *not* the Williamsburg of the West."

To get away from the main tourist action, head over to B Street and drive up to the top of the hill. Here you can get an overview of the town, the same view the rich mine owners had when they built their mansions above the workers and mines below. Also on B Street you can visit an admission-free museum, located in the Fourth Ward School, a striking-looking Victorian building.

While in Virginia City, you can visit a mine, ride a steam train, and stroll through the weathered old cemetery. Virginia City is a small town on the verge of yet another comeback. Until the day someone opens a great restaurant, I recommend Virginia City as a day outing destination from Lake Tahoe.

VIRGINIA CITY, *Route 341. For more information, contact the Chamber of Commerce, P.O. Box 464, Virginia City, NV 89440. Phone: (702) 847-0311. During winter, be sure to call ahead to be sure the roads are open.*

HOW TO GET HERE: *From North Lake Tahoe, take Route 28 to Nevada. Continue until you come to Route 341. Turn right onto Route 341 and take it into*

Virginia City. From South Lake Tahoe, take Route 50 East to Nevada and continue past Carson City to Route 342. Turn left onto Route 342 and take it into Virginia City.

CHAPTER **14** Mendocino County

With all the wonderful possibilities in exploring the area within 3 or 4 hours of San Francisco, if I had time for only one trip, it would be to Mendocino. Actually, the famous seaside town of Mendocino is just part of the lure; the drive up and the stops along the way make it all the more worthwhile. It's a trip that combines the rocky cliffs of the Pacific, redwood forests, another wine country, arts and crafts, rare museums, and good places to eat and spend the night.

There are three ways to get to the village of Mendocino. One is to drive straight up the coast. This is not only the longest route but also the most trying for those who tend to get carsick when driving on constantly curvy narrow roads while hugging the ocean's edge. However, this shoreline road does take you to some lovely areas, including Sea Ranch and the old coastal town of Gualala. Sea Ranch is a private community of modern homes designed to blend in with the landscape. The homes are architecturally significant, and many of them are available for weekend rentals. There is also a lodge that offers overnight accommodations and a restaurant. Around Gualala the main features are the Old Milano Hotel, which still looks like it did when it was new in 1905, and, a bit north of town, St. Orre's, an inn and restaurant that looks like a small Russian palace.

A quicker and less winding way to get to Mendocino is by going north on Highway 101 to the intersection of Route 128 in Cloverdale, then taking Route 128 through the Anderson Valley to the coastline. This joins Route 1 near the town of Albion for the short ride up to Mendocino. The third way is to continue on Highway 101 to Ukiah and then come over on the Ukiah-Comptche Road. I recommend going up via the last route, then returning through the Anderson Valley and the community of Boonville.

The main reason my wife, Catherine, wants to visit Hopland as often as possible is to visit Mendocino Woolens as often as possible. Not only is the clothing to her liking, but there's a good story behind the shop.

The area surrounding Hopland has many sheep. Once upon a time this was a major apple, lumber, hops, and sheep area, but by the late 1970s the economy was sagging. A very clever woman named Rose Killian came up with an idea that could benefit everybody. Her plan was to set up a major textile operation, creating a market for all the sheep farmers in the area, as well as a workplace for the artistic types who had fled the city to live a more bucolic life. Her grand scheme involved major grants and community support, with jobs for everyone. Even though the right people seemed to love the idea, the foundation and government funds never came, so she decided to go ahead on a smaller scale. The result was Mendocino Woolens, a small shop and mail-order company that buys local wool, dyes it in the most fashionable colors, weaves it into cloth, and sews it into lovely clothing, toys, and afghans.

Casual visitors can drop in and not only see the latest creations but also watch Rose and her colleagues put the finishing touches on items. More important, they have a unique opportunity to see the process from scratch at the company's barn out in the country, about five minutes from the store. Here, on a farm, you can see the wool brought in from the nearby Hopland Field Station Farm. You can feel and smell the wool, right off the sheep. You can watch dyeing, see weaving on old-fashioned looms, and probably even get a chance to get behind the controls and do a little weaving yourself. If you've never tried it, you'll be surprised at the amount of coordination required. It's another one of those chances to be reminded that all clothes aren't made from synthetics in a factory. Tours are offered during the spring shearing season.

A nice side story for you incurable romantics: When Rose was trying to set up her business, someone put her in contact with a local carpenter who could build her looms. You guessed it—Frank not only did the job but went on to become her husband and partner.

MENDOCINO WOOLENS, *U.S. 101, Hopland. Phone: (707) 744-1110. Retail outlet open 10 A.M. to 5 P.M. daily; tours of the dyeing and weaving facility by prior arrangement.*

HOW TO GET HERE: *From San Francisco, cross the Golden Gate Bridge and take Highway 101 about 90 miles north to Hopland, the place where it changes from a four-lane highway into a busy country road. Caution: Logging trucks seem to appear from nowhere on this stretch of road; be careful whenever entering the highway. When approaching Hopland from the Bay Area, Mendocino Woolens will be on your left.*

SOLAR-POWERED WINERY

The McDowell Valley is a gorgeous stretch of Mendocino County, just outside the town of Hopland. It is named for Paxton McDowell, who came west to make his fortune in gold. He settled for gold from grapes, and nearly a century later his former spread is the site of the nation's first solar-powered winery.

In the purest sense of the phrase, this is a family-operated business. Richard Keehn, a former military pilot who came to the valley for peace after serving in Vietnam, is assisted by his wife, Karen, and their eight children. They have built a showplace of a winery, with a large and inviting wood-and-glass tasting room overlooking the valley and their ranch home. They also run a second tasting room out by Highway 101 for those in a hurry.

The idea of a solar-powered winery is a good hook in an industry that requires some attention-grabber. But Keehn says this is not a mere gimmick; his state-of-the-art solar operation saves enough on the cost of heat for sterilization, bottle washing, and building comfort that he can reduce his prices by a dollar a bottle. If you call ahead, you can arrange for a tour of the operation (which is much like every other winery), and you will probably get a short lesson in solar energy.

Another unique facet of the McDowell Valley operation is the attempt to simplify the language of wine tasting. Winemaker John Buechenstein is working with other enologists to create a tasting wheel that identifies the various qualities of wine, putting it into language that everyone can understand, as opposed to terms like *impudent* or *naive*. The wheel spells out such wide-ranging possibilities as "essence of roses" and "wet wool socks" to aid the taster in identifying his or her own experience of the wine. Who knows, after they perfect the wheel, it may start showing up in wine stores.

This is the kind of low-key winery that merits staying awhile to enjoy the grounds and the attractive building. Keehn and his family are friendly folks who love to play hosts.

MCDOWELL VALLEY VINEYARDS, *3811 Highway 175, Hopland. Phone: (707) 744-1053. Tasting room open daily 10 A.M. to 5 P.M. Tours of the winery operation by appointment.*

HOW TO GET HERE: *From San Francisco, take the Golden Gate Bridge to Highway 101 and continue north until you come to the town of Hopland. On the outskirts of town, turn right onto Highway 175 and continue for 4 miles until you come to the winery. The other tasting room is right on Highway 101 before you get to town.*

SUN HOUSE

Unless you're a resident of Mendocino County and need to conduct government business, it is easy to bypass the city of Ukiah. For travelers, Highway 101 whisks us by the county seat on our way to the redwoods farther north. What a shame it would be to miss the Sun House and Grace Hudson Museum. This is a world-class facility just a few minutes from the freeway.

The Sun House was the dream home of Ukiah's most famous couple, Grace and John Hudson. They were wealthy, avant-garde residents who were world famous in the early 1900s. Grace was a painter; John was an ethnographer who had worked at the Field Museum in Chicago. Both of them were devoted to the study of the Pomo Indians, the original occupants of this part of California. Named for the Hopi sun symbol, their home was built on a large lot in the center of town. It is a warm, six-room, Craftsman-style redwood house, filled with items that reflect the Hudsons' bohemian lifestyle and their devotion to their work.

The nearby Grace Hudson Museum was added on the property in 1986. It is a spacious and dramatically lit gallery, and though the building is modern, it complements the Sun House.

The best way to take it all in is to go on a docent-led tour of the Sun House, then wander around on your own in the gallery. At one time all the items on display were inside the Hudsons' home, crammed to the rafters. Now, with the items more spread out, you can get a sense of their personal lives inside the Sun House.

Most of the collection is next door at the museum, where you will also see a magnificent display of Grace's artwork. And though her paintings are remarkable works of art, it is easy to overlook their social and moral importance. Grace Hudson was painting portraits of Indians at a time when most artists were painting aristocrats. She was the first to show Indians, often poor and downtrodden, as beautiful. As you gaze on her canvases, you can see how she was challenging the stereotypes about Indians, capturing their humanity for all to see. Grace Hudson changed the way many people around the world viewed Native Americans.

John Hudson collected baskets, and the Pomo Indians are masters of basketry. Hundreds of baskets are on display, along with thousands of artifacts from the Pomo and other Indian cultures.

As museum director Suzanne Abel-Vidor points out, one thing that makes this collection unique is the fact that it all comes from one family. Most museums contain the contents of lots of people's attics; this one family collected and saved everything of historic and artistic importance.

Don't try to rush a visit here. Save time to allow yourself to savor the entire collection and be transported back to another time.

SUN HOUSE AND GRACE HUDSON MUSEUM, *431 South Main Street, Ukiah. Phone: (707) 462-3370. Open Wednesday through Saturday, 10 A.M. to 4:30 P.M.; Sunday, noon to 4:30 P.M. Closed holidays. Docent-led tours of the Sun House are offered from noon to 4 P.M. Admission: Free.*

HOW TO GET HERE: *From San Francisco, cross the Golden Gate Bridge and take Highway 101 North to Ukiah. Exit at Gobbi Street. Go left (west) on Gobbi to State Street. Turn right onto State and continue to Mill Street. Turn right on Mill, go one block, then left on Main. The house and museum are a block or so away, on the right.*

Now here's something you don't see everyday: a giant water-powered millstone at work, grinding corn, oats, wheat, and other grains into flour, meal, and cereal. A special display area is set up for folks who are interested in this sort of thing. Not only can you drop by and see this nineteenth-century wonder of technology, from the outside waterwheel to the inside workings of the grinding process, but you can also purchase sacks of freshly ground ingredients for your next baking extravaganza. Moore's is basically a large retail store, selling many packaged goods as well as some fresh-baked delights, such as cookies and muffins, of the healthy variety. It's also an informal visitor's information center.

MOORE'S FLOUR MILL, *1550 South State Street, Ukiah. Phone: (707) 462-6550. Open Monday through Saturday, 9 A.M. to 6 P.M.*

HOW TO GET HERE: *From San Francisco, cross the Golden Gate Bridge and take Highway 101 North to Ukiah. Exit at Gobbi Street. Go left (west) on Gobbi to State Street. Follow it through town, south, until you come to Moore's. From Hopland, take the first Ukiah exit off Highway 101 and turn left (west) to State Street. Turn right to Moore's.*

MOORE'S FLOUR MILL

Centuries ago, the Pomo Indians who inhabited this area made an annual trek to the coast to hunt for food. The ritual included a stop at the sparkling spring, which they believed had healing powers. The Indians named it the "living waters." In the 1880s white men starting bottling the stuff. The first brand name was G. W. Henderson's Bonanza Mineral Water. Of course, it took the French with Perrier to turn bottled water into gold. Today the naturally carbonated water from this spring is bottled by the Mendocino Beverage Company. You may have seen it in stores and restaurants around northern California.

This is not a visit to your average bottling company. Sure, there are production lines here, too, but the reason to make the trip is for the beautiful country setting. First of all, you get there by driving along the Mendocino backroads and down a long private driveway through a pine forest. In a clearing you will see a small industrial-looking building where the water is bottled. Your guide will then take you on a walk through a redwood forest to the source of the "living waters." It is delineated by a fountain—a small statue of a young woman carrying a water bucket. The water spills over into another basket; put a cup under this, and you can drink carbonated water right out of the earth. Careful—the taste has an edge to it. If you dare to stick your face into the well near the fountain, you'll probably suffer whiplash when the natural carbonation hits your nose.

If you're like me, you're probably wondering what mineral water is. The answer you'll get here is that mineral water absorbs calcium, magnesium, potassium, iron, and other minerals from the rocks under the earth's surface. Not only do our bodies need these minerals, but the natural source means that they will

MENDOCINO BEVERAGE COMPANY

be readily absorbed. This is also one of the few places on earth where mineral water is naturally carbonated (most bottled waters get their fizz at the factory).

Be sure to allow enough time to continue the tour across a meadow to the "Far West's smallest museum"—a quaint little shack where you'll see a small collection of Indian artifacts found on the property and a remarkable if small collection of the world's mineral water bottles, from G. W. Henderson's Bonanza Mineral Water to Perrier (and, of course, Mendocino Mineral Water).

MENDOCINO BEVERAGE COMPANY, near Comptche. Phone: (707) 996-6114. Call in advance to be sure someone will be available to give you a tour.

HOW TO GET HERE: From San Francisco, head north on Highway 101. Continue to Ukiah, and then take the Ukiah-Comptche Road toward the ocean. This is also called Orr Springs Road for a stretch. After you hit the small village of Comptche, continue for about 1 mile, and go over a small bridge (all you will see is a railing to indicate that you are on a bridge crossing a creek); right after this bridge you will find a dirt road that follows the creek through the redwoods. It has a sign that says "Private Road—Do Not Enter." This is the road you want; follow the dirt road for 2½ miles until you will see the large industrial plant and parking lot on your left.

MENDOCINO COAST BOTANICAL GARDENS

This is one of the most complete and extensive gardens in the West. Unfortunately, you'd never know it from the road. It is camouflaged by an unattractive entrance, café, and other roadside clutter that make it look like a tourist trap. Don't be discouraged. Once you get inside, your eyes and soul will be treated to a series of inner gardens that stretch all the way to the ocean.

That the garden exists at all is a remarkable story. It started in 1961, when Ernest and Betty Schoefer retired from the nursery business in Burbank and moved north. They bought 47 acres of Mendocino Coast wilderness just south of the town of Fort Bragg. The forest and brush were so thick that a person could barely walk through it. But once a gardener, always a gardener; the Schoefers cultivated a garden and kept it going. Ernest cleared and planted and built trails; Betty operated a little gift shop and nursery out front.

In 1977 the maintenance of the property became too much for the elderly couple, so they sold the land to a real estate group with plans for major development. After much legal hassling, 12 acres were sold to the California Coastal Conservancy to be run as a public garden. The real estate group still owns the rest of the property, including the aforementioned road frontage; the gardens are managed as a nonprofit organization, supported entirely by donations, memberships, grants, and the work of dedicated volunteers.

As you can imagine, the garden suffered during all the legal squabbling. But in the past five years it has undergone an incredible transformation. More than

150 volunteers have come in to clear, plant, and create a living showplace. They planted thousands of native and exotic plants in separate showcase areas. There's a heather garden, a Mediterranean section, a cactus and succulents garden, a fern canyon, a camellia area, a heritage rose garden, and, perhaps the most spectacular, the rhododendron display, consisting of big-leaf varieties from China, dwarfs, new hybrids, and shrubs developed by local plant breeders and collectors.

The spectacular rhodie display is at its peak in April and May, but no matter what time of year you visit, there will be something to see. No doubt you will see volunteers at work: retired contractors building benches and bridges, doctors tending to drooping fuchsias, former schoolteachers weeding flowerbeds. Someone will always be on hand to tell you about the plants and the many plans for the gardens, which have become a community center of sorts for residents.

The Mendocino Coast Botanical Gardens have attracted the attention of horticulturists from around the world. Due to the ideal climate conditions—mild rainy winters and cool, foggy summers—the gardens have become a testing ground for the survival of some endangered plants. You are sure to see some plants you have never seen before. Wear good walking shoes; you may be inspired to take the short hike to the cliffs above the beach.

MENDOCINO COAST BOTANICAL GARDENS, *Route 1, Fort Bragg. Phone: (707) 964-4352. Open every day, 10 A.M. to 4 P.M. Admission: Free, but donations are requested. Wheelchair accessible.*

HOW TO GET HERE: *From Mendocino (see directions to Mendocino in Area Overview on page 177), follow Route 1 North and look for the gardens on the southern outskirts of Fort Bragg. The entrance will be on the left side of the road.*

HENDY WOODS STATE PARK

Here is a good stop on your way back to the Bay Area from Mendocino via Route 128 and Boonville. If you plan your trip well enough, you can wander through the park at your leisure, maybe visit a winery in the Anderson Valley, and pull into Boonville in time for lunch or dinner at the Boonville Hotel. What Hendy Woods offers is a chance to take a stroll through one of California's lesser-known redwood groves. Within the 905-acre park are actually two groves, called Big Hendy and Little Hendy. Little Hendy is 20 acres and has a trail. Big Hendy is 80 acres and features the ½-mile wheelchair-accessible Discovery Trail.

This is an old-fashioned state park. There's no fancy visitors' center, no swimming pool. The ranger says that every so often he has to break up a noisy Trivial Pursuit game at the campground, but that's the rowdiest it gets around here. This is a real family-oriented place, with lots of wildlife (black-tailed deer, raccoons, rabbits, gray foxes, bobcats, skunks, horned owls, woodpeckers, thrushes), picnic areas, swimming in spring and early summer (by late summer the water level is usually too low for anything but wading), and fishing in fall and winter.

The stars of the show are those magnificent redwoods. The original 405 acres of the park were purchased in the late 1800s by foundry owner Joshua Hendy. He helped preserve the pristine quality of the area, as did the Masonite Corporation, which bought the property from Hendy and later turned it over to the Save the Redwoods League. The additional 500 acres were added later. It's easy to zip by the park without even realizing the giant redwoods are there. Try to save time for at least a brief walk in the forest.

HENDY WOODS STATE PARK, off Route 128, 6 miles northwest of Philo. Phone: (707) 937-5804 or (707) 895-3141. Gates open during daylight hours. Day use fee: $3 per vehicle. You can reserve campsites by calling (800) 446-PARK.

HOW TO GET HERE: From San Francisco, cross the Golden Gate Bridge and continue on Highway 101 North to Cloverdale. Head west on Route 128 past Philo, turn left on Greenwood Road. The entrance to the park is on this road. From Mendocino (see directions to Mendocino in Area Overview on page 177), take Route 1 to Route 128 and continue to Philo.

CHAPTER **15** Redwood Empire

AREA OVERVIEW

For many visitors to California, number 1 on the list of things to see is the giant redwoods. Even though extensive logging reduced the supply before the preservation movement got under way, we are fortunate that many groves remain. The largest of these is in the area south of Eureka, about four hours north of San Francisco, straight up Highway 101.

In our first book, we wrote about the Avenue of the Giants, the company town of Scotia, the Victorian town of Ferndale, and the city of Eureka. All these are good places to visit on a trip to the Redwood Empire. Here are a few more good choices for seeing this special part of the country.

CONFUSION HILL

This is the northern equivalent of the famous Mystery Spot in Santa Cruz, only more elaborate. Not only do you scale a hill that appears to defy gravity and walk cockeyed in a house that puts you on a 45-degree angle, but there's also a train ride through the redwoods and several displays illustrating this miracle of gravity. Confusion Hill also features such baffling sights as water that runs uphill (or at least appears to do so), marbles that seem to be rolling uphill, and other phenomena they call "confusing but amusing." Warning: Watch what you say as you stumble around in this magnetic fun house; there's a microphone on one wall so that the folks down below in the garden can chuckle at your reactions.

The train ride is a much calmer attraction, provided for those who can't stomach the strange effects of Confusion Hill. It simply takes you for a spin through the redwoods on top of the hill.

CONFUSION HILL, *Highway 101, 18 miles south of Garberville, near Piercy. Phone: (707) 925-6456. Open in winter 10 A.M. to 4 P.M. every day; in summer (after Memorial Day) 8 A.M. to 7 P.M. Train runs only in dry weather. Admission: $2.50 to go inside. Train ride is an additional $2.50. Reduced rates for children.*

HOW TO GET HERE: *From San Francisco, take Highway 101 North. Watch for signs.*

LAND OF THE HOBBITS

About 20 minutes to the north of Confusion Hill, just after you enter the Avenue of the Giants, you'll come to a gift shop in a tree, called the Chimney Tree. That tells you you have approached a must stop for dyed-in-the-wool Tolkien fans. This is where you can begin a walk back through the woods on a fantasy trail filled with dioramas from *Lord of the Rings*. There are redwood carvings of characters from the story with piped-in narration. Apparently, Tolkien fans find it authentic. Frankly, I am a total alien in that territory and cannot speak with authority. I can tell you that the ½-mile trail runs through beautiful country and that everyone seems to be having a good time. It is clearly an attraction for kids, although they appear to be just as interested in the animals roaming around the ample ranch on which the attraction is located.

LAND OF THE HOBBITS, *off Highway 101, south of Phillipsville. Phone: (707) 923-2265. Open May 1 through mid-October during daylight hours. Admission: Adults, $2.50; children, $2.*

HOW TO GET HERE: *From Confusion Hill (see previous entry), continue north on Highway 101 and exit to the right at the start of the Avenue of the Giants. Look on the right for the Chimney Tree.*

THE LOST COAST

If you are really feeling adventurous and want to explore one of the most remote sections of northern California, head for the Lost Coast. This is an 80-mile-plus stretch of land so rugged that the coastal highway had to be moved inland to get around it. It's the longest section of California coastline without a paved road. There have been attempts to tame this wild land, but none has succeeded. Depending on your car and the weather conditions, there are roads that will take you in to various roadheads. Parts of the Lost Coast are the westernmost points in the continental United States. Within the area are the Sinkyone Wilderness Park and the King Range National Conservation Area, both accessible only on foot, horse, or llama. The land is full of exceptional contrasts here, from black sand beaches to thick forests. Some parts of the Lost Coast are higher than Big Sur, and the elevation in places changes from sea level to more than 4,000 feet in less than 3 miles.

One of the nicest drives is through the Mattole River Valley and on out to the Mattole River recreation site, which does offer a parking lot and an area for barbecuing. There are also portable chemical toilets. That's about as elaborate as services are likely to get. This is a good starting-off point for a hike down the coast or up a nearby hill to get a higher view. The Mattole River is good for fishing and has plenty of sandy access before it empties out into the ocean.

On the long drive after leaving Highway 101 (plan on at least an hour), you'll pass tiny rustic villages and beautiful country, after passing through the center of the Rockefeller Forest. Although some of the towns look quaint and charming, like Honeydew, be advised that this is also reputed to be the center of northern California's highly profitable and illegal marijuana-growing trade. If you see a "No Trespassing" sign, take it seriously. Growers do not welcome guests or snoopy photographers.

After wandering around the coast, you can continue the adventure with a drive to the town of Petrolia, where oil was first discovered in California. It's a friendly, remote village with a few stores, nice scenery, and about 500 residents who want to keep the Lost Coast lost. The scenic ride continues as you follow the road all the way along the ocean and then inland into the town of Ferndale.

HOW TO GET HERE: *From San Francisco, take Highway 101, then exit for the Rockefeller Forest at Weott and continue west. You will pass the magnificent redwoods, then enter a fertile valley. As you drive along the valley, you will be on Mattole Road, which you can follow all the way to the ocean. For Petrolia, look for the signs as you leave the Mattole River recreation site. There are very few roads to choose from, and directions to Petrolia and to Ferndale are marked.*

TRINIDAD One day while we were shooting a "Backroads" television story in Eureka, a couple in a camper pulled over and informed me that I ought to visit Trinidad. I made the usual feeble joke about Calypso music, which they took with patient good humor. They handed me a brochure about the town and their bed-and-breakfast inn, I promised to try and get there someday, and that was that.

Two years later Catherine and I finally got around to taking the half-hour drive north of Eureka to this beautiful village, and we could have kicked ourselves for not having done it sooner.

Trinidad is one of my favorite stops on the backroads. It looks like an undeveloped Mendocino. You can catch a glimpse of the town's dramatic coastline as you travel north on Route 1. Once you get to the Trinidad harbor, it's like no other spot on the coast. The ocean flows directly up to a cove that is ringed by high cliffs. It's not uncommon to see mother whales and their babies frolicking in the protected waters. There's a lighthouse in a parklike setting with paths leading down to the water and a monument to the Indians and to sailors who lost their lives at sea.

Overlooking it all is the bed-and-breakfast place where our original tipsters live. Even though they only have a few rooms, which are usually booked well in advance, Carol and Paul Kirk also act as the town's unofficial Chamber of Commerce. They have brochures on attractions in the area and can steer you to places of interest.

What's to do in town? First and foremost, savor the many views. There are coastline trails for hiking, with benches thoughtfully placed along the way for resting and admiring the ever changing ocean. You can walk or drive out to Trinidad Head, a huge hill or small mountain that is the highest point in town, at the edge of the harbor. There's a small Indian Heritage Museum, chronicling the lives of the Yuroks, some of whom still live in Trinidad. Museum hours are irregular, however, so you'll have to ask around town to find out when it will be open. If you're lucky, you will run into the guiding force behind the museum, Axel Lindgren, whose Swedish great-grandfather married the Yurok medicine woman. Last time we were in town, Axel was in a small park demonstrating the craft of canoe-making.

Humboldt State University also runs a marine laboratory that is open to visitors. It's a small place, but you can see several aquarium tanks filled with fish and dip your hands (or let your kids dip theirs) into a touchy-feely tank to experience the feel of sea urchins, starfish, and other sea life.

Fewer than 500 people live in Trinidad. This is a very small town, and specific directions to places are unnecessary. The best way to visit is to park your car at the ocean and walk around. You might also enjoy visiting Trinidad State Park and nearby Patrick's Point State Park, where you can camp and picnic.

TRINIDAD, *off Route 1, 30 miles north of Eureka. You can reach Carol and Paul Kirk at the Trinidad Bed and Breakfast Inn at (707) 677-0840, or you can write to the Trinidad Tourist Information Center at P.O. Box 847, Trinidad, CA 95570. The Telonicher Marine Laboratory run by Humboldt State University is on Ewing Street, off Edwards. Phone: (707) 677-3671.*

HOW TO GET HERE: *From San Francisco, head north on Highway 101. There is a Trinidad turnoff about 20 miles to the north of Eureka. You'll enter on Main Street. Then turn left on Trinity and head for the harbor, which is on Edwards Street.*

CHAPTER **16** Shasta

AREA OVERVIEW The name Shasta turns up throughout the state of California. There's the Shasta daisy, Shasta Cola, and, to the north, Mount Shasta, Lake Shasta, and Shasta Dam. These last three are the main focal points of a vacation area that offers a bit of everything for those who prefer backroads-type living. This is hiking, camping, boating, swimming, and skiing country, with little or no traces of sophisticated urban life. Surprisingly enough, you don't travel a backroad to get here. Interstate 5 is the only logical route, and it's an easy four- to five-hour drive from San Francisco. Fortunately, the freeway is much more scenic in this direction than it is when you are heading south toward Los Angeles.

OLD SHASTA Certainly the least known of all the Shastas is the town of Old Shasta, most of which is a state historical park, located about 6 miles west of the city of Redding.

This restored town was once the seat of Shasta County and at the heart of the northern California Gold Rush. Major Pearson B. Reading, who discovered gold in these parts in the 1850s, found an estimated $5 million of bullion in them thar hills. But when the railroad came, it bypassed Shasta and went instead to Redding, taking the county seat and population growth with it. (By the way, Redding is not named for Major Reading but for a representative of the Southern Pacific Railroad.)

Today, Old Shasta is an impressive sight, especially after you drive past the modern suburbs on the outskirts of Redding, before happening upon a town that looks much as it did in the 1850s. The whole town is lovely, only a few blocks long, surrounded by rolling hills and high trees.

A visit here might begin in the old courthouse, which is now the town museum. The building has been well restored and features a variety of exhibits. On the first floor are artifacts from the bustling Gold Rush days, including mining equipment and farm machinery. There is also an exhibit depicting the lives of the many Chinese miners who flocked to the area. The most impressive part of the building is the old courtroom, which looks out onto some sobering gallows. You can also visit the jail cells occupied by some long-suffering mannequins. If your timing is right, you can have a docent-led tour.

Unrelated to any of this is an impressive collection of paintings donated by a benefactor of the museum, who wished for her art to be stored on the premises.

After touring the courthouse, just wander around the town in any direction you choose. You'll find picnic sites, a peaceful historic cemetery, a Masonic hall that's still in use (the oldest one in the state), abandoned buildings in various states of arrested decay, and a re-created mercantile store (open in the summer only) that features a collection of goods one might have wanted to purchase in Shasta circa 1855.

OLD SHASTA STATE HISTORICAL PARK, *Route 299, 6 miles west of Redding. Phone: State Park Office, (916) 243-8194. Open daily 10 A.M. to 5 P.M. Admission: Free.*

HOW TO GET HERE: *From San Francisco, cross the Bay Bridge and take Route 80 East to Route 505 North to Interstate 5 North. Exit onto Route 299 at Redding. Continue through town and go 6 miles to Shasta.*

SHASTA DAM

I have a vivid childhood memory of visiting a giant dam while on vacation in the West with my parents. Frankly, I don't remember which dam it was, either Hoover or Grand Coulee, but I distinctly remember feeling like a tiny speck next to the mammoth structure, built to harness a major river. Looking down from the top and up from the bottom, the sheer immensity of the dam left a lasting impression.

That feeling came back in a flash when I visited Shasta Dam, about 12 miles north of Redding. It is one of the largest concrete gravity dams in the United States, second only to the Grand Coulee in Washington. It was built over six years, between 1938 and 1944, with materials moved on a 9-mile conveyor belt in Redding. Whatever your opinion of damming rivers is, you can be impressed by the feat of human imagination and engineering necessary to construct such a thing. The Shasta Dam is the key to the California farm industry, serving the Central Valley from Redding to Bakersfield with water, flood control, and electric power.

Here are some facts about Shasta Dam:

- It was built with 6.5 million cubic yards of concrete, enough to build a 3-foot-wide sidewalk around the world at the equator.

- It is 602 feet tall, the height of a 60-story building.

- It weighs 15 million tons.

- The spillway is the highest artificial waterfall in the world. When the lake is full, the water cascades from three times the height of Niagara Falls.

Unfortunately, the extent of your tour is uncertain at this time. Until a few years ago, regularly scheduled tours were offered inside the dam. But budget cuts during the Reagan administration reduced the number of tours to two a year, one in spring and another in fall. If you do get the full tour, you will be taken from the visitors' center down an elevator to the power plant; you'll walk past the giant turbines and generators to the bottom of the spillway. Perhaps by the time you have this book in hand, some tours will have been added to the schedule.

Fortunately, the visitors' center at the top is open year round, and most of the time there will be an information person on duty to answer any questions you might have. In the visitors' center you'll find many displays and exhibits, including a free 20-minute movie about the history of the dam. Also, from the dam you will get a stunning view of Lake Shasta, Mount Shasta, and the surrounding valley.

Although it's a good place to stop off for only an hour or so, if you are nearby at night, plan to take the time to pull over at an overlook on Interstate 5; the dam is lighted and is a spectacular sight.

SHASTA DAM, *Shasta Dam Boulevard, near Redding. Phone: (916) 275-1554. Open 7:30 A.M. to 4 P.M. all year. Admission: Free.*

HOW TO GET HERE: *From Redding, continue up Interstate 5 to the Project City exit. Drive 10 minutes west on Shasta Dam Boulevard to the visitors' center.*

LAKE SHASTA CAVERNS

Lake Shasta was formed by the Shasta Dam. It is a large body of water that you'll see for several miles on both sides of Interstate 5. It is the largest artificial lake in California, with more than 370 miles of shoreline. Here you'll find several beaches, recreation areas, camping, boating, fishing, and hunting.

There are several caves around the lake, and one is open to the public for tours. Lake Shasta Caverns is a privately owned attraction that could be a bit expensive for a family of four. A visit costs $9 for adults, $4 for kids, but for this admission price you get a two-hour adventure. It begins with a 15-minute boat ride across the lake, then a bus trip to the cave entrance, then a guided tour inside. The caverns have been left in their natural state, meaning plenty of stalagmites and stalactites, with the addition of paved walkways, hand railings, and lighting. During very hot or very cold weather, keep in mind that it's always 58 degrees inside the caves.

LAKE SHASTA CAVERNS, *P.O. Box 801, O'Brien. Phone: (916) 238-2341. Open all year. From October to April, tours at 10 A.M., noon, and 2 P.M.; summer tours begin at 8 A.M. Admission: Adults, $9; children, $4.*

HOW TO GET HERE: *From Redding, follow Interstate 5 North for about 15 minutes and look for the exit to Shasta Caverns Road. Follow that road to the reception area for the caverns.*

On a clear day, you know well in advance that you are heading for Mount Shasta. Shasta is the largest freestanding peak in the world, rising some 14,000 feet above the town of Mount Shasta City. The mountain glistens in the distance, towering over Siskyou County, the place where California ends before the Oregon border. Mount Shasta's snow-capped peak inspired the poet Joaquin Miller to describe the mountain as being "Lonely as God and white as a winter moon." It is also supposed to be one of the world's seven sacred mountains *and* a live volcano, though it hasn't erupted in modern times. It is also very accessible; you can drive several thousand feet up the mountain in less than a half hour.

The drive up the mountain is on a good, wide road that you pick up just outside Mount Shasta City. Mount Shasta City is a small, modern town with sport and ski shops, motels and restaurants, plus a resident population of ex-hippies, spiritualists, and folks who choose to live where there's lots of clean air and wide-open spaces.

You will hear lots of fantastic stores about the mountain. The tale told most often is that Mount Shasta is inhabited by Limurians, ancient intelligent beings said to stand 7 feet tall and to possess seven senses, which allow them to escape efforts by humans to find them. As the story goes, the Limurians discovered that their continent was sinking, so they moved to a high point on ours. Many folks claim to have caught a fleeting glimpse of these creatures and to have heard chimes up near the peak. Since the mountain is often topped by a circular cloud, it's been said that flying saucers are able to land undetected.

My first experience on the mountain was a bit more earthly, but certainly spiritual. On a wonderfully clear day one summer, I drove my convertible to an overlook high on the mountain. With no one else around and only the sound of the breeze to accompany me, I looked out toward Mount Lassen to the east, cranked up my cassette deck, and conducted a Bach concerto with more flourish than Leonard Bernstein could dream of. (The mountain made me do it.)

The mountain is a haven for hikers, who can wander up to caves, waterfalls, and breathtaking views, and for skiers, who will find the slopes less crowded than in the Tahoe area and who can reach the ski area without worrying about road closings and tire chains; most of the time you don't reach the snow line until you ascend the mountain.

Within 15 minutes of Mount Shasta City are a number of other attractions. You'll find small lakes for swimming on the western side of Interstate 5. To the north are several woodsy parks, campsites, and small lodges. To the southeast is the old company town called McCloud, which has a lovely river; this is where the Hearst family went for vacations when San Simeon became too crowded (their mansion, called Wyntoon, is still a family getaway but not open to the public). On all sides is the beautiful Shasta-Trinity National Forest.

You will find an information office on the main road as you come into the center of Mount Shasta City from Interstate 5; here you can pick up brochures on the many attractions and services in the area.

HOW TO GET HERE: *From Redding, take Interstate 5 North. Look for signs.*

CHAPTER **17** Clear Lake

AREA OVERVIEW   If you take Route 29 North beyond Calistoga, the fashionable and the chic give way to less glamorous surroundings. In Lake County, wineries are few and far between, pickup trucks and campers are more prevalent than Mercedes' and BMWs. Yes, there are some wineries and other attractions, but the main draw here is the largest lake entirely within California, Clear Lake (Tahoe is a bigger body of water, but part of it is in Nevada).

Clear Lake is 18 miles long and 8 miles wide. According to scientists who spend their time figuring out such things, Clear Lake is the oldest lake in the Northern Hemisphere and possibly the world. It takes about two hours to drive all the way around it. It's a family vacation spot, with one large and pricey resort, the Konocti Harbor Inn, plus lots of small motels and campsites for folks on tight budgets. People flock here for a variety of reasons, all of them aquatic: fishing, sailing, windsurfing, water skiing, swimming, parasailing, and the like.

There are two main towns on the lake. Clearlake (the town is one word) is to the east, just up Route 53 from Route 29. It's a blue-collar town with a few services such as groceries, gas stations, and restaurants. On the west side, Lakeport is prettier and offers more attractions and amenities. This is the county seat and has a nice park and local museum. On the northern side of the lake are the towns called Nice and Lucerne, but don't expect the French Riviera or Switzerland.

What you should expect is a very blue lake, surrounded by hills (green in winter and spring, brown in summer and fall), many golf courses and tennis courts, and a guaranteed escape from San Francisco's summer fog. In fact, temperatures here frequently soar above 100 degrees Fahrenheit.

Like so many places around the Bay Area, there are wonderful surprises near and around Clear Lake. I'll tell you in detail about two. One is a destination, Anderson Marsh State Park; another is an activity, rockhounding.

When you pull into Anderson Marsh State Park, it looks like you are about to visit someone's kindly Aunt Em out on the farm. The driveway leads to a lovely old farmhouse, and as you head up the walkway, chances are a nice lady in a turn-of-the-century dress will greet you with a plate full of hot biscuits. Frankly, at first I thought this was a gimmick they set up when TV crews come around, but I was assured that volunteers at the historical home are always cooking something on the old-fashioned stove inside. You might think the refreshments are reason enough for a visit, but there is much to see and learn here. In fact, it's worth the hour-plus drive up from Calistoga, even if you're not going on to Clear Lake.

The miracle of Anderson Marsh is that it was almost turned into a housing development. But thanks to a citizens' group spearheaded by a young archaeologist named John Parker, this is now a 900-acre state historical park that preserves more than 40 Indian village sites dating back thousands of years. In 1976 Parker was hired by the U.S. Corps of Engineers to make an environmental study for a water project. He found the area to be filled with endangered species, plus one of the highest densities of prehistoric Indian sites anywhere in California. He set out to gather community support to save the area from development. Evidently he was successful; in 1982 Anderson Marsh became a California state park.

Parker, who was completing his doctorate when I met him, still runs seminars in the summer and leads work crews doing archaeological digs. If you see a young Indiana Jones look-alike roaming around, chances are it's the man who saved the marsh.

Most tours, however, are run by the state Parks Department folks, plus the local volunteer brigade. Visits are organized to take you back in time, beginning with the Victorian farmhouse, which is furnished with period pieces and is organized around the kitchen. Here you'll get an idea of what farm life was like, circa 1900. Take a short walk out past the barns and into the field, and you will step back several hundred years to a typical Indian village. There you'll see demonstrations of basket weaving, acorn grinding, and other aspects of village life. As a bow to modern life, this area has several picnic tables, so you can enjoy a packed lunch.

As you continue toward the marsh, you will be on the site of an Indian culture 10,000 years old. This is still mostly open space with a few barns set up to store artifacts that have been uncovered. Since this is an area still under study, the rangers will have to tell you which parts are open for wandering around.

Anderson Marsh begins where the farmland ends and continues up to the southern tip of Clear Lake. This 500-acre preserve is home to hundreds of species, including otters, mink, many fish varieties, and even an occasional bald eagle and mountain lion. No boats, motorcycles, or other noisy machines are

ANDERSON MARSH STATE PARK

allowed here, just the wilderness as it might have been thousands of years ago when it provided all the necessities of life for the original inhabitants.

ANDERSON MARSH STATE HISTORICAL PARK, *Route 53. Phone: (707) 994-0688. Open Friday through Sunday, 10 A.M. to 4 P.M.; other times by appointment. Admission: Free.*

HOW TO GET HERE: *From San Francisco, take the Golden Gate Bridge to Highway 101 North to Route 37 toward Vallejo and Napa. At Route 29, turn left and continue north all the way through Calistoga. Continue on Route 29 to Route 53, which join together for a stretch. Stay on Route 53; shortly after Route 29 branches off to the left, look for the entrance to Anderson Marsh State Park, on the left side of the road.*

ROCKHOUNDING

One of the things people do around Clear Lake is search for rare and unusual rocks. Thanks to volcanic activity eons ago, this area is a veritable garden of delights for rock collectors, aka rockhounds. The most popular item around here is the Lake County diamond, which is actually a high-grade quartz that greatly resembles the more valuable gem. One can also find obsidian, jade, calcite, jasper, and chert, if you know where to look.

The best way to learn is to stop in at one of the several rock shops around the lake. These stores often double as meeting places for local gem and mineral clubs; at the very least you can get some information or arrange for a guided tour.

I was taken for an excursion by Pat Bernstead, who runs the Rock Shop in the center of the town of Clearlake. First he showed me some store displays of what we might find out in nature. Then he provided the equipment we would need, which amounts to a good hammer and chisel, a magnifying glass, and a strong bag for carrying the bounty home. If you want to get really serious, you can head out equipped to the gills with field guides and the like, but I think the main things you need, in addition to the ones just mentioned, are a pair of sturdy shoes, a supply of water, and a lot of patience.

You can go out on your own, or you can spend a few bucks to hire a guide. Information about guides and rock clubs can be found in the rock shops. They also provide cutting and polishing services, and most important, they display beautiful rocks. If you're like a lot of fishermen I know, you can pick up a gem and then take it home and tell the neighbors tales about how you "found" it.

ROCK SHOP, *14590 Lakeshore Drive, Clearlake. Phone: (707) 995-9219.*

MANZANITA HILL ROCK SHOP, *7325 Pyle Road, near Nice. Phone: (707) 274-4489. Be sure to call ahead to be sure the owners are not out rockhounding.*

HOW TO GET HERE: *From Anderson Marsh (see previous entry), continue on Route 53 to the town of Clearlake. Turn left on Lakeshore Drive.*

The Central Coast is usually included on any visitor's list of places to see outside San Francisco, mainly because of Hearst Castle. As long as you're in the neighborhood, take the time to enjoy this area, which combines some of the best of the features of northern and southern California. There are picturesque and inexpensive coastal towns like Morro Bay. There's an artsy quality to Cambria. San Luis Obispo offers the energy of a college town, with its combination of Beach Boys and Deadheads. Pismo Beach provides not only memories of Jack Benny radio routines but also some of the widest stretches of usable beach on the coast. There is even a new and thriving wine industry in the nearby hills.

The area is easily reached by taking Highway 101 South to Paso Robles, then Route 46 to the coast, or the more scenic route, Route 1, all the way down along the coast. It's just about halfway between San Francisco and Los Angeles, a comfortable four-hour drive.

AREA OVERVIEW

About 2½ hours south of the Bay Area, inland off Highway 101, is a lovely place to stop to stretch your legs and take a self-guided tour of one of the first California missions. Mission San Miguel is probably the best example of a mission in its original condition; a visit here is an opportunity to see how people lived in these parts nearly 200 years ago.

Mission San Miguel, established in 1797 and named for St. Michael the Archangel, was the third mission established in the 21-mission system in California. Construction of the adobe church began in 1816. Though the look is simple and severe from the outside, inside you will see the colorful murals applied in 1820 by Estevan Munras, an artist who traveled from Catalonia, Spain. With the help of Native American assistants, Munras painted simulated balconies, doors, archways, and, of course, religious figures.

The mission, however, did not prosper, and for a while it became the site of such secular enterprises as a tavern and a Howe sewing machine agency. The place even has a dark past involving a family murdered by bandits vainly attempting to steal some gold.

Eventually the mission buildings returned into the cradle of the Catholic Church and since 1928 have been run by the Franciscan order. For a while the place was used as a monastery, but now it is an active parish church, the site of community events and annual religious celebrations. There's a wonderful at-

MISSION SAN MIGUEL

mosphere to the mission, serene and humble. The buildings are immaculately maintained, and the public is welcome. You will see a sprawling cactus garden, a historic cemetery, and a museum with historical artifacts plus some rather elaborate models of various California missions constructed by inmates at San Quentin. On a more practical note, this is a nice place to use the rest rooms, and there's a picnic table or two for your convenience.

If you're lucky, you'll encounter Brother Quintin, who calls himself the janitor. His tonsure and robe will more quickly identify him as a Franciscan. Brother Quintin has been at Mission San Miguel on and off for the past 35 years, continuously for the past 12, though he hasn't managed to lose his Bostonian accent. He's in charge of maintaining the mission and possesses not only a wealth of knowledge about the place but also a sense of humor and a warmth that makes all welcome.

MISSION SAN MIGUEL, *Old Highway 101, San Miguel. Phone: (805) 467-3256. Visitors welcome 9:30 A.M. to 4:30 P.M. daily and at Sunday mass. Donation requested.*

HOW TO GET HERE: *From San Francisco, get on Highway 101, take the Tenth Street exit and head east, back under the highway. Turn right on Mission Street and continue south for about 2½ blocks to the mission.*

HEARST CASTLE Entire guidebooks are devoted to the history of this American palace, so I won't bother with the details here. What I will tell you, however, is that this is one of the most popular tourist attractions in California, and you should not expect to see the castle without a reservation and without spending some time waiting in line. Even if you don't have the time for a tour or if you happen to be in the neighborhood without prior planning, you can stop by the visitors' center where there's plenty to see. And it's free.

For years, visitors to Hearst Castle had to hang around in the parking lot and makeshift trailers waiting for their tour to begin. Recently a sparkling, neo-mission-style visitors' center was constructed, complete with historical photos and artifacts (not to mention a snack bar and souvenir stand). You can look around while waiting for your tour to begin, or you can make this a stop in itself.

On display are such items as original drawings by architect Julia Morgan and art from Hearst's giant collection, including an ancient Roman mosaic and two Italian Renaissance paintings. Through a wall of windows you can watch art restorers at work, refurbishing items from the castle. There's even a window with telescopes to provide a view of the house on the hill from the center.

If you want to take the full tour, you have a choice of four options. Tour 1 is designed for first-time visitors and includes the ground floor of the castle, one of the three guest houses (bigger and certainly more luxuriously appointed than most people's year-round homes), plus some of the gardens. Tour 2 includes the kitchen, the library, and the Hearsts' private suite, occupying the entire third floor. Tour 3 is good for architecture buffs, featuring a comparative look at the structural and decorative techniques that changed over the various decades during which the castle was built. Tour 4 (not available in winter) emphasizes the grounds and gardens of San Simeon.

You will be sold a ticket for a specific day and time. All tours are walking tours; you must be prepared to walk at least ½ mile and up at least 150 stairs. Visitors confined to wheelchairs may make special arrangements by calling the visitors' center.

HEARST SAN SIMEON STATE HISTORICAL MONUMENT, *Highway 1, San Simeon. Phone: Visitors' center, (805) 927-4622. Tickets: In California, call MISTIX at (800) 446-PARK; from outside California, call (619) 452-1950. Visitors' center open 8 A.M. to 4 P.M. daily, except major holidays. Admission: Visitors' center is free; tickets to tour Hearst Castle are $10 for adults, $5 for children 6 to 12.*

HOW TO GET HERE: *From San Francisco, take Highway 101 South to Paso Robles, then Route 46 West to Route 1; continue on Route 1 North to the castle. Driving time from San Francisco is approximately four hours.*

NITWIT RIDGE

It's doubtful that William Randolph Hearst and Art Beal ever met each other, yet their homes are the most famous around these parts. The connection between these two men goes beyond location. Hearst spared no expense importing materials and hiring the best architect and craftsmen to build his San Simeon Castle. Well, Art Beal was a trash hauler in those days, and he collected Hearst's throwaways plus a few finds of his own to build his own castle (of sorts), now known as State Historical Landmark 939, or "Nitwit Ridge."

The main difference between these two men is that Beal built his castle all by himself.

You won't find a visitors' center or organized tours at Beal's place. At this writing, Beal is in his nineties and ailing. A group of neighbors and admirers has formed a society to preserve the unique home and gardens, but for now you can only see the place from the road. Fortunately, even at this distance, there is much to see and marvel at.

Nitwit Ridge is a showplace of folk art, a monument to individuality built from bedrock Beal blasted from the mountain nearby and hauled to the site. Embedded in the many walls, stairways, and walkways around the house are not only Hearst's throwaways but also the artifacts of a consumer society: soda cans, shells, an old TV here, a pair of eyeglasses there, even part of a toilet seat. Touches of humor abound throughout, statements of some kind from Beal, who liked to call himself "Captain Nitwit" and "Der Tinkerpaw."

This is no bungalow, either. The home itself is on three levels with porches overlooking the road on one side and a 2½-acre garden on the other. And even though the appearance is whimsical, there is function in the design. For example, the handrails for the outside stairways are all working water pipes.

Cambria is a community that has recognized the importance of honoring its folk artists while they are still alive. The hope of the Art Beal Society, the group trying to preserve the property, is to raise enough money to fix the crumbling stairs and walkways to make them safe for visitors. In his younger days, Beal loved to show folks around. He was an Olympic swimmer, a published poet, and a jack-of-all-trades. Most of his life, though, he hauled trash; from the items no one wanted he made his home. In a weird way, much of the community is represented here, embedded in the stone landmark that is Nitwit Ridge.

The director of the Art Beal Society is Jim Fajardo, a researcher at Hearst Castle. Jim says both homes are monuments to two creative men. One had money and a world view; the other had no funds and a local view.

NITWIT RIDGE, *Hillcrest Drive, Cambria. Visible from the road only.*

HOW TO GET HERE: *From Hearst Castle (see previous entry), continue south on Route 1 into the town of Cambria. Turn left on Cambria Road, then left on Main Street. Take the next right to Cornwall, then take the second right to Hillcrest. Nitwit Ridge is about 100 yards up Hillcrest on the left.*

HARMONY

Driving along the coastal route south of Cambria, you will pass a town with one of the most appealing names in all of California. Harmony is worth a quick stop, even if just to have your picture taken by the city limits sign. But some people take months to plan their visit; these are the hundreds of couples in love who decide to get married in Harmony, obviously trying to buck the odds on the current divorce rate.

To the casual drop-in visitor, Harmony offers several attractions. For one thing, you can meet the entire town; at last count, the population was 18. You'll probably encounter the mayor, Jim Lawrence, who also happens to own the town. You see, several years ago, Jim and his wife, Kaye, came to Harmony to buy a piano they had seen advertised, only to discover that the entire town was for sale. So they bought the piano and the town (a clever way to avoid piano-moving expenses, if you ask me).

Gradually the Lawrences have been turning Harmony into a crafts center. The only street sign is a pole with several boards, each pointing the way to the town's glassblower, potters, painters, and jewelry makers. The town also sports a restaurant that often offers entertainment on weekends, and, of course, there's the town wedding chapel. It's all rather quaint with its brick walkways, court-yards, and nicely restored wooden buildings. The crafts people, by the way, are serious and talented; this isn't a schlock selection of tourist stuff you'd find in any souvenir shop.

The town was named during an era that was less than harmonious. This used to be busy dairy country with many feuding farmers. Some diplomatic soul decided to call the town Harmony in the hope that it would set a more peaceful tone. The old dairy barns are now used as the crafts area.

If you like the idea of buying a little town to call your own, you might be interested to know that the Lawrences paid $650,000 for Harmony in 1981. Today, if you're lucky, that sum might buy a dandy three-bedroom fixer-upper in Palo Alto.

By the way, if you want to get married in Harmony, that takes some advance planning; no drop-in nuptials are performed.

HARMONY, *Route 1, 5 miles south of Cambria. For more information, call City Hall (also the Lawrence residence) at (805) 927-8288.*

HOW TO GET HERE: *From Hearst Castle or Nitwit Ridge, continue south on Route 1 for about 5 miles and look for Harmony on the left (east) side of the road.*

GIANT CHESSBOARD

Anyone who has read *Through the Looking Glass* remembers the giant chessboard and the living pieces—the White Knight, the Red Queen—that Alice encounters there. In the Central Coast town of Morro Bay, you can encounter a giant chessboard and perhaps some life-size chess pieces of your own.

Morro Bay is a sweet little town, a seaside fishing and resort community famous for a huge rock that sits offshore. It's a laid-back place to visit, with several nice motels and good places to eat. There's not a lot of night life, or that much activity during the day, either. One place you can meet some locals is at the giant chessboard, located in the town square at the harbor.

On Saturday afternoon the Morro Bay Chess Club turns out for a game of team chess. Each square on the board is about 2 feet square; the wooden pieces they move around weigh about 40 pounds each (no wonder this is a team game). Each fall the entire community turns out for a celebration around the chessboard, with people playing the various pieces. Sometimes a game is set up between adults and children (I'm told the kids usually win); at other times someone will write a play and the chess game is dramatized, expressing a message about world peace.

You can visit the chessboard any time; it just sits there as a part of the town park. If you want to make arrangements to play during the week, you can call the local Parks and Recreation Department.

MORRO BAY CHESSBOARD, *Near Market Street and Morro Bay Boulevard, Morro Bay. Phone: Parks and Recreation Department, (805) 772-1214.*

HOW TO GET HERE: *From Hearst Castle or Harmony, continue south on Route 1 and look for the turnoff to Morro Bay. The center of town is only a few minutes from the highway and one block from the ocean.*

THE FIRST MOTEL

Most Californians consider San Luis Obispo the halfway point between San Francisco and Los Angeles. Without verifying that claim with exact measurements, it is certainly the biggest town before you hit Santa Barbara, and it's the first town where you feel like you're approaching southern California. The air is different here, the college kids look blonder and tanner, and there's always a feeling that half the residents are getting ready to head for the beach. The pace, though, is more like northern California, with plenty of good places to eat, several coffeehouses, and lots of leftover hippies.

San Luis Obispo also has an unusual claim to fame: It's the home of the world's first motel, or, more accurately, the place where the word *motel* was invented.

Back in the early days of automobile travel, old Highway 101 was a popular route, so "the most delightful and complete Motorist's Hotel in the world" was constructed in 1925 at the foot of the steep Cuesta Pass. Lots of cars broke down along this stretch of highway; next door to the motor hotel was a mechanic's garage, and more than one set of pioneer motorists ended up spending the night in the conveniently located lodging.

Where did the word *motel* come from? There are several versions to the story. One is that sometime in the 1920s, a giant wind knocked off some the letters on the "Motor Hotel" sign so that it read "Mo tel." Rather than fix the sign, the owners started calling their place a motel. Another story is that the painter hired to make a new sign talked the owners into saving some pennies by combining the two words. Another theory is that he simply ran out of paint. Regardless of how it came to be, the word *motel* became part of our language.

Betty Grau bought the motel in 1976. She had grown up in San Luis Obispo and knows all the stories and legends about the place, including the rumor that Marilyn Monroe and Joe DiMaggio stayed there on their honeymoon. The place still looks much as it has for the past couple of decades, with a series of separate cabins surrounding well-manicured lawns and a swimming pool. Rooms are small and Spartan, with rates starting at $40 a night. You also might want to take note of the restaurant, which is famous for its steaks.

MOTEL INN, *2223 Monterey Street, San Luis Obispo. Phone: (805) 543-4000. Be sure to call ahead if you'd like to take a look at the place.*

HOW TO GET HERE: *From Morro Bay (see Giant Chessboard), head south on Route 1 to San Luis Obispo, about 15 minutes away. Route 1 becomes Santa*

Rosa Avenue once you get into the city. Continue on Santa Rosa to Monterey Street. Turn left on Monterey and head north to the motel, which is on the right, shortly before you reach Highway 101.

MADONNA INN

If one cares to see what the first motel hath wrought, up the road from the Motel Inn is what many consider the ultimate roadside hostelry, the hard-to-miss Madonna Inn. Why hard-to-miss? First of all, billboards will inform you that you are approaching the place. But beyond that, the color: a shade of pink that could wake you up faster than a cup of coffee.

No, the Madonna Inn was not named for the pop singer with a penchant for lingerie. The Madonna Inn was built more than three decades ago by one Alexander Madonna, who made his fortune building the roads around here. There are more than 100 rooms in his inn, each one unique and displaying his penchant for rocks.

For example, one of the most popular rooms is the Madonna Suite, complete with a cavelike shower and a fireplace carved out of a 45-ton boulder. Other rooms have streams running through them; all of them have flourishes of the incredible Madonna pink. Rooms go for about $60 to $150 a night, and returning fans book their favorite rooms up to a year in advance.

However, I think the best way to visit is simply to tour the lobby, where you'll get the idea. Upstairs in the gift shop you can look at picture postcards of the rooms for free. Then if you feel like hanging around, stop in the coffeeshop, where you can get enormous portions of better-than-average road food. My mother-in-law never passes up the opportunity to stop in and have a slice of the Madonna Inn's mile-high banana cream pie. Gentlemen won't want to miss the one-of-a-kind men's room downstairs from the coffeeshop; if the coast is clear, let your female companions in to have a look.

MADONNA INN, *100 Madonna Road, San Luis Obispo. Phone: (805) 543-3000.*

HOW TO GET HERE: *From San Francisco, take Highway 101 to the Madonna Road exit and follow the signs.*

GUM WALL

Have you ever had the unpleasant experience of finding someone else's gum under your theater seat? Or has your shoe stuck to the sidewalk thanks to someone's used Juicy Fruit? Well, the town of San Luis Obispo has come up with a clever solution: Make art, not gum wads.

I don't know if this was somebody's plan or if it emerged spontaneously, but in downtown SLO you can see a mural painted with gum. The "artists" have written messages, created designs, and drawn pictures, both abstract and figurative, on two facing walls that line a narrow walkway from the street to a parking lot. You'll see Double Bubble, Beeman's, all colors, and, I suppose, all flavors. Depending on your viewpoint, it's quite charming or utterly disgusting.

GUM WALL, *in the alley off the 800 block of Higuera Street, San Luis Obispo.*

HOW TO GET HERE: *From Route 1 (see Hearst Castle), follow Santa Rosa Street to Higuera, which is the main downtown thoroughfare. Turn left on Higuera and continue to the 800 block, which is between Chorro and Morro streets. Park anywhere you can, and walk through the narrow walkway that contains the gum wall.*

CHAPTER **19** Backroads to Los Angeles

AREA OVERVIEW One of the most popular programs we ever broadcast on "Bay Area Backroads" was called "The Road to L.A." We presented an alternative, little-traveled backroads route from San Francisco to Los Angeles. Each year, millions of Americans travel between California's two most famous cities, by air, train, or car. The main auto routes have drawbacks. Interstate 5, which is the fastest route, is as boring as heck. Route 1, along the coast, is beautiful; but it is also curvy and slow and you can age visibly by the time you finish the journey. Inland Highway 101 is in the process of being improved, but it can be busy, and the stretch near San Francisco is almost as dull as Interstate 5.

Here is a backroads route to Los Angeles that is beautiful, leisurely without being dull, and full of interesting stops along the way. It's a trip that will take you back to the feeling of travel before superhighways, when you actually went through towns and villages and saw something of the kind of daily life that goes on there, rather than buzzing down a highway that could be anywhere. The obvious drawback is that you have to have time to enjoy it: A leisurely two-day trip is preferable to a six- to eight-hour rush between the two cities. You could make it in one long day by skipping some of the stops.

We will begin at San Juan Bautista, our first exit off Highway 101 onto the backroads. San Juan Bautista is a lovely old California town, with a main street that is a state historical park built around the eighteenth-century mission. San Juan Bautista also has a lot of nice shops and several good Mexican restaurants. This is a good place to get out of the car, stretch your legs, have a bite to eat, and get used to the pace of the backroad to L.A. Along the way are several detour destinations, which will be described in detail.

The route is as follows: From San Francisco, head south on Highway 101 past

Backroads to Los Angeles

San Jose

152

San Juan Bautista

5

101

25

198

Coalinga

1

46   2

41

5

3

33

1

4

Ojai

Santa Barbara

101

1

Malibu

Los Angeles

San Jose to Route 156 and the exit for San Juan Bautista. Take Route 156 out of San Juan Bautista to Route 25 at Hollister. Switch to Route 25 South and continue past the east entrance to Pinnacles National Monument and on down to Route 198. Turn left (east) on Route 198 to our main route south, Route 33. The stretches of road on Routes 25 and 198 are uncrowded, very scenic passages through small villages and beautiful country. You'll then take Route 33 all the way through the flatlands and over the mountains to Ojai.

For the last leg of the journey, you will rejoin Highway 101 into Ventura. If you wish, watch for the signs to Route 1. If you take this coastal route, also called Pacific Coast Highway, you will enter the Los Angeles area via Malibu and Santa Monica. If you prefer, you can stay on Highway 101 and head into Hollywood, but it's less scenic and likely to be crowded, especially around rush hour.

At various points on the trip there are worthwhile detours, which may take you another 30 to 60 minutes out of your way but should interest you.

IRON ZOO
① Here's a little detour around the town of Coalinga. If the name rings a bell, perhaps you are recalling the famous 6.5 earthquake that rocked this small town in 1983. Or perhaps you are familiar with the annual Great Horned Toad Derby, which takes place Memorial Day weekend. However, the locals are particularly proud of their contribution to art in America, which is affectionately known as the Iron Zoo. You see, a lot of unsightly oil rigs used to dot the landscape around here. Then, in 1973, local artist Jean Dekessian had an idea. Perhaps she could turn an eyesore into an attraction.

Jean got permission from one of the oil companies to use her imagination, paints, and welding materials to add a touch of whimsy to the ugly, rust-colored pumps. First she painted one device to look like a moving rabbit, then another to look like a skunk, then others to look like horses, raccoons, insects, and birds —all very colorful and fun to look at. The oil pumps became a source of local pride, and the town of Coalinga had something new to brag about.

Jean continues to touch up her creations each year or so, keeping them looking fresh; the oil companies pay for the upkeep. This idea has spread to other towns, so you may see some Dekessian-inspired pumps in places like Texas and Oklahoma. In fact, Jean has devised a handy kit to send to painters in other oil communities to help them spruce up the landscape.

There is no formal tour or meeting place to observe this collection of 50 or so fanciful rigs called the Iron Zoo. They're simply along the road on Route 198, before you come to the major intersection of Interstate 5. By the way, this junction is the site of the best restaurant and inn around these parts, the Harris

Ranch. If you're here around mealtime, this is the place to stop for excellent beef dishes.

IRON ZOO, *Route 198, near Coalinga.*

HOW TO GET HERE: *As you approach Coalinga on Route 198 (see Area Overview), you'll see a sign to Route 33 South. That will be your ultimate turn, but for now continue on Route 198 toward Route 5. The Iron Zoo continues for several miles along that stretch of road.*

JAMES DEAN MEMORIAL

This destination is a bit of a detour from our between-the-freeways backroad to L.A., but it is well worth the half-hour drive to the town of Cholame (pronounced "show-lam"). You drive down the route James Dean was speeding along on the fateful evening of September 30, 1955, the night America's most idolized rebel crashed and died.

The night he died, Dean was driving his Porsche up from Los Angeles to Salinas for a race. At age 24, his life ended outside Cholame: the boy from Indiana pinned behind the wheel of a European sports car. It took more than 20 years for someone to erect a monument, and amazingly, that someone was a businessman from Japan. Seita Onishi saw *Rebel Without a Cause* and became a Dean devotee; he visited Hollywood but could find no memorial. He went to Cholame and found only a post office and a diner. So he took it upon himself to design a fitting memorial. Onishi, who speaks no English, went to the Hearst Corporation, who owns property near where the crash occurred, and received permission to erect his tribute: a 30-square-foot monument, stunning in its simplicity. A reflecting sculpture is accented by an oleander tree ("the tree of life"), a gravel garden, a cement bench, and plaques with several inscriptions, including one of Dean's favorites, from *The Little Prince:* "What is essential is invisible to the naked eye." This fan from Japan pays the folks at the diner to maintain the monument.

Most of the time, highway travelers zip by, then turn around and pull over to have a look. The effect the monument has on people is dramatic. Good ol' boys in pickup trucks become solemn and reverent. Families stare at the shiny aluminum sculpture, the moms and dads remembering the first time they saw *Rebel Without a Cause* and *East of Eden,* the kids wishing they could be as cool as James Dean was in his day.

Sometimes people are so moved that they feel they have to talk to somebody, so they head over to the post office, where Lilly Grant works. She says she had never been much of a Dean fan, but after listening to the stories and memories of the faithful, she has come to understand his appeal. Lilly has amassed several scrapbooks of James Dean mementos that have been sent to her over the years by fans, most of whom regard Dean as the ultimate American dreamer, always unsatisfied with the present and hoping to find something better down the road. "He was the original fast kid," says Lilly.

The diner next door to the post office has a display of Dean memorabilia, including the ticket he received for speeding just a few hours before his fatal accident. Postcards and souvenirs are for sale.

JAMES DEAN MEMORIAL, *Route 46, Cholame. Phone: Post office, (805) 238-1390.*

HOW TO GET HERE: *Take Route 33 South of Coalinga (see Area Overview) until you come to Route 46. Turn right and head west for about 30 minutes to Cholame.*

OIL MUSEUM After your detour to the James Dean Memorial on Route 46, rejoin Route 33, where the road is straight and uneventful. You can peacefully drive at the speed limit without worrying about huge trucks roaring by. The view consists mainly of farm country with some mountains in the distance. But when you cross into Kern County, through the waves of heat rising up from the highway, you may see an eerie dance in the distance.

As you near the town of Taft, you will realize that this surreal ballet is being performed by hundreds of oil rigs, pumping away as far as the eye can see. This is the heart of California's oil country, not as well known as Texas or Oklahoma, but gushing nonetheless. The story of the oil industry in this area is told by graphic displays in the West Kern Oil Museum, at the southern end of the town of Taft.

Why would anyone want to visit this oil museum? Jane Kinsey, a former schoolteacher who is the museum's volunteer curator, is blunt about it. "First of all, it's air-conditioned," she says, and if you're in the area on a typical day when the thermometer hovers around 90, you'll appreciate the value of her answer. But creature comforts aside, the oil museum is a surprisingly interesting place with some 7,000 square feet of displays and exhibitions. The museum building is on the site of a well that was drilled in 1917 and is surrounded by yards full of drilling equipment and rigs, displayed amid a landscape of cacti and other native plants.

Originally Taft was a company town, named simply Site 2. The oil company provided homes, parks, and other town services for their workers. After a fire, the town was rebuilt and named after the U.S. president at the time. Unlike Dallas and other towns where great numbers of people struck it rich in the oil fields, the wealth in Taft was kept within the oil companies; workers came and went, moving on to other sites every few years or so.

Taft is proud of its legacy in oil, and the museum is staffed by volunteers who seem to be everywhere, eager to tell you about their town, the oil, and the Yokut Indians, who lived on this land for centuries. According to Jane, in 1915 one out of every two barrels of California oil came from Kern County, which still leads the state in oil production.

While we're on the subject of oil, Taft is a good place to fill up the car with gas. Soon you'll be heading up the mountains and into forest land, which is the most beautiful leg of the backroads trip to L.A. but without a lot of opportunities to fill 'er up.

WEST KERN OIL MUSEUM, *Route 33 and Wood Street, Taft. Phone: (805) 765-6664. Open Tuesday through Saturday, 10 A.M. to 5 P.M.; Sunday, 1 to 4 P.M. Admission: Free.*

HOW TO GET HERE: *As you head out of town on Route 33 (see Area Overview), look for the sign to the museum on the right.*

One of the main reasons to take the backroad to L.A. is to go over the pass on Route 33 through the beautiful Los Padres National Forest. Granted, this is much slower than going over the Grapevine on Interstate 5, but it is also infinitely more pleasant. The road takes you along streams and through woods and mountain valleys, with several sites for picnicking, camping, and hiking along the way. And when you come out the other side, you will see Shangri-La.

No kidding: The Ojai Valley was the spot chosen for the 1937 film *Lost Horizon,* the classic in which Ronald Colman and company survive a plane crash and stumble into a land of love, peace, and longevity. There's even a bench where you can rest and take in the view on the site where the movie was filmed (it's on East Ojai Avenue).

The town of Ojai is a modern-day Shangri-La of sorts. Less than two hours from Los Angeles by car, it is eons away in spirit and style. Ojai is part health resort, part spiritual retreat, part artists' community, part home of expensive boarding schools, and part hippie hideout, with several other parts mixed in. Whatever part interests you, it's worth spending some time here, at least to see the spectacular light at sunset over the mountains. Locals talk of seeing a purple aura over the hills; perhaps you'll see it too.

In the center of town is a lovely plaza and park where several seasonal festivals are held. Summer is prime time in the park, with a series of jazz, classical, and dance events, plus a major tennis tournament. Across the street you may hear the collective grunts and sighs of the folks staying at the Oaks, a spa where guests come to slim and aerobicize (often you will see guests in Oaks sweat suits jogging around town). As you drive through town, you'll see evidence of the

SHANGRI-LA

theosophists and other spiritual groups who believe the land around Ojai to be blessed. This is the town where Krishnamurti established the Krotona Institute, which is still in operation.

One "only in Ojai" experience is to be had at Bart's Books at 302 West Matil-lija, just a few minutes from downtown. This local institution was modeled after the open bookstalls of Paris; visitors wander through a courtyard filled primarily with used books. At night, presumably for those who must read at all hours, a selection of books lines the sidewalk, and payment is on the honor system.

You can visit several art galleries in Ojai; occasionally studio tours are available. The sculptor-potter Beatrice Wood—"the *grand dame* of the art world," some call her—still works daily in her studio and gallery outside town. In 1989 when I last visited, Wood was a very hospitable and spry 92-year-old; it's definitely worth checking to see if her studio is still open to the public.

If you are in a hurry to arrive in L.A., at least be sure to spend a few minutes driving around Ojai, past the orange groves, kiwi farms, mansions, and vistas. It'll make you hungry to visit another time.

OJAI, *Route 33. For general information and a map, stop at the Chamber of Commerce on the main drag of town, Ojai Avenue, or write P.O. Box 1134, Ojai, CA 93023. Phone: (805) 646-3000.*

HOW TO GET HERE: *Take Route 33 through the Los Padres National Forest (see Area Overview).*

Index

209